"So many people are desperately searching for love, whether consciously or unconsciously. May Ram Dass's intimate and heartfelt account inspire others to find their own path of true love, compassion, and joyful service."

—Thich Nhat Hanh, author of *Savor*

"*Be Love Now* reveals the true meaning of yoga, the union of the open heart—this is required reading for anyone who follows a path of devotion. As always, Ram Dass shares his journey with eloquence, wit, and depth of being."

—Daniel Goleman, author of *Emotional Intelligence* and
Ecological Intelligence

"The awakening power of love shines on every page of this wonderfully inspiring book. With insight and engaging humor, Ram Dass shares with us a lifetime of spiritual practice. This book is a rare treat."

—Joseph Goldstein, author of *A Heart Full of Peace*

"Read this delicious, ecstatic journey and be awakened, be pulled body and soul into the heart of love."

—Jack Kornfield, author of *A Path with Heart*

"A gift of love from the man who introduced me to the idea of higher consciousness and became one of my greatest teachers."

—Dr. Wayne Dyer, author of *The Power of Intention*

"If the West even approaches enlightenment in the twenty-first century, there's no way to overestimate the role of Ram Dass in making it happen. He planted seeds that turned into a million trees; if and when they blossom, they will exude the fragrance of his teaching forever."

—Marianne Williamson, author of *The Age of Miracles*

"There is no one better than Ram Dass to transmit the essence of Eastern religion and philosophy to Westerners. He has made the journey and from the depth of his Joy and Wisdom he shares with us the journey of so many great Beings."

—Krishna Das, kirtan wallah

"Ram Dass is one of our greatest teachers. With *Be Love Now,* he shares his profound discovery that 'love is a state of being, not a trip from here to there.' "

—Deepak Chopra, author of *Buddha* and *Muhammad*

"Few are those who have given us such access into the intimacy of their evolving spiritual journey as has Ram Dass. In *Be Love Now* he sets an example of what it means to have an ecstatic romance with the Infinite, to be a faithful disciple of one's teacher, and a humble practitioner of the highest meaning of love."

—Michael Bernard Beckwith, author of *Spiritual Liberation*

be love now

ram dass

with rameshwar das

the path of the heart

be love now

HarperOne

An Imprint of HarperCollins*Publishers*

HarperOne

HarperCollins books may be purchased for educational, business, or sales promotional use. For information please write: Special Markets Department, HarperCollins Publishers, 10 East 53rd Street, New York, NY 10022.

HarperCollins website: http://www.harpercollins.com

HarperCollins®, 📖®, and HarperOne™ are trademarks of HarperCollins Publishers

FIRST HARPERCOLLINS PAPERBACK EDITION PUBLISHED IN 2011

Library of Congress Cataloging-in-Publication Data
Ram Dass.
Be love now: the path of the heart / by Ram Dass, Rameshwar Das. — 1st ed.
p. cm.
ISBN 978–0–06–196138–0
1. Love—Religious aspects. 2. Spirituality. 3. Spiritual life.
I. Das, Rameshwar. II. Title.
BL626.4.R36 2010
205'.677—dc22 2010022211

11 12 13 14 15 RRD(H) 10 9 8 7 6 5 4 3 2 1

To Maharaj-ji

A man in a blanket who died but lives within me
and always knows my heart,
a cosmic playmate whose laughter goes beyond time,
who always loves me more,
more than a lover, father, or mother,
more than I love myself,
even when I forget to love him,
whose presence is like a sweet
silent mistlike energy in my heart,
who showed me a path
with no direction
and illumines every step along the way,
without whom none of this would exist.
Through him I met my real self.
He wouldn't take credit for this book, but it is his.

contents

Foreword: Getting Here from There,
by Rameshwar Das   ix

1. The Path of the Heart   1

2. Excess Baggage   24

3. To Become One   43

4. Darshan   62

5. Guides   85

6. Remover of Darkness   111

7. The Way of Grace   156

8. A Family Man   192

9. One in My Heart   212

Credits and Permissions   297
Notes   301

getting here from there

rameshwar das

S PRING, 1967. I was twenty, a sophomore at Wesleyan University in Middletown, Connecticut. I had just spent my first extended time out of the country on a semester abroad in Franco's Spain. The Vietnam War was raging, and there was upheaval on campus.

Freshman year I took a seminar, "Freedom and Liberation in Ancient China and India," that stirred an interest in Taoism and Buddhism. At the same time, I started smoking pot and experimenting with mescaline, DMT, and LSD. The visual and lyrical effects of psychedelics stimulated my artistic, philosophic, and poetic intuitions and expanded my inner and outer horizons. They didn't improve my academic standing.

That spring a flyer appeared for a guest lecture by Richard Alpert, Ph.D., formerly a psychology professor at Harvard, who had done some of his graduate work at Wesleyan. Two of his former students, Sara and David Winter, were teaching psychology at Wesleyan and had invited him to speak.

Alpert was vaguely notorious to me as an associate of Timothy Leary, a counterculture icon. They had both been fired from Harvard in connection with their psychedelic activities. Alpert had the distinction of being the only tenured professor ever publicly exorcised from Harvard's Ivy League faculty. They didn't go quietly. Dr. Leary's infamous 1960s commandment "Tune in, turn on, and drop out" had become a media mantra and a cultural strategy. Pot and acid made rapid inroads, displacing alcohol as drugs of choice. The Beatles and the Stones tripped out, and there was an atmosphere of intrepid inner exploration and raucous fun mixed with political outrage. Some of it was hedonism, some was dumb, and some of it became the bones of a generation.

Dr. Alpert's talk began at 7:30 P.M. in one of the student lounges. I expected a pep talk on "better living through modern chemistry" (then an ad slogan for DuPont Chemical). About fifty people attended, mostly students, spread out on couches, chairs, and the carpet. Instead of a tweedy Harvard psychedelic psychologist, the speaker entered wearing a scraggly beard, sandals, and a kind of white robe or dress. Dr. Alpert had just returned from India, where his name had been changed to Ram Dass. He said it meant "servant of God." He looked like a soapbox prophet in Hyde Park, which I'd just seen in London.

Instead of an opening paean to psychedelics, he began to relate his experience of living for six months in an ashram in the foothills of the Himalayas. He described meeting a guru who had a cataclysmic effect on his consciousness, so much so that he sequestered himself for six months in the guru's ashram to learn yoga and meditation. This was too weird for a portion of even this avid audience, and before long some departed. After a while, someone turned out the lights, and Ram Dass continued to talk in womblike darkness. In the dark, his disembodied voice fairly crackled with a kind of energy that permeated the room. He combined the excitement of a scientist with a new discovery and an explorer in *terra incognita*. He continued describing his experiences and responding to questions until 3:30 A.M.

As Ram Dass spoke of the interior transformation he had undergone, I began to experience one too. Subjectively it was like a figure-ground flip when, in one of those high-contrast images, you suddenly see the space instead of the shape. In my case I went from being the center of my universe to seeing myself as just one spark of awareness among billions. I understood in that moment that we are all on an evolutionary journey toward realization through infinite time and space.

It was more than a conceptual understanding. There was a feeling of meeting together in a deep space of love, and compassion for what Ram Dass called "our predicament." Two and a half years later, when I traveled to see the guru in India, I experienced precisely this feeling again, like déjà vu. However it happened, an old man in a blanket, whom I also came to call Maharaj-ji, came through Ram Dass that evening. The abode of love, compassion, and oneness in which the guru lived had moved temporarily to Connecticut.

To a twenty-year-old on an intensely personal quest for identity, this was revelatory. The idea that there were other beings who had actually made and completed this journey of inner exploration that I had only imagined was astounding. Maybe the journey wasn't quite so personal after all.

The next day I sought out Ram Dass and visited with him at the Winters' home. Something had clicked that needed further exploration. Whatever I had experienced, I wanted more of it. I have almost no recollection of what was said between us in that exchange. I know I felt awe and gratitude, though as we talked I realized Ram Dass was very much on his journey, as I was on mine. Later I came to realize he sometimes had a difficult time when people associated him with the transmission of that state. What could he say? "Sorry, that wasn't me talking"? I think it drove him to work harder on his own "stuff."

He was always completely, refreshingly out front about his own desire system and need for approval, and he used his neuroses as "grist for the mill." Rather than sweep things under the rug, he used the meanderings of his psyche as humorous fodder for his talks. There was no "holier than thou." It was more wholly than holy, more practical than pious. I think other people, too, appreciated how Ram Dass used himself as a case study for his inner research. The confluence of his psychological training, his openness from psychedelics, and his synthesis of Eastern religion made him a perfect resource for consciousness evolving during the upheaval of the 1960s. He managed to bring it together in under-standable language. And it didn't hurt that he told a good story.

Over the next two years I drove up periodically from Wesleyan to visit Ram Dass, following I-91 from Connecticut through Massachu-setts to where he was staying at his family's summer place, a farm on a lake near Franklin, New Hampshire. In warm weather he stayed in a tiny guest cottage without water or plumbing that he made into a cozy retreat, or *kuti,* where he meditated, practiced yoga, and cooked a daily pot of *khichri,* rice and lentils mixed together. In the winter he moved into the servants' quarters of the main house in the attic over the kitchen.

Ram Dass taught me the basics of yoga and meditation and recom-mended some of the writings of the saints and yogis he had come to know of in India. *Pranayama* (breath energy practices) and saying *mantras* (sacred syllables) became part of my routine. I learned to cook *khichri* and make *chapatis,* Indian flatbread.

Ram Dass's father, George Alpert, was a lawyer who had been presi-dent of the New York, New Haven, and Hartford Railroad. He and his fiancée, Phyllis, were often at the house when I came up to visit Ram Dass in Franklin. They were extraordinarily hospitable, and I felt like extended family. Clearly Ram Dass's new manifestation had left them at a loss after his career at Harvard, but they loved who he had become, and they didn't really care why. George continued to call him Richard and seemed bemused by the assortment of mostly young people who kept turning up. It was all a bit of a mystery, but the love had infected them too.

Although he was mostly a hermit that year, in 1967 Ram Dass also gave a talk at the Bucks County Seminar House in Pennsylvania. In Franklin, along with his daily *sadhana,* or spiritual practice, he worked on a manuscript about his experience in India. In the winter of 1967–68 he gave an extended series of talks at a sculpture studio on the East Side of Manhattan. The same people showed up night after night, often with friends. Others were beginning to be affected by the extraordinary energy and presence that accompanied his talks.

Ram Dass spoke with self-deprecating humor, using his own missteps as counterpoint to the intensely serious journey he was illuminating. His self-revealing honesty in facing his personal demons and his delight in the absurdity of a Harvard psychologist encountering Eastern mysticism became hallmarks of his presentations. He linked his psychedelic drug experiences, which many of us had experienced by then, to the dissolution of the ego in Eastern philosophy. And he used his encounter with the guru as a model for attaining the higher consciousness he now saw as the goal, enlightenment.

Soon after graduation from college in 1969 I was drafted and called in for a physical. Bearded and hirsute, I stood in my underwear with a string of prayer beads repeating a Hindu *mantra* during the entire day of prodding and poking. The psychologist was the last station along the line, and by the time I arrived at his station I had been praying with such intensity I could hardly see. The psychologist, who looked as though he was unhappily doing his alternative service himself, disqualified me. I was put in a 1-Y and later a 4-F classification, which meant unfit for service. That left me free to join the young people, students, hippies, flower children, and others who had heard Ram Dass in person or by word of mouth and were arriving at the driveway in Franklin. My younger brother and sister went to the rock festival at Woodstock while I meditated at yogi camp with Ram Dass.

Outdoor weekend *darshans*, spiritual gatherings with Ram Dass, evolved under a tree in the yard, with George's gracious permission, into summer camp. We were a ragtag group of twenty to thirty on an "Inward Bound" adventure. Tent platforms and a *darshan* house went up in the woods above the farm, and Sufi dances and yoga classes were held on George's beloved three-hole golf course. Group meditations and yoga were part of the daily schedule, as Ram Dass sought to transfer his experience in India to this motley cadre of would-be yogis. We made up with enthusiasm and love for what we lacked in disciplined renunciation. By summer's end the weekend crowd under the trees numbered in the hundreds. Some of the campers were like ships passing in the night, some have perished, and others are still in touch, now grandparents.

Ram Dass's painstakingly written manuscript about his India trip found no takers in the publishing world. He continued giving public talks, and that fall he drove cross-country to California to teach at a nascent center for psychological and spiritual growth in Big Sur called Esalen. Esalen assigned him housing with a writer and his wife, John and Catty Bleibtreu. John noticed the transcripts from Ram Dass's talks at the New York sculpture studio as he pulled the suitcase out of his car. He asked if he could take a look. He thought there were some good stories, and he checked off the ones he liked.

From Esalen, Ram Dass drove to the Lama Foundation near Taos, New Mexico, a back-to-the-land commune of artists and hippies that he had helped found before his trip to India. Steve Durkee, a visionary artist who had spearheaded an art group called USCO in New York, was a friend and the main man at Lama. He also noticed the transcript and asked what it was. Over dinner with five or six of the resident artists at Lama, they brainstormed ways that the passages John Bleibtreu had checked could be illustrated.

During the fall and winter of 1969–70, Ram Dass, Steve, and the Lama commune went to work on making Ram Dass's words into text art. At his talks Ram Dass gave out postcards that people could send in to Lama to get a copy of whatever emerged. I even did my part and copied some of the photos of saints Ram Dass had brought back from India.

In early 1970 the Bountiful Lord's Delivery Service at Lama mailed out several thousand copies of a twelve-by-twelve-inch corrugated box, the contents and printing of which were financed from the proceeds of Ram Dass's lectures. It was distributed at no charge. In the box was a core book from the transcripts called *From Bindu to Ojas* (Sanskrit for "From Material to Spiritual Energy"). It was printed on brown paper and hand bound with twine. Included were a booklet about Ram Dass's journey to the guru titled *HisStory*, a section of spiritual practices called the *Spiritual Cookbook*, holy pictures to put up on your refrigerator or altar (some of which are reproduced in this volume), a book list called *Painted Cakes*, and an LP record of chants and spirituals from the contemporary scene. It was a true do-it-yourself kit for a spiritual journey.

The summer of 1970 saw a brief revival of the yogi camp at Franklin. After Ram Dass had been on the road and lecturing for a year, the numbers began to be overwhelming for George's farm. But from those evanescent groups came the genesis of a Western *satsang,* a community of seekers.

Ram Dass continued to lecture and travel, but was mindful that Maharaj-ji had told him he could return to India in two years. (*Maharaj-ji* is a common honorific in India that literally means "great king." In this book *Maharaj-ji* usually refers to Ram Dass's guru, Neem Karoli Baba, because most of the time that's how he was addressed.) Finding himself beginning to burn out after all the public exposure, Ram Dass was thinking about going back to continue his work on himself. Demand for the *Bindu to Ojas* box quickly exceeded the supply from the original printing. Steve Durkee was working on turning it into a book with distribution by Crown Publishers, with an editor named Bruce Harris. It was titled *Be Here Now.*

Ram Dass's guru, whom he had referred to only as Maharaj-ji in his talks and the box, had told him not to tell people about him. However, Ram Dass gave permission for three of us "students" to write to a devotee in India to see if Maharaj-ji would allow us to come see him. Jeff Kagel (later Krishna Das), Danny Goleman (who later became the psychology editor at the *New York Times* and wrote a bestseller, *Emotional Intelligence*), and I wrote to K. K. (Krishna Kumar) Sah asking him to please request Maharaj-ji's blessing on our journey to India to see him.

When K.K. was growing up, Maharaj-ji was a kind of foster parent to him, and he still considers himself something of a child in relation to Maharaj-ji. When Ram Dass first met Maharaj-ji, Maharaj-ji sent him to stay at K.K.'s home, so K.K. felt a special responsibility for Ram Dass. Years later K.K. related what happened when he took our letters to Maharaj-ji. He laid the letters on the bed where Maharaj-ji was sitting, and Maharaj-ji inquired what they were.

K.K. said they were from students of Ram Dass who wanted to come see him. Maharaj-ji said, "What do I have to do with these people? Tell them not to come!"

K.K. had been lovingly feeding Maharaj-ji slices of apple. Now he stopped. He put his head down and pouted. Maharaj-ji went on talking to other people and finally looked down at K.K.

"What's the matter?"

"I can't tell them that, Maharaj-ji. They are Ram Dass's students."

This went on for a while. Finally, Maharaj-ji said, "Tell them whatever you want."

We got a letter back from K.K. in his exquisite hand. It said, "Maharaj-ji doesn't invite anyone to come, but his doors are always open. If you should find yourself near Kainchi Ashram while in India. . . ." That nuanced response was enough to start us buying tickets and securing visas.

Instead of the expected culture shock on arriving in India, I felt completely natural. Everything was out on the street without pretense, nothing hidden. Even the beggars with deformities were part of some seamless, fragrantly decadent whole. We traveled from Bombay (now Mumbai) to Delhi, and then from Delhi to Nainital, where we hoped to find K. K. Sah. The last leg of the trip was a twelve-hour ride up to the mountains on a gear-grinding, diesel-spewing U.P. Roadways bus. Nainital is a "hill station" constructed around a scenic lake by the Brits to escape the summer heat of the plains. The atmosphere literally changes as the bus ascends miles of switchbacks from the dust and traffic below.

From Nainital, coming down the last switchbacks from the hamlet of Bhowali into the valley of Kainchi, we caught glimpses of the orange spires of the ashram *mandir* (temple). I experienced a profound feeling of coming home, a little like the last miles to my grandparents' place on Long Island, where we would go for the summer after school let out.

As we arrived K.K. said, "Maharaj-ji, they are here now."

Maharaj-ji said, "Feed them," and sent a bunch of bananas.

It was a good sign. We were asked to take *prasad,* food. We sat down to piles of spicy potatoes and *puris,* deep-fried bread, on leaf plates. I ate three mounds of potatoes and seventeen *puris.*

After eating, K.K. brought us to where Maharaj-ji was sitting on a wooden *tukhat,* or bed, in his "office." There was no hesitation, no unfamiliarity.

Maharaj-ji told K.K., "They are good persons."

K.K., who was glad the newcomers were being treated so well, replied without missing a beat, "I never bring bad people to you."

Everyone laughed, and he proceeded to interpret for us. Maharaj-ji said we came from good families, and he played a bit with our clothing. Later we went back to Nainital to stay at a family hotel owned by K.K.'s cousins and were permitted to come back to the ashram every few days.

Meeting Maharaj-ji was a total flashback to that first night at Wesleyan. The feeling inside was the same, the same figure-ground reversal; I became a speck floating in the ocean of existence instead of the focal point of my own egocentric universe. Maharaj-ji's overflowing love and affection made me feel completely safe. I was soaking it up like a sponge. Though I was meeting him for the first time, I felt as if I had known him and he had known me forever. I had come home, to a real home in the heart, to a family that transcended blood relationship.

Ram Dass eventually joined us in Nainital after accompanying Swami Muktananda on a world tour. By the time he arrived, it was nearly Thanksgiving, and Maharaj-ji had left the hills, which got very cold in winter, for the warmer plains. We didn't know where he had gone, and we didn't find him for more than a month. Actually he found us.

In 1972 after a year in India, Ram Dass stopped off in London and gave several lectures. Back in the United States, he found himself a spiritual celebrity because of the publication of *Be Here Now,* which struck a cultural chord and had sold out several printings.

He traveled and lectured constantly. The year 1973 saw the publication of a six-record box, *Love Serve Remember,* which I and a number of those in

the recent Indian cohort worked on. It was based on a series of talks with Paul Gorman on WBAI radio in New York and produced at a media commune called ZBS in upstate New York.

I delayed returning to India to complete the record project, and in September 1973 I had just arrived at Franklin for a visit with Ram Dass when a telegram arrived with news that Maharaj-ji had left his body—he had died. I went through a cascade of reactions one after another: grief, regret that I had not made it back, gratitude that I was among "family" when the news came, and a realization that the bath of love was still there. Any of the Buddhist teachings on impermanence that had not taken hold were now being reinforced big time. It was all changing. Maharaj-ji's new teaching was, "Sink or swim."

Some of us made a brief pilgrimage back to India to visit the Indian family and view Maharaj-ji's ashes. When we resumed our lives back in the States, there remained a strong presence of the guru, yet there was no form, and it was difficult to describe. Many in the *satsang* were inspired to service in some shape or form.

Ram Dass continued lecturing and teaching, published several more books, and worked to change models for social service, dying, and consciousness in the culture. He helped start a group called the Seva Foundation (*seva* means "service" in Sanskrit) meant to bring the values of *karma yoga* (the yoga of selfless service) to social action. I saw him periodically, though he was based on the West Coast and I was still living on Long Island.

Ram Dass had a *murti* (statue) of Hanuman, the monkey god of service and devotion, carved in Jaipur, India, and shipped to the United States through the port of Los Angeles. While devotees searched for land for a Hanuman temple, this beautiful fifteen-hundred-pound white marble flying monkey took up temporary residence in Arroyo Hondo, New Mexico, on land belonging to one of our India crew.

There was disagreement among the devotees about how to consecrate the *murti*. Some wanted to do it with a Brahmin priest and full Hindu *puja* (worship rituals). Others were ready to open the box and just say hello. One of us, tripping on LSD, jumped into the crate with Hanuman and plowed through all the wood shavings, newspaper, and chips until finally he brought Hanuman into the light. Hanuman was then set up in a barn on the land. Later he moved with his host to a shed on the outskirts of Taos. Gatherings began to happen there to commemorate the annual anniversary of Maharaj-ji's death (final merging or *mahasama-dhi*). Eventually the land was purchased from the *satsang* member, and it became Maharaj-ji's ashram in America.

In 1975 Hilda Charlton, a teacher in New York who had introduced us to Swami Muktananda, met a housewife from Brooklyn who had experienced a transformation while learning yoga at a Jack LaLanne studio and was (supposedly) in communication with Maharaj-ji. Her name was Joyce; Hilda called her Joya. Hilda introduced Ram Dass to her by telling him Maharaj-ji was living in Joya's basement in Brooklyn. Ram Dass was soon inducted into the inner circle and began receiving the accelerated esoteric course.

Joya was able to induce euphoric states in those around her, and she certainly seemed to enter into extraordinary out-of-body states herself too. Sometimes they were hard to distinguish from the constant melodrama that went on around her. The Joya saga continued for a couple years.

Ram Dass was spending time in New York. He and I began work on this book along with a photographer friend, Peter Simon. At the time it was envisioned as a photographic tour guide to spirituality in the West. Thirty-five years later it has become a deeper and more joyful reflection on the journey than either of us could have expected.

Ram Dass came to the belated conclusion that Joya's secret teachings were more hypocrisy than esoteric revelation, and he left. He gave a chagrined account of his experience in a front-page mea culpa in *New Age Journal* titled "Egg on My Beard." I stayed on longer in the Joya scene out of a misplaced sense of loyalty, and the manuscript sat on a shelf, forgotten for a couple decades. Joya caused many bridges to burn, and the one between Ram Dass and me took a while to rebuild. Gradually we resumed contact through the Seva Foundation, the ashram in Taos, *satsang* gatherings, events like the Home-Aid benefit in New York, and generally sharing Maharaj-ji's love, which remains the constant glue in our lives.

Ram Dass was back on tour, speaking and leading retreats. When he wasn't on the road, he lived in northern California with an artist he had formed a bond with, working on book and video projects, and a prototype for a radio call-in show.

In 1993 I met Kate. She attracted me, and our karmic stars were clearly and inevitably crossing. In November 1996, Ram Dass married us at her family's summer place atop a hill on Martha's Vineyard. As my newly betrothed danced with Ram Dass at the reception, he seemed to pass out and collapsed on the dance floor. I was engaged with other guests and didn't notice. He revived quickly and sat out the rest of the party. Kate said he was surprised at what had happened. The band played on, but later the incident seemed like foreshadowing. The next day he departed to lead a retreat in the Caribbean.

In February 1997 I had a call from Dr. Larry Brilliant, a *satsang* brother in California, who said Ram Dass had suffered a devastating hemorrhagic stroke, a bleed in his brain, and might not survive. It had probably happened during the night, and he had not been able to summon help until his manager, Jai Lakshman, called from New Mexico. Ram Dass managed to knock the phone off the hook. Jai, hearing no coherent response, said, "Are you in trouble? Tap once for yes, twice for no." After a single tap he called Ram Dass's secretary, Marlene, who lived nearby. She found him on the floor and called 911. Ram Dass's survival and recovery were in doubt. People were praying for him on both sides of the world.

The next years were a Sisyphean struggle to adapt to disability and to regain first his speech and then as much body function as he could. His storytelling gift had disappeared into aphasia, and his right side was paralyzed. Fortunately, he is left-handed. His mind, his consciousness, remained completely intact, if not expanded. His heart, his sense of compassion, became a glowing jewel of pure presence.

Before the stroke Ram Dass had been working on a book about aging. Needless to say, his understanding and approach changed. Laboriously, and with assistance from another writer, Mark Matousek, Ram Dass completed *Still Here,* which was published in 2000. Few readers were aware of the magnitude of accomplishment required just to complete the manuscript. Mickey Lemle, a documentary filmmaker, made an amazing film about Ram Dass during this period called *Fierce Grace.* It chronicles Ram Dass's passage to a deeper place in himself—an evolution that continues as he uses his own suffering as grist for the mill.

Ram Dass began traveling intermittently, lecturing and speaking at retreats, though on a much curtailed schedule. The aphasia punctuated his talks in new ways, so they ran slower and deeper. His old friend Wavy Gravy, of the Hog Farm commune, said, "He used to be the master of the one-liner. Now he's the master of the ocean liner."

In October 2004 Ram Dass once more undertook a journey to India, to revisit the temple in the hills where he had first immersed himself in yoga and Hinduism and learned to search within without chemical enhancement. Kate and I and our by now two children, ages five and seven, made the journey independently, and we all met there for the harvest festival of the goddess, Durga Puja. It was an emotional and deeply moving pilgrimage for Ram Dass, one that he had thought he might never be able to make again. The simplicity, silence, and maternal affection of the surroundings were a source of great renewal and, even with the relatively inaccessible steps and doorways of the ashram and its bare-bones comforts, he thrived.

He stayed for about ten days, and our family remained for the rest of a three-month sojourn while he journeyed back to California via Singapore. It was a lengthy trip with stopovers, some thirty-six hours. When he got back to California he was home for a day, then flew to Hawaii to conduct a long scheduled retreat on Maui. At the end of the retreat he developed a high fever and at the emergency room on Maui was diagnosed with an acute urinary infection that had migrated to his kidneys and into his bloodstream. Pope John had died from a similar infection.

We corresponded by worried e-mails from Rishikesh in India with Ram Dass's caregivers. He was in the hospital for nearly a month. Once again he almost bought the farm. The bug he had was resistant to most antibiotics and made urinating exquisitely painful. By the time he got out of the hospital, he was weak and further travel was out of the question. Sridhar Silberfein, an old friend who had organized the Maui retreat, found him a house and helped set up a household so he could recover. It was slow going. Since then, with the exception of one trip to the mainland to visit the Hanuman temple in Taos, Ram Dass has stayed on Maui. The tranquil atmosphere and tropical climate are conducive to health and profound healing, as is a supportive community.

When he wound up in Maui in November 2004, his finances, long dependent on lecturing and touring, were depleted. Maharaj-ji had told him not to accept his inheritance from his father, and Ram Dass had always raised funds for others' causes. Friends, students, and supporters, notably author and teacher Wayne Dyer, a fellow Maui resident, rallied to raise money so Ram Dass could live there without traveling.

Having returned to New York, I went to visit Ram Dass in Maui in early spring of 2005. He was slowly regaining strength, eating better and working with an acupuncturist and Chinese herbal doctor, who thirty years before had been a student when Ram Dass taught the first summer at Naropa Institute in Boulder, Colorado. He was doing serious physical therapy again for the first time since he'd stopped a year after the stroke. Annual retreats began to be held in Hawaii. Another of Ram Dass's first students, Krishna Das, now the chant master of the yoga circuit, joined him leading retreats that brought students from the mainland. A new website was set up at www.ramdass.org.

When we met again the following fall, we recalled the long dormant manuscript sitting in my basement. We decided it was time to bring it to light and see what was there. As we tried to make sense of what we said in the 1970s, reworked it, and brought it into the present moment, a kind of joy suffused the process. The 1960s and 1970s are long gone, yet the sense of unconditional love that was awakened then—the ocean tide of the guru's compassion, the journey set in motion within us—is still the beacon of our shared universe.

Over the years something has crystallized in Ram Dass. Elements from the rainbow of his experiences in academia, psychology, psychedelics, India, and the stroke have coalesced into a clear white light of wisdom. Working with him, I have new appreciation for the nuance of his perceptions about the layers of consciousness. When I wax pedantic, he brings it back to the heart. When I am mired in ego, he subtly changes the point of view to the soul.

Our karmic calamities, the grace notes of circumstance, the twists and turns of this path, are an unfathomable mystery. Exploring its dimensions with Ram Dass, chuckling over the illusions, missteps, and potholes along the way, is a delight. Change is the only constant; the more things change, the more they stay the same.

It's only love. There is nothing more. May we all be loved, and be love, now.

the path of the heart

IMAGINE FEELING MORE LOVE from someone than you have ever known. You're being loved even more than your mother loved you when you were an infant, more than you were ever loved by your father, your child, or your most intimate lover—anyone. This lover doesn't need anything from you, isn't looking for personal gratification, and only wants your complete fulfillment.

You are loved just for being who you are, just for existing. You don't have to do anything to earn it. Your shortcomings, your lack of self-esteem, physical perfection, or social and economic success—none of that matters. No one can take this love away from you, and it will always be here.

Imagine that being in this love is like relaxing endlessly into a warm bath that surrounds and supports your every movement, so that every thought and feeling is permeated by it. You feel as though you are dissolving into love.

This love is actually part of you; it is always flowing through you. It's like the subatomic texture of the universe, the dark matter that connects everything. When you tune in to that flow, you will feel it in your own heart—not your physical heart or your emotional heart, but your spiritual heart, the place you point to in your chest when you say, "I am."

This is your deeper heart, your intuitive heart. It is the place where the higher mind, pure awareness, the subtler emotions, and your soul identity all come together and you connect to the universe, where presence and love are.

Unconditional love really exists in each of us. It is part of our deep inner being. It is not so much an active emotion as a state of being. It's not "I love you" for this or that reason, not "I love you if you love me." It's love for no reason, love without an object. It's just sitting in love, a love that incorporates the chair and the room and permeates everything around. The thinking mind is extinguished in love.

If I go into the place in myself that is love and you go into the place in yourself that is love, we are together in love. Then you and I are truly *in* love, the state of *being* love. That's the entrance to Oneness. That's the space I entered when I met my guru.

Years ago in India I was sitting in the courtyard of the little temple in the Himalayan foothills. Thirty or forty of us were there around my guru, Maharaj-ji. This old man wrapped in a plaid blanket was sitting on a plank bed, and for a brief uncommon interval everyone had fallen silent. It was a meditative quiet, like an open field on a windless day or a deep clear lake without a ripple. I felt waves of love radiating toward me, washing over me like a gentle surf on a tropical shore, immersing me, rocking me, caressing my soul, infinitely accepting and open.

I was nearly overcome, on the verge of tears, so grateful and so full of joy it was hard to believe it was happening. I opened my eyes and looked around, and I could feel that everyone else around me was experiencing the same thing. I looked over at my guru. He was just sitting there, looking around, not doing anything. It was just his *being,* shining like the sun equally on everyone. It wasn't directed at anyone in particular. For him it was nothing special, just his own nature.

This love is like sunshine, a natural force, a completion of what is, a bliss that permeates every particle of existence. In Sanskrit it's called *sat-cit-ananda*, "truth-consciousness-bliss," the bliss of consciousness of existence. That vibrational field of *ananda* love permeates everything; everything in that vibration is in love. It's a different state of being beyond the mind. We were transported by Maharaj-ji's love from one vibrational level to another, from the ego to the soul level. When Maharaj-ji brought me to my soul through that love, my mind just stopped working. Perhaps that's why unconditional love is so hard to describe, and why the best descriptions come from mystic poets. Most of our descriptions are from the point of view of conditional love, from an interpersonal standpoint that just dissolves in that unconditioned place.

When Maharaj-ji was near me, I was bathed in that love. One of the other Westerners with Maharaj-ji, Larry Brilliant, said:

How do I explain who Maharaj-ji was and how he did what he did? I don't have any explanation. Maybe it was his love of God. I can't explain who he was. I can almost begin to understand how he loved everybody. I mean, that was his job, he was a saint. Saints are supposed to love everybody.

But that's not what always staggered me, not that he loved everybody—but that when I was sitting in front of him I loved everybody. That was the hardest thing for me to understand, how he could so totally transform the spirit of people who were with him and bring out not just the best in us, but something that wasn't even in us, that we didn't know. I don't think any of us were ever as good or as pure or as loving in our whole lives as we were when we were sitting in front of him.[1]

Welcome to the path of the heart! Believe it or not, this can be your reality, to be loved unconditionally and to begin to become that love. This path of love doesn't go anywhere. It just brings you more here, into the present moment, into the reality of who you already are. This path takes you out of your mind and into your heart.

> When someone asked Maharaj-ji how to meditate, he said, "Meditate the way Christ meditated. . . . He lost himself in love."

Love is a natural human inclination. People in other times and places have found this path in many different cultural situations. In India it's called *bhakti yoga,* finding ultimate union through love, a tradition that stretches back many centuries. *Bhakti yoga* practices are a way to enter into unconditional love, into the radiant heart, to dissolve oneself in the ocean of love, in the One. Later in the book you will meet a few of the Indian "saints" who have become that love. We will look at ways you can also tread on that path. There's no formula. Each of us has our own key to unlock the reality of our heart.

Falling into Love

The first time you experience unconditional love as an adult, it may be a gentle melting of a glacier. Or it may be more of a cataclysm, like a giant earthquake that shakes you to your inner core. You are falling in love, but the act of receiving love that intense and all-encompassing changes your conception of yourself. You can't swim in such a vast ocean and remain entirely in the small pond of your limited self. Even if that opening is only for an instant, even if it goes away and is apparently forgotten, that moment of realization, of the heart opening, colors the rest of a lifetime. There's no going back. The lingering taste of that ultimate sweetness remains and won't be denied.

Jesus used the metaphor of a fisherman. When you first feel that depth of joy, you are caught in the net of pure love by the divine fisherman; you're hooked on that love.

My guru is like a fly fisherman. The ego twists and pulls and runs out the line trying to escape, but each time the hook of divine love sets more deeply until finally the little you, the personality and all its habits, the bundle of thoughts and desires, surrenders to the greater Self, that being of pure love and consciousness that keeps pulling you in to merge.

When I was first got to India, I abhorred the idea of gurus. I was attracted to Buddhism, which appealed to the psychologist in me. How did I end up sitting in front of a Hindu guru? When I first met him, I hardly knew what I was doing there myself.

But when Maharaj-ji immersed me in his unconditional love, it altered the course of my life. My view of myself completely changed. That meeting opened my heart. In that moment I opened up to the guru—not just to the old man in the blanket sitting in front of me, but to a place within him that reflected my true Self. That spiritual Self is the source of unconditional love.

When I returned to the States after that first time in India, I felt as though I was carrying a precious jewel in my heart and I wanted to share it. I could talk about my heart opening and the new awareness it had brought. But the guru—I didn't really talk much about the guru, because the idea seemed so inappropriate for the West.

For one thing, there is always a mixed reaction to the notion of surrendering to another person. Surrendering in our culture is almost always seen as negative. We don't like being told what to do; we like to figure it out for ourselves. Surrendering means giving up our power, and it usually has to do with ego power or sexual dominance.

The term "guru" evokes images of con men and hucksters rather than spiritual masters. Of course, we are right to be cynical when we see so-called gurus get entangled in money, sex, and power. Seductions, tax evasion, expensive cars, high-priced *mantras*—even Hollywood had its fun with gurus and cults (e.g., *The Love Guru*). The image of charismatic corrupters preying on weak-minded followers is hard to avoid. Most people wouldn't know a real guru if they fell over him or her, and certainly few have ever met one.

At first Maharaj-ji seemed almost like a magical being to me. He had incredible spiritual powers, but slowly I began to appreciate that it was the ocean of his love that had truly hooked me. And that was the real thing. Here was a flesh-and-blood being who was living in a state of unconditional love all the time. That love allowed me to surrender, to accept his guidance on the inner journey to find that love in myself.

Later I encountered other beings, some living and some gone from the body, who helped me see more of the road map for this path of the heart. These beings come in all shapes, sizes, and manifestations, as we all do. They are signposts and guides to help us on the *bhakti marg*, the road to love, even though we each have to travel it ourselves. Some of the beings who have inspired me are the ones who have also inspired this book. I hope they will help you on your way too.

Unconditional love dissolves any rational hesitation as we become drunk on its sweetness. We are like moths circling a candle flame, immolating ourselves in a fire of living love.

LIVING FLAME OF LOVE

Oh, living flame of love,
how tenderly you penetrate
the deepest core of my being!
Finish what you began.
Tear the veil from this sweet encounter.

Oh, gentle fiery blade!
Oh, beautiful wound!
You soothe me with your blazing caress.
You pay off all my old debts,
and offer me a taste of the eternal.
In slaying me, you transform death into life.

Oh, flaming lantern!
You illuminate the darkest pockets of my soul.
Where once I wallowed in bitter separation
now, with exquisite intensity,
I radiate warmth and light to my Beloved.

How peacefully, how lovingly
you awaken my heart,
that secret place where you alone dwell within me!
Your breath on my face is delicious,
calming and galvanizing at once.
How delicately, how lucidly
you make me crazy with love for you!

—St. John of the Cross,[2] translated by Mirabai Starr

Whatever your metaphor (and you can choose—and mix—your own), whether it's succumbing to the softness of the ultimate romance, being submerged in a tidal wave of love, or being pulled into the gravitational field of a star, once you have experienced unconditional love, you have nowhere to go. You can run, but you can't hide. The seed is planted, and it will grow in its own time. You can only grow into who you truly are.

You may think you're free to come and go and play where you will, but the Beloved has taken you for his or her own, and in reality you can only surrender more and more to that divine attraction. Slowly but surely, in a moment or over thousands of lifetimes, the Beloved reels you in until you merge back into the unitary state of *sat-cit-ananda,* the truth-consciousness-bliss of the Self.

Family and Friends

The first day I met my guru, Maharaj-ji, a bond formed with him that changed my life irrevocably. A man from the nearby town of Nainital was translating the conversation into English for me. His name was Krishna Kumar, or "K.K.," Sah. At the end of that encounter Maharaj-ji asked him to take me to his home. He told him to feed me "double *roti,*" or toast, presumably because I was a Westerner unfamiliar with Indian food.

K.K. first saw me as an uptight Western stranger and didn't know what to make of me. Yet he had received an order from his guru and, out of deference reaching back to his childhood, he obeyed without question. Without hesitation he and his sister and brother absorbed me into the loving world of their family. They treated each other playfully as spiritual beings, not just as siblings, and they treated me as a family member. Four decades later we're still in that relationship.

Overnight I was introduced to a world where miraculous beings, saints and gurus, are part of the warp and weft of everyday life. It was nothing overt or messianic. These people were just living their lives. What to them was their ordinary routine allowed me to assimilate a sea change in my outlook for which I had no previous reference points.

K.K. and his family had grown up with Maharaj-ji. In India traditional families carry on *bhakti* practices that suffuse every part of life. Love is the unspoken language. With multiple generations living in joint homes, that living transmission provides a bridge for pure love from infancy into childhood and over the hormonal roller coaster of adolescence into adulthood. A family guru or a spiritual elder gives younger generations glimpses of unbounded love. Maybe you've had a grandparent or someone like that in your family too.

K.K.'s sister, Bina, who like him remains unmarried, squatted in the kitchen over a wood fire making *chapatis*. I had just reached the point of stuffed satisfaction from one of her amazing meals when K.K. engaged me in conversation. As soon as I turned my head to talk to K.K., Bina whisked another *chapati* and a helping of *subji* (vegetables) onto my brass *thali* (plate). There was no chance to say, "Thanks" or "No thanks." They had the routine down. I ate it all. In India it's an insult if you don't eat everything served to you, because food is so valuable. This happened a couple more times, and pleasure began to become pain. But K.K. and Bina were teasing me with such innocent delight I couldn't help but enjoy it all, even the digestive discomfort.

K.K. is about my age, a few years younger. His connection to holy beings reaches back generations. Maharaj-ji first came to visit his home when he was a child. K.K.'s father, Bhawani Das Sah, was a Circle Inspector of Police for the Kumaon hill district of the British Raj. Part of his duty was to open and close the great temple at Badrinath high in the Himalayas at the beginning and end of the summer season and to keep track of police matters throughout the sprawling district. In the early twentieth century, motor roads were almost nonexistent in the hill area, and he traveled on horseback or on foot. He was a deeply spiritual man, and on his tours of duty K.K.'s father took the opportunity to visit the remote ashrams of many saints and yogis for whom the hill area is a traditional retreat.

He became a devotee of several great saints, known and unknown, and they came to his home when they passed through the town. Neem

Karoli Baba—Maharaj-ji—was one of them. K.K. remembers it as an occasion for sweets and celebration. The first time Maharaj-ji came to the house, he asked where the bed was that another great saint, Hairakhan Baba, had slept on, and he lay down on it.

K.K.'s father died when K.K. was still quite young, and Maharaj-ji as the family guru became in many respects his father figure—but an unusual one! K.K. would skip school to hang out with Maharaj-ji on his rambles in the hills. His schoolteacher, a devotee, would mark him present as long as K.K. would in turn arrange for him to see Maharaj-ji. On an infrequent occasion when K.K. was actually in class, his teacher said, "You have been absent so much, now that you are present I am going to mark you absent!"

K.K. not only translated the language for me (his English was very good, working as he did as a clerk for the Municipal Board), but conveyed through his being the love flowing between him and Maharaj-ji, and from Maharaj-ji to me. Living with K.K., eating his sister Bina's cooking from the wood fire, watching their daily *puja,* or worship, at the family altar, and feeling the love and respect they had for the saints gave me a cultural context for the changes I was going through. They reinforced the heart connection that Maharaj-ji had opened like a tunnel into the profound depth of my being. The way that K.K. honored and loved the saints gave me a framework for what was happening inside me.

Even so, that experience of the heart was at first too unfamiliar for me. In retrospect, forty years later, I see how I interpreted what occurred with Maharaj-ji through my mind. During our first encounter, he told me my thoughts about my mother from the previous night, which he could not possibly have known. It blew me away. Initially I focused on the fact that Maharaj-ji had read my mind. It took ten years before I began to realize that what had actually changed me was the opening of my heart.

At the time I was totally shaken up by that experience of his reading my mind. I looked down at the ground, thinking that if he could read that part of my mind, then the many shameful secrets I was enumerating to myself must be plain to him too. I hadn't reckoned on the consequences of meeting someone who knew everything about me!

Filled with guilt, I finally looked up at Maharaj-ji. His face was only a few inches from mine, and as I looked into his eyes, he looked back at me with so much love, love that was unconditional, all-knowing, and completely accepting. It was like a shower or a bath of love that cleared away all the impurities I was carrying from the past.

Because I knew that he knew everything about me, I felt forgiven. He knew all of it, and he still loved me. It was so beautiful.

His love washed away all the guilt and shame I had been holding, feelings that were the unconscious props of my personality. With that one glance the house of cards of my ego collapsed, and suddenly for the first time in my adult life I saw myself as a pure soul.

For ten years after that, people asked me what it was in that meeting that had changed me, and all I could tell them was that he was a mind reader. It took a decade for me to realize that wasn't it. The mind reading softened me up, no doubt, but it was the love that opened my heart.

Up Close Impersonal

When we talk about the heart, it's easy to confuse the emotional heart and the spiritual heart, because, though they are both the heart, they represent different levels of consciousness. There's the emotional heart we're all familiar with, the one that romance and poetry are usually about (except mystic poetry). Emotional love encompasses all the dramatic feelings of attraction and hate and jealousy and sweetness and tenderness that make your heart throb, all these emotional states. It is laden with the hooks that continually create attachments and constantly affirm our egos.

Most emotions like fear, anger, lust, and envy are connected to our personality and the impulses from our conscious or unconscious mind, instincts for survival and procreation. Love is part of the emotional spectrum, but it is different because it emanates from our soul. Even when it becomes confused with our ego projections, love is actually from the higher essence of our being, the part that begins to merge with the spirit and approach the One.

Emotions come into being and are interpreted in our mind, arising and dissipating. If we're angry, we feel anger in our mind. The emotion and the external stimulus or internal impulse that triggers it (usually some frustration that leads to anger) comes into the mind and stirs the thoughts like a gust of wind passing through.

Siddhi Ma is an amazing woman who holds Maharaj-ji's ashrams together. She's had a great affinity for saints since childhood. After she was widowed and her children grown, she's lived continuously at Maharaj-ji's ashrams. She said about anger, "Once the fire starts, it will burn itself out." If you don't catch it at the impulse stage, it will only dissipate after causing distress for you or others.

Emotions do seem to have a life of their own, whether they come from habitual patterning or spontaneous reactions. Emotions give you multileveled information about your environment. Sensations stimulate emotions as you interact with people and situations. It's like a wave that lifts and carries you and sets you down again.

When we feel emotional love, we ride the wave, and when it recedes, we need love all over again. Our Western psyche is built on the need for emotional love. Our mind creates a whole reality around it. We *think* that's the way it is, that everybody needs emotional love, and that if we don't get it, we are deprived or insecure. Our minds tell us the more emotional love we get, the better off we are.

Our culture treats love almost entirely in connection with interpersonal relationships and interactions. Emotional love is based on external gratification, having our love reflected back to us. It's not grounded in feeling love from inside. That's why we keep needing more. When we love somebody emotionally, that need for feedback creates a powerful attachment. We get so caught up in the relationship that we rarely arrive at the essence of just dwelling in love.

Once I was deeply in love with a woman who broke up with me. I was in great emotional distress, but after some weeks I realized I was still in love. But I was no longer in love with her. She had left, we were permanently parted, and I had (unwillingly) come to terms with that. But I still felt love within me, I was carrying it around, and my heart was still wide open. I found I could be in love, with or without someone to receive it—a painful but deep realization that love is inside me, that love and the object of love aren't necessarily the same thing.

Love is actually a state of being, and a divine state at that, the state to which we all yearn to return. The outer love object stimulates a feeling of love, but the love is inside us. We interpret it as coming from outside us, so we want to possess love, and we reach outside for something that is already inside us.

The equation changes when we understand love in a more universal way, as a way to get to the One. We can try to possess the key to our hearts, to our Beloved, but sooner or later we find that is impossible. To possess the key is to lose it. Paradoxically, we have to let go of emotional love to find the soul love that illuminates us from within.

There's a story about the sixteenth-century poet-saint Tulsi Das, who wrote the vernacular Hindi *Ramayana* and many great devotional works. Tulsi Das was deeply in love with his wife. She said to him, "If you were *half* as attached to Lord Rām, to God, as you are to this impure body, you'd be liberated by now." That woke him up.

Maharaj-ji showed me the possibility of transforming personal into impersonal love. I experienced the extraordinary magnitude of his love, but I saw he didn't need anyone to love him back. At first I brought along all my old habits of emotional love. He became the object of my affections; I fell in love with him. From the first I could feel he loved me more than any other person who had ever loved me. It gave me a new dimension of love, something I had never felt before. And it persisted. It was love on another plane.

His presence was something I could only recognize from inside my soul. The deeper I went in my own being, the more fully I could feel his love, the more the spigot opened and the more the love flowed. No matter how deep I went, there was more love. Finally it was too much for my normal waking consciousness.

Gradually, I began to see how impersonal his love was. I realized it wasn't directed at me, but I could bathe in it, and when I bathed in it, all my negative thoughts and feelings were nullified. I felt it in me, and I thought, "Wow, this is someplace I've never been before." My neurotic ego had never allowed me to go there before.

The need for emotional gratification and the accompanying anxiety about losing it slowly fell away. Whenever I became afraid of losing it, I found I was still enveloped in more love than I'd ever felt. I would watch him mouthing, "*Rām, Rām, Rām,*" and feel a wave of love.

> I love you more than you can ever love yourself.
>
> —*Meher Baba*

The more I gave up my desire for personal love, the less distance there was between his being and mine, and I felt much closer to him. Since he left his body, my love for him has not been limited to his form. We are sharing the same love. We can just be, in love.

If I go deeper in myself, the love is greater. It's not just superficial. It didn't go away when he died. I used to feel I could only get that love in India, but now all I have to do is plumb the depth of the moment. At first I used Maharaj-ji as the source of love, but slowly I became sure that the same love is in me. It is a constant joy.

Now he's just here, laughing behind it all. And it's still all love. Maharaj-ji's teaching is just love. He's not critical. The more open I am, the more I can receive the love. It's the whole trip, the beginning, the middle, and the end.

Heart-Mind

For a moment let's call the place from which soul love emanates the heart-mind. When Ramana Maharshi, one of the Indian saints you will meet, experienced the Self in the middle of his chest, it wasn't his physical or emotional heart. It was his spiritual heart, in Sanskrit the *hridayam*, the seat of consciousness, what the Quakers call the "still, small voice of God."

The heart-mind is not the ego. Our ego is a constantly changing bundle of thoughts about who we *think* we are. We build an edifice of thought forms and feelings that we identify with. It's like a concept of self overlaid on a group of thoughts and emotions that we take as real. There's nothing bad about having an ego. Those thoughts and feelings are necessary for a healthy personality. But if you identify so strongly with the ego that you think that's all there is, that limited view can keep you from your deeper Self.

As a psychologist I was always dealing with that constellation of thought forms. My Western psychological self is based on the premise that I am my mind. It never opened a door to my heart-mind, not even through Freudian training and years of psychoanalysis.

I couldn't get to my spiritual heart through my rational mind. My mind had to stop for my heart to open. Or as Patanjali, in the *Yoga Sutras,* the foundation of the system of yoga, puts it, *"Yoga citta vritti nirodha,"* or, roughly translated, "The union (*yoga*) arises when the waves of thoughts (*vritti*) in consciousness (*citta*) cease (*nirodha*)."

When at our first meeting Maharaj-ji recited to me the intimate thoughts I had been having about my mother, who had died six months before, it brought my mind tumbling down. I hadn't voiced them to anyone. There was no way he could have known those things, and yet he knew my heart. The impossibility of his knowing my inmost thoughts and feelings,

> The reality about the cord of love that binds you and me, dear, is known to my soul alone; and my soul ever abides with you. Know this to be the essence of my love.
>
> —*Rām's message to Sita, in the* Ramayana[3]

coupled with my primal love and grief for my mother, just ripped me open. I couldn't think. He opened the door to my spiritual heart, to my heart-mind, through my love for my mother and his love for me. He loved me more than I had ever been loved before, though, as I have said, even after that heart opening for years I focused on the mind reading.

As I did spiritual practices, I began to witness my own mind from inside. I was aware of my eyes seeing, aware of feelings in my body. That witness consciousness is part of the heart-mind. The heart-mind is awareness turned inward, awareness of the spiritual universe within, and the quality of that awareness, the feeling that accompanies it, is love.

The Ātman, or divine Self, is separate from the body. This Ātman is One without a second, pure, self-luminous, without attributes, free, all-pervading. He is the eternal witness. Blessed is he who knows this Ātman, for though an embodied being, he shall be free from the changes and qualities pertaining to the body. He alone is ever united with Me.

—Srimad Bhagavatam 74

People instinctively identify with their awareness. When you ask people who they are, they point to their chest. That's where that awareness resides, not in the thinking mind in the head. That's the heart-mind. Cognitive psychology has never been able to find the mechanism of consciousness. Our awareness is individual in us, and it is also part of the larger awareness of God. It's not different. We are fingers or tendrils of God consciousness.

In the West people treat awareness as a thought process rather than a heart-mind process. But our awareness actually comes from the heart-mind. Shifting our identification from the ego to the heart-mind is the beginning of individual spiritual work. That pure awareness is the territory of the soul. One way to understand spiritual work within an individual incarnation is to see it as a process of shifting from identifying with our ego to identifying with the soul or spiritual self. The quality of the soul is not just awareness, but also love and compassion, peace and wisdom.

In India they distinguish more clearly between levels of the mind. There are three levels from the thinking mind to the heart-mind. The thinking mind is *manas*. The intuitive intellect and the faculty of discrimination is *buddhi*. Individual awareness, the pure sense of I-ness, is *ahamkara,* which is the heart-mind and the witness. All of these levels of mind emanate from the individual soul, or *jivatman,* which is our connection to the all-pervading, universal soul, the *ātman.*

It may be helpful to see these planes as a series of veils or illusions (*maya*) that keep us separate from the *ātman,* or universal soul. In another sense they are a schematic of the conscious universe. The universal consciousness of the *ātman* is localized in the *jivatman,* our individual soul. Our most basic experience of selfhood is the individual awareness, the *ahamkara.* The higher mind, or *buddhi,* is the discriminating wisdom that mediates between pure awareness and the world of form. The everyday continuum of disparate thoughts and feelings that keeps us identified with sensory experience is the *manas,* the thinking mind. Of course, these are just labels.

When I first took psilocybin, I experienced the *ātman* and witnessed all the layers of my identity, of my incarnation. But I couldn't maintain my identity with it; I couldn't stay in it because of the power of my attachment to my thinking mind. I was still identified with myself as a psychologist. Coming down from those psychedelic trips was coming down into the thinking mind from a realm of direct experience of the Self that was unmediated by thought. When I got to India that experience allowed me to meet Maharaj-ji on his level in the *ātman.*

Home Is Where the Heart Is

During my initial experience with Maharaj-ji, I focused on two aspects of his being: that he knew everything and that he was loving me unconditionally. It took me a long time to put the two together in myself, to understand the depth of a being who could do that. I had to go from identifying in my head to identifying in my heart-mind.

I keep coming back to what Maharaj-ji did that first morning I was with him. It was not just mind reading. It was not only that he loved me unconditionally, although maybe it was that love that took me into the One. Now I think it was grace. That graceful love allowed the awareness and love to merge in the heart-mind, allowed the horizon of the sky of consciousness to open, allowed me to experience the One. Grace is at the nexus of love and awareness. There it's all open and it's all love. I could *see* everything as One, but to *become* One is grace. He gave me that grace to experience that for a moment. It was such a deep sense of being home. The One is awareness and love, but together they add up to more than the sum of their parts: home.

At the time this all happened in a rush of feelings and experiences, which, as you can tell, I am still integrating forty years later. But what allowed me to trust Maharaj-ji and enter into this path of the heart with him as a guide was the love. Within his love I felt so completely safe, I was able for a moment to let go of my fears and unworthiness and enter into my soul, my *jivatman.*

When I was with Maharaj-ji, I felt very loving toward the world. I realized that was created by his presence. He was a doorway to God. His consciousness was so playful with mine, it pulled me in, like the gravity of a larger body pulling in a smaller one. Our relationship is my journey within. Maharaj-ji is my inner Self.

Maharaj-ji instructed me to love everybody, and that has reverberated in me for years. Gradually, I've begun to be aware that I do love everything and everybody, not necessarily their personalities, but their essential being, because that is my essential being too. That's soul perception, perceiving from the *jivatman.* When love comes together with awareness, the door is opened to the heart-mind and the soul. He brought that together for me. The heart-mind, the spiritual heart, is awareness and love.

My path is to continue to deepen that love for everyone and everything. That's how I can serve Maharaj-ji and help others attune to their souls. And when I'm radiating the love and the joy that reside in my soul, that's also what comes back to me. When I'm in touch with my soul, I live in an environment of the soul, which gives others the opportunity to enter their soul too.

If someone calls and you open a door and go out into the sun, you feel its warmth too. It's not a concept. You can't know it. You can only be it.

I Am Loving Awareness

I have a practice in which I say to myself, *I am loving awareness.* To begin, I focus my attention in the middle of my chest, on the heart-mind. I may take a few deep breaths into my diaphragm to help me identify with it. I breathe in love and breathe out love. I watch all of the thoughts that create the stuff of my mind, and I love everything, love everything I can be aware of. I just love, just love, just love.

I love you. No matter how rotten you are, I love you because you are part of the manifestation of God. In that heart-mind I'm not Richard Alpert, I'm not Ram Dass—those are both roles. I look at those roles from that deeper "I." In the heart-mind I'm not identified with my roles. They're like costumes or uniforms hanging in a closet. "I am a reader," "I am a father," "I am a yogi," "I am a man," "I am a driver"—those are all roles.

All I am is loving awareness. *I am loving awareness.* It means that wherever I look, anything that touches my awareness will be loved by me. That loving awareness is the most fundamental "I." Loving awareness witnesses the incarnation from a plane of consciousness different from the plane that we live on as egos, though it completely contains and interpenetrates everyday experience.

When I wake up in the morning, I'm aware of the air, the fan on my ceiling, I've got to love them. *I am loving awareness.* But if I'm an ego, I'm judging everything as it relates to my own survival. The air might give me a cold that will turn into pneumonia. I'm always afraid of something in the world that I have to defend myself against. If I'm identified with my ego, the ego is frightened silly, because the ego knows that it's going to end at death. But if I merge with love, there's nothing to be afraid of. Love neutralizes fear.

Awareness and love, loving awareness, is the soul. This practice of *I am loving awareness* turns you inward toward the soul. If you dive deep enough into your soul, you will come to God. In Greek it's called *agape*, God love. Martin Luther King, Jr., said about this *agape*, this higher love: "It's an overflowing love which is purely spontaneous, unmotivated, groundless and creative...the love of God operating in the human heart."⁴

It's the love Maharaj-ji spreads around, the unconditional love. He loves you just because, just because. *Spontaneous, unmotivated, groundless.* He's not going to love you because you're an achiever or a devotee or a yogi, or because you're on the path. He loves you just because. Can you accept it? Can you accept unconditional love?

When you can accept that kind of love, you can give that love. You can give love to all you perceive, all the time. *I am loving awareness.* You can be aware of your eyes seeing, your ears hearing, your skin feeling, and your mind producing thoughts, thought after thought after thought. Thoughts are terribly seductive, but you don't have to identify with them. You identify not with the thoughts, but with the *awareness* of the thoughts. To bring loving awareness to everything you turn your awareness to is to be love. This moment is love. *I am loving awareness.*

If you put out love, then you immerse yourself in the sea of love. You don't put out love in order to get back love. It's not a transaction. You just become a beacon of love for those around you. That's what Maharaj-ji is. Then from the moment you wake until the moment you go to sleep, and maybe in dreams too, you're in a loving environment.

Try using *I am loving awareness* to become aware of your thought forms and to practice not identifying with them. Then you can identify with your soul, not your fears and anxieties. Once you identify with your spiritual being, you can't help but be love.

It's simple. I start with the fact that I'm aware, and then I love everything. But that's all in the mind, that's a thought, and loving awareness is not a thought. Or if it's a thought, it's pointing to a place that's not a thought. It's pointing at a state of being the way the concept of emptiness is pointing at emptiness, which is really fullness.

Souls love. That's what souls do. Egos don't, but souls do. Become a soul, look around, and you'll be amazed—all the beings around you are souls. Be one, see one.

When many people have this heart connection, then we will know that we are all one, we human beings all over the planet. We will be one. One love.

And don't leave out the animals, and trees, and clouds, and galaxies—it's all one. It's one energy. It comes through in individual ways, but it's one energy. You can call it energy, or you can call it love. I like to look at a tree and see that it's love. Don't you?

> *Deny the reality of things*
> *and you miss their reality;*
> *Assert the emptiness of things*
> *and you miss their reality.*
> *The more you talk and think about it,*
> *the further you wander from the truth.*
> *So cease attachment to talking and thinking,*
> *and there is nothing you will not be able to know.*
>
> *To return to the root is to find the essence,*
> *but to pursue appearances or "enlightenment" is to miss the Source.*
> *To awaken even for a moment*
> *is to go beyond appearance and emptiness.*
> —Seng-ts'an, Third Patriarch of Zen[5]

excess baggage

A HUMAN LIFE IS A SERIES of experiences. When we have little awareness of our predicament, experiences feed our attachments and condition our desire for more experiences. Our perspective changes when we begin to sense, even momentarily, the unity of all things and our identity with the Self.

We start to see each experience as a teaching to be brought into awareness and loved until we are free from being captivated by the experience. As we begin to awaken, experiences lead to reflection and contemplation. Then as we become more aware, experiences become a fire of purification, a burning ground of the ego, grist for the mill of developing consciousness, food enabling the emerging soul to break free of its bonds.

What is the nature of the mind stuff that keeps us in our egos? Ego attachments may be habits of thought, the residue of experiences, desires we've developed and reinforced or that have been implanted, even unconscious urges and tendencies.

Attachments conspire to create this stuck-together bundle of changing thought forms and feelings we label a self, our ego.

This sanguine idea of self is just that, an idea, a description of how we're doing at the moment, self-inflated or disappointed, a conglomeration of thoughts, feelings, and concepts that changes all the time. One morning I wake up thinking about enlightenment. The next morning I wake up thinking about world politics and environmental disasters. The next day I'm anxious about getting this book done. These temporal experiences that form our ego are like flickering images of a passing show. Each one seems real at the time, but they keep changing.

> The Self is the witness, all-pervading, perfect, free, one consciousness, actionless, not attached to any object, desireless, ever tranquil. It appears through illusion as the world.
>
> —*Ashtavakra Gita I:12*

One of the first steps in getting free of the attachment to this ego idea is to develop a witness. We have thousands and thousands of me's, but there is one me that is separate and watches all the other me's. It's on a different level of consciousness. It's not just another role; it's part of the heart-mind.

This witness is your leverage in the game. The witness me isn't trying to change any of the other me's. It's not an evaluator or a judge; it's not the superego. It doesn't care about anything. It just observes. "Hmmm, there she or he is doing that again." That witness place inside you is your centering device, your rudder.

The witness is part of your soul. It's witnessing your incarnation, this lifetime, from the heart-mind. It's the beginning of discrimination between your soul and your ego, your real *Self* and your *self* in the incarnation. Once you begin to live in this witness place, you begin to shift your identification from the roles and thought forms. As you witness yourself, the process becomes more like watching a movie than being the central character in one.

As you begin to dwell in Self-awareness, the old identifications with ego roles begin to just fall away. You shift your identification from the external roles and attachments to internal awareness. It's a *being* thing, not a *doing* thing.

You don't *do* anything. I once asked Dada Mukerjee, one of Maharaj-ji's oldest and closest devotees, how to give up attachments. He said, "Well, you can give things up, or you can wait until they give you up." Dada was a lifelong smoker, and though smoking was definitely not allowed in an ashram environment, Maharaj-ji very lovingly allowed him time and space to drop out of sight for an occasional cigarette. After Maharaj-ji left the body, Dada just stopped smoking.

The ego is based on fear, but the soul is based on love. Maharaj-ji is teaching us about soul. He's acknowledging our souls. As you witness your ego stuff, one way to release it is to constantly offer it into the fire of love in your heart. *I am loving awareness.*

Another *mantra* I have used to get into witness awareness and see the ego from the God perspective is: *I am a point of sacrificial fire held within the fiery will of God.* I received this *mantra* from Hilda Charlton, a teacher in New York who was a *chela,* or disciple, of Nityananda, whom you will meet later. She held a weekly class at St. John the Divine in Manhattan that helped countless people keep their spiritual heads above water. In her youth Hilda was a modern dancer. She traveled to India in the 1940s and danced in maharajas' courts to support herself. She was a strong teacher, and this is a fierce *mantra* to work with. Nityananda, her guru, was a great Shaivite *siddha,* a realized being who followed Shiva, the destroyer. He was also full of boundless love and compassion.

As you continue with your *sadhana,* as meditation deepens, you identify less and less with the ego and begin to touch and enter more deeply into the space of love. You begin to experience love toward more and more people and find love in the experiences that come into your field of awareness.

When Maharaj-ji said, "Ram Dass, love everybody," I said, "I can't." That was my ego talking. He said, "Love everybody." He wasn't listening to my ego. In that moment I saw my dying ego and who I was becoming. I looked between him and me and had a vision of a coffin, and my old self was in the coffin. I had to give up. He just wasn't going to honor my ego any longer.

As you keep giving up the habits that hold you back from loving, the ego's fear of letting go dissolves in the love. From the ego's vantage point you surrender into love. From the soul's vantage point you are coming home, the boundaries of separation are fading, and the two are becoming one. As you begin to enter into Oneness and to become love, instead of perceiving from your ego, you're perceiving from your soul. You are shifting your identification from ego to soul. You don't kill your ego; you kill your identification with your ego. As you dissolve into love, your ego fades. You're not thinking about loving; you're just being love, radiating like the sun. That last step requires Grace.

The Pressure Cooker

Although it often seemed like nothing was happening around Maharaj-ji, a lot was going on for everyone. It was an incredible space where most of what was happening was internal and little of it external. It was like a great river, like the Mississippi or the Colorado—beneath a calm opaque surface turbulent waters carry great rocks and tons of sediment and mud, carving out entire landscapes. As we sat around seemingly doing nothing, the changes beneath the surface felt truly geological, or neurological, as if Maharaj-ji was rewiring us on a subtle level.

Most of the time while we were sitting with Maharaj-ji, he was carrying on mundane conversations with devotees about families, jobs, weddings, or health. Meanwhile I might be going through an exquisitely painful memory or riding an emotional roller coaster. Every once in a while there would be a twinkle of recognition from Maharaj-ji, a piece of fruit thrown directly at me, a penetrating glance, an acknowledgment that told me he still knew everything that was going on. This happened a lot.

Many of us had come to him from transformative experiences with psychedelic drugs. However, our faith in him was not built on episodes of being high, which have inherent within them the seeds of disappointment and loss, because you always come down. Instead, he kept us down as he kept burning out our fears and neuroses and attachments, and at the same time we kept seeing the depth of our love for him. It built a base of love and trust, which you might call faith.

For example, I was carrying a burden of doubt when I returned to India to see Maharaj-ji in 1970. In America a boy who had been my student had died. He was a deeply spiritual kid whose father was a foreign scientist. The family was well off and had homes in New Hampshire and Arizona. The boy lived in New York, but had gone to do *sadhana* in a cave on their place in Arizona. Later I heard from his mother that he had died.

The mother said, "My son has achieved *mahasamadhi* (final merging)." She showed me the diary that he had kept. He wrote that he was taking *samadhi,* that she should not worry, and that he would be watching over her. She asked me, "Is everything he said true?"

I said, "Well I don't know, but I'm going back to India in the fall to see my guru, and he will certainly know."

I had my doubts. No student of mine had gained *mahasamadhi,* and I said to myself that it must be drugs. Later I learned he had indeed taken LSD. There had been blood on the walls of the cave, and I assumed he had tried to do *pranayama* (yogic breath control) while on LSD and had overdone it.

One day we were all showing our photos to Maharaj-ji, passport photos and pictures from our wallets. I remembered I had this boy's photo and went to get it. It was his high-school graduation picture. It didn't look much like the way I remembered him, but I put his picture next to Maharaj-ji, who said, "He left his body." Then he proceeded to quote from the boy's diary: "Tell Ram Dass I have finished my work. I will be watching over you, Mother," and he gave me all the information from the diary. Maharaj-ji said, "He's one with Christ. He has finished his work. He's watching over his mother."

Then he said, "Your medicines weren't the cause of his death." His death had been weighing on my mind. I wrote to the mother and told her that Maharaj-ji had affirmed what her son had written to her. This is just one instance of how Maharaj-ji worked with the subtleties of our lives beyond appearances to confirm our faith.

He also worked on us through our relationships with one another, sometimes calling one or two or all of us down during the day for some conversation or teaching or to use us as examples in some teaching or melodrama with the Indian devotees. Late in the afternoon we would see him for a final gathering before catching the last bus back to town.

One day Maharaj-ji appointed me "commander-in-chief" of the Westerners. I was supposed to keep everybody in line and get everybody on the bus. It was like herding cats. Somebody like Krishna Das would want to stay at the temple. So he asked Maharaj-ji, and Maharaj-ji gave his blessing for him to stay over. What was going on here? My authority was being thwarted! My feeling of importance as commander-in-chief deflated like a balloon.

Once when we were in Allahabad, Maharaj-ji told me to bring everyone to the house where he was staying at 6 P.M. Some rascals went early. When I got there with those who had dutifully followed my lead, the early birds were all having a great time with Maharaj-ji. Upon our arrival he promptly went into his room, and we didn't see him the rest of the evening.

He kept pulling the rug out from under me every time I tried to establish my power. It was playful, but it left my ego nowhere to stand. I had to choose between my ego pride and my love for him. I struggled with the pride, before my heart made the choice. I continued along with the commander-in-chief farce, but I stopped taking it seriously.

We spent the most time with Maharaj-ji at Kainchi, a beautiful temple in the Himalayan foothills. On my first visit, in 1966–67, I was there almost alone through the winter months learning yoga and absorbing a new worldview. It was intensely solitary.

When I returned in 1970, a group of Westerners was already there. From the outside the scene must have seemed idyllic. The temple was in a valley with a river, quiet countryside, good food, warm sun. But it was not a restful scene. There was a quality of nervous tension and the tremendous energy of Maharaj-ji's presence, whether we were physically with him or not. It was like a pressure cooker.

Our tensions with one another were incredible too, some from the discomforts of dysentery, hepatitis, and other ailments and some from the difficulty of adjusting to Indian culture. Maharaj-ji kept the pressure going. There were jealousies, rivalries, and feelings of competition for Maharaj-ji's attention and affection among the Westerners. As if we had any ability whatsoever to influence that! It was all his *lila*, his dance! The closer we got to those higher states of energy and consciousness, the more it seemed as though our imperfections gained energy too. We started to call it the Grace Race.

Relations between Westerners and Indians were sometimes tense too, whether from our inadvertent transgressions of cultural mores or possibly their feelings that the crazy *videshis* (foreigners) were usurping Maharaj-ji. You couldn't tell; everybody was always going through something. Maharaj-ji usually acted as if he had nothing to do with it, but we knew he was behind it all.

These situations kept hitting us where we lived. If there was a place where we were holding on, it soon became obvious. Sometimes Maharaj-ji was very fierce, sometimes cold, sometimes warm and humorous, as if to tell us not to take ourselves so seriously. And all of it was part of his *lila* and his work with each of us to get us free. Maharaj-ji was present for many people on many levels at the same time. He could be talking with one person, and we would each be receiving the teaching we needed and interpreting it according to our own situation.

Dealing with Our Stuff

We can't mask impurities for very long. When we suppress or repress them, they gain energy. Eventually we all have to deal with our same old karmic obstacles. Maharaj-ji used to enumerate them with regularity: *kama, krodh, moha, lobh*—lust, anger, confusion, and greed. It's the spectrum of impulses and desires that condition our interior universe and our view of reality. We have to take care of this stuff, so we can climb the mountain without getting dragged back down.

This clearing out opens the door for *dharma*, for being in harmony with the laws of the universe on both a personal and social level. If you do your *dharma*, you do things that bring you closer to God. You bring yourself into harmony with the spiritual laws of the universe. *Dharma* is also translated as "righteousness," although that evokes echoes of sin and damnation. It's more a matter of clearing the decks to be able to do spiritual work on yourself.

The *niyamas* and *yamas*, the behavioral dos and don'ts of Patanjali's yoga system, are a functional approach to *dharma* that is useful without being judgmental. You do what will take you closer to God, the One, and don't do what takes you further away. The dos, the *niyamas*, are: *sauca*, cleanliness or purity; *santosha*, contentment; *tapas*, austerity or religious fervor; *swadhyaya*, study; and *ishwara pranidhana*, surrender to God. Even the don'ts, the *yamas*, are framed as positive qualities to be cultivated: *ahimsa*, nonviolence or harmlessness; *satya*, truthfulness or nonlying; *asteya*, nonstealing; *brahmacharya*, continence or not being promiscuous; and *aparigraha*, noncovetousness or freedom from avarice.

There are many subtle issues surrounding these practices, of course, but those are the basics.

When I was first at the temple in the Himalayas, I was taught these practices by Hari Dass Baba, whom Maharaj-ji assigned to teach me yoga. He wrote on a chalkboard, because he kept silence. He was very sweet, but the *niyamas* and *yamas* seemed like an almost Victorian moral code. As I learned more of yoga though, I began to see how these spiritual disciplines fit into the puzzle.

By the time I had practiced the *niyamas* and *yamas* for six months, I felt much lighter. In my eyes I was beginning to become a true yogi. By directing my attention away from the distractions of the outer world, the *niyamas* and *yamas* were helping me to be more one-pointed in my inner journey.

This was a period of intense practice for me, in relative solitude in an ashram. But this stuff never really goes away. When I returned to the "marketplace" of the West, all the usual distractions were there. Maybe they didn't pull me quite as much, and I was no longer as completely fascinated by every desire. This is what the *niyamas* and *yamas* do—they create a perspective and help you focus on the deeper satisfaction from the spirit. For instance, *brahmacharya,* which is often translated "celibacy," actually means "linked to God." You might be celibate, but it's because you're into God, not because there's anything negative about sex. It gets subtle, and the work is ongoing. Even now, I am still wrestling with contentment in my old age.

My Spiritual Scrapbook

As you pass through life on the way to God, what's important is not what you experience, but how you identify with or cling to what you experience. Depending on your method, an experience may be figure or ground on your individual path. An experience may become a dominant theme, or it may be irrelevant. For example, when I was studying *vipassana,* or insight meditation, in Bodh Gaya, where Buddha became enlightened, with S. N. Goenka and Anagorika Munindra, pressure began to build up in my forehead. I thought it was a big spiritual advance, and I was thrilled at the prospect that my *ajna,* my third eye, was opening.

Goenka said, "That's just blocked energy. It's no use to you. Go out into the garden, run it down your right arm and out through your fingertips, and send it into the earth."

I followed his instruction. I saw a blue light come out of my fingertips, and the pressure was gone from my forehead. I missed it. But in the *vipassana* system it was irrelevant. In a *shakti*, or energy-oriented, system you would focus on it, push it higher, and work with the energy.

Ultimately every method gets you to the same place. There are many paths up the mountain, but the peak is the same. You don't notice this at the bottom. We don't hear much about the advanced part of most systems, because few people get to the peak.

An experienced Buddhist meditator told me that only after he meditated for many years was he ready to do *metta*, the meditation of loving-kindness, which opened his heart. He was only ready for the heart after he had quieted his mind. That was my experience too. After I got to a degree of concentration in *vipassana*, I was able to return to Maharaj-ji with a more one-pointed love.

On the other hand, if you are a *bhakti* practitioner, only when your heart is so absorbed in loving the Beloved does your mind become capable of merging. You get there from another direction. You go up the mountain from a different side, but the view from the top where love merges with awareness is One.

To a subtle diagnostician of spiritual progress these experiences are all clues to where you're not—yet. From the summit all these states are available, but you're not clinging to any of them. You don't define your-

> I have built my house in the stainless. I am merged in the formless. I am one with the illusionless. I have attained to unbreakable unity. Tuka says, now there is no room for egoism. I am identified with the Eternally Pure.
>
> —*Tukaram*[1]

self in terms of any of them. You're all of them, and you're none of them. You're no longer stuck in being the experiencer. It's all just here.

Merging into Oneness transcends experience. That scares the hell out of people who are stuck in their ego. The ego doesn't want that. The ego just wants to keep collecting more and more subtle experiences as a separate self. It makes people think the journey is just one subtle experience after another. The spiritual journey isn't like that.

It's scary for the ego when you start to merge. When I sat with Maharaj-ji once and the energy started to rise, I started shaking so hard, I was afraid I'd break my neck. He said, "He's not ready," and the energy or whatever it was stopped. I saw the way my mind was holding me back. I still had work to do.

Our human conditioning makes the ego react against threats to survival. The experiencer experiences fear when the experiences disappear. That's why there aren't very many liberated beings—because you have to let go. Lots of people like to be seeking God, but not too many want to actually get there.

The Five-Limbed Yoga

When we were with Maharaj-ji in India at Kainchi, generally we would go out to the temple on the early morning bus from Nainital. Only a few of us at a time were ever allowed to stay at the temple when Maharaj-ji was there. More Westerners did later, but I didn't. On arrival we would enter and *pranam,* or greet, the temple deities, and if Maharaj-ji was out on his *tukhat,* or wooden bed, under the portico, we would go up, *pranam,* and give him the apple or whatever offering we had brought.

With regard to practice, that time with Maharaj-ji defies easy description. Maharaj-ji gave few specific teachings, and our routine was largely a formless improvisation that revolved around him. There were the daily rituals in the temple, but for the Westerners the days would pass in a blissful cloud focused on him. Western minds being irrepressible, eventually one of our number dubbed this unscripted play "Maharaj-ji's Five-Limbed Yoga" (the classical *raja,* or *ashtanga, yoga* is eight-armed). The five limbs were Eating, Sleeping, Drinking Tea, Gossiping, and Walking About.

> To a poor person God appears in the form of food.
>
> —*Maharaj-ji*

Although the intent of such a description was humorous, these simple daily acts were charged with significance in the intense atmosphere that pervaded the little temple in the Himalayan valley. Maharaj-ji might be talking to somebody, ignoring us, and we'd just sit there quietly and look at him. Sometimes he'd accept the apples and throw them back to us or start a conversation about something that was going on in our lives at that moment. Sometimes he'd just sit quietly with us. Those were precious moments. After a little while he might order tea for us, one of the ashram staff would bring a teapot, and we would drink it in front of him. Once, someone asked Maharaj-ji how to get rid of attachments, and he answered, "You want tea? Don't take it."

Usually he would send us to rooms in the back of the temple, where we stayed much of the day. At lunch we were fed copious quantities of *puris* and spicy potatoes and sometimes Indian sweets. That food satisfied an inner hunger besides nourishing our bodies.

Maharaj-ji officiated from a distance over the kitchen, checking and overseeing everything. Food would be offered to him before being served to anyone else, and he would bless it. He taught us that food had to be cooked with love or it would be poison. He often said people had to fill their stomachs before they could think about God.

Maharaj-ji made sure just the right amount of food was prepared every day. Nothing was wasted, everything was consumed, and nothing was kept for the next day. Maharaj-ji told the cooks in the kitchen how many people to expect. He ran a tight ship. Feeding people was a big part of his teaching.

After lunch there was often a rest period or nap time. Some would read and others would snooze; sometimes the urge to sleep was overpowering. Those naps often became forays into the unconscious and astral planes. Vivid dreaming was common. Sleep wasn't time off, but a kind of teaching on other planes. We were just wrapped in the embrace of all that *shakti,* or cosmic energy. Then we'd see Maharaj-ji again in the afternoon for *kirtan* chanting or *darshan* before we took the last bus back to Nainital.

> "Serve the poor,"
> Maharaj-ji said.
> "Who is poor,
> Maharaj-ji?"
> "Everyone is poor
> before Christ."

Occasionally Maharaj-ji would call one or another of us up to demonstrate for the Indian devotees how we had come all the way from America on a true spiritual quest, often holding us up as absurdly pure examples to tease the Indians about their supposed impurities. Sometimes he would have us perform the Hindu prayers or songs we had learned to show how devout and holy we were. Everyone delighted in this charade, which would sometimes be repeated for days on end as new audiences arrived and we learned the chants. Wanting to perform well, we learned the prayers quickly.

Once I was called in while Maharaj-ji was talking with a High Court judge. I was introduced as the Harvard professor. The judge invited me to visit the High Court, which, of course, I had no desire to do. My father and brothers were all lawyers, and I knew the lay of that land. Trying to be polite I said, "Oh, delightful!"

Maharaj-ji mimicked my response. "Delightful!" he said. "If Ram Dass says it will be delightful, of course, he'll come."

At the High Court I visited the lawyers' room, and, having read *Time* magazine, I held forth about Nixon's visit to China. This was just after

India's brief border war with China, and it was a hot-button topic. The next day one of the lawyers came and asked if I would like to speak to the Bar Association.

Finally catching on, I said, "Well, you'll have to ask my guru."

So he asked Maharaj-ji if I could speak to the Bar Association about Nixon and China.

"Oh no," said Maharaj-ji. "You can't trust Ram Dass to talk about important things. He only can talk about me or spiritual things."

Then the lawyer said, "Oh. Well, then we won't have him come. He'll come to my house sometime to talk to a few lawyers about spiritual things."

Tea, or *chai*, served milky and sweet in unfired earthenware cups, appeared every few hours. It was strong and tasted slightly of the clay dust in the cups. It kept us in a state of high alert, or at least more alert than we would have been otherwise. I think India runs on *chai* and betel nut. One of Maharaj-ji's old devotees, "Hemda" Joshi, was fond of saying, "There's always time for tea!" Sipping tea was also an opportunity to socialize and exchange stories, deepening those mysterious bonds of spiritual family.

Gossip, mostly about Maharaj-ji, helped create and sustain the mood; it was a thread that held together the disparate band of Westerners, some of whom had strong personalities. Comparisons to other spiritual scenes, rumors of interpersonal attractions, not so subtle rivalries—it all came out in the wash of words and thoughts we exchanged.

In the summer of 1971 a few of us planned to undertake a rainy-season meditation retreat with Anagorika Munindra, a Buddhist teacher, at Lakshmi Ashram, where he used to stay every summer on a hilltop in the Himalayan village of Kausani. Before we left for Kausani, I proudly told Maharaj-ji we were going to study Buddhist meditation. He said, "As you like," leaving us to follow the winding path of our own desire.

Kausani has an incredible panoramic view of the Himalayan peaks, but they were almost always obscured by monsoon clouds at that time of year, so there were few tourists. Every few days there was a revelatory view when the clouds parted or played peak-a-boo with the mountains beyond. Plentiful mud and leeches completed the environment.

There were originally five of us, and we were going to study privately with Munindra-ji. After some days in Kausani a letter arrived from Munindra-ji saying he regretted not being able to come. He had to take care of his mother, who was ill. It was going to be a self-directed retreat.

The house soon proved too small. One day we looked down the hill and saw a group of Westerners getting off the bus. Maharaj-ji kept sending more Westerners to join us, telling them to study meditation with

Ram Dass. Maharaj-ji had set me up. Now with about twenty people, we moved to the main hotel in Kausani, the eponymous Gandhi Ashram, where Mahatma Gandhi was briefly sequestered by the British.

Besides meditation and early morning chanting, I began devising exercises to help people lighten their karmic load. I would sit with each individual, and we would look into each other's eyes. After we had established contact and watched the passing clouds of our mind stuff for a while, I would say, "If there's anything that makes you uncomfortable, if there's anything that you feel you can't tell me—tell me."

I was trying to re-create the way that Maharaj-ji worked with people's "stuff." But he knew everything in people's heads, and I didn't. I was aiming for that unconditional love. I was loving people after they had shown me their greatest shame or pain.

Rivers of anxiety, insecurity, suppressed rage, and sexual feelings, secret tales of shame and regret all poured out from people in deepest confidence, all to be released into love. Except, as it turned out, there was an unseen hole in the ceiling. The young woman in the room above could hear everything. Before long everyone knew everyone else's inmost secrets. There was nowhere to hide. Everyone's secrets were cosmic gossip. It was just another reminder that Maharaj-ji knew everything.

It was a relief to finish the "meditation retreat" and return to the confines of Maharaj-ji's temple. When we got back, Maharaj-ji pointed to me and said, "Here comes the Buddhist meditation teacher!" He laughed joyously. Still mortified at having had to give up my studies, I had to laugh too. It was another reminder that there was nothing to learn or do; I could only become it.

Walking about. Many of us had learned Buddhist walking meditation, and though we were by no means formally practicing, our strolls indeed became meditative in the environs of the ashram.

You could also walk overland to the ashram. The distance by taxi or bus on the twisting hill road from the nearby town was some fourteen kilometers, but you could take a more direct route to the ashram by walking on footpaths. You would trek up the hill behind our hotel to a high point called Snowview, where you could see the Himalayan peaks, then walk down footpaths (there were no roads) through valleys and tiny farm villages for a couple of hours before arriving (if you hadn't made a wrong turn) at the back side of the ashram. It was a journey into another world, simple and pastoral, what the Hobbit Shire might have been like in Tolkien's mythical world with the added rough edges of hardscrabble farming and Himalayan winters. That excursion from the modern world into timeless village India was a beautiful way to quiet the mind before arriving at the ashram.

chapter three

to become one

T HE *I am loving awareness* practice from the first chapter is a *mantra,* or what we in the West might call a prayer or an affirmation. *Mantras* work in different ways. One kind engages your conceptual mind to take you into a new space, in this case dissolving your mind into your heart by constantly reminding you to view everything with love. The Tibetan *mantra OM MANE PADME HUM* is similar. If you stay with it, the mind just sinks into the heart. Using a *mantra* is one practice in which more is better. Repetition furthers.

Other *mantras* are more purely vibrational, using seed syllables, like *OM*, that reverberate on many levels of consciousness. Rām is one of the Hindu names of God that combines both the vibrational and conceptual spheres. You can channel your yearning for God through the practice of *Rām Nam*, reciting or chanting Rām's name over and over until it brings you into the soul, opening into the unified state. You create a vibrational field that starts in your heart and eventually becomes the universe, taking you into the One. You open a door so that grace can enter in. *Rām Rām Rām*

Rām Rām Rām Rām Rām Rām Rām Rām Rām Rām Rām Rām Rām Rām Rām Rām Rām Rām Rām Rām Rām Rām Rām Rām Rām Rām Rām Rām Rām.

When I'm out in the marketplace, I finger my beads silently, repeating *Rām Rām Rām*. As I look around me everything is Rām, all is one. I Rām-ize whatever situation I'm in; I bring it into Rām's vibrational field. There are two planes of consciousness operating here. I'm fingering my beads in the grocery store, and the beings around me are in their roles as customers or clerks, but I see them as souls. Because I'm in my soul, I can see their souls. If you can be a soul, identify with your soul, then you can see other beings as souls. Maharaj-ji was introducing us to our souls. He rests in his soul and that creates a sympathetic vibration with other souls. That's how you really serve God, by bringing others into their souls.

The Rām *mantra* works on vibrational and conceptual planes at the same time. Repetition of the *mantra* brings you into the vibrational field of the divine Name. Devotion to Rām opens you to the heart space of Rām's being. For Hindus the many layers of stories and symbolism about Rām from the *Ramayana* enrich their devotion. The *Ramayana* is the Bible of North India.

For example, in the *Ramayana,* Hanuman, the monkey god, epitomizes service and devotion by carrying Rām's ring (representing God's love) to Sita, Rām's wife (the soul), who has been kidnapped by Ravana, a ten-headed demon who represents the power of ego running amok in the world of the senses. She's been singing the separation blues in Sri Lanka, and is she ever glad to get a hit of God's love from Hanuman during her dark night of the soul! All those thoughts and emotions are part of *Rām Rām Rām Rām Rām Rām Rām Rām Rām.*

The name that Maharaj-ji gave me, Ram Dass, means "servant of Ram," which is another name for Hanuman. So I'm named after Hanuman. It's just a constant reminder to me of how Maharaj-ji keeps on saying, "Love everyone and serve everyone!" It reminds me to keep looking to see how I can serve.

More complex prayers like the forty verses in Hindi of the *Hanuman Chalisa* (*chalis* means "forty" in Hindi) combine the conceptual and the vibrational in an intricate tapestry. The long prayer describing Hanuman's exploits brings up the story with its emotional content and the vibration, bringing me into the presence of Hanuman. It's also a prayer for Hanuman to stay with me, to help and protect me.

We sang to Maharaj-ji in India, and those verses evoke a memory that brings me to him again. Whether or not you understand the Hindi words, chanting with a yearning for God will bring you into the moment and open that vibrational door. That's what a *mantra* does.

When I first heard the *Hanuman Chalisa* in India, I couldn't imagine people practicing it in the West. Now, thousands in the West have learned to recite it. I marvel at how so many have committed it to memory. The *Chalisa* opens you to Hanuman, who opens the door to Rām, to God.

Music has a unique ability to convey emotion, and when it combines with the vibrational quality of a *mantra,* there is nothing like it to bypass the mind and open a direct route to the heart. In the *Ramayana* it says that chanting Rām's name is more powerful than Rām himself, because it has the ability to take you to Rām—not Rām, the character in the *Ramayana,* but Rām, the state of being, God.

Kirtan, singing the Hindu names of God, Rām and Krishna, and the mother goddess, Durga, was one of the only things we could *do* for Maharaj-ji. He loved even the musically inept renditions that we performed for him. For us it was a way to express our yearning and love for God, opening a sweetness that continues to be there whenever we gather to sing the Name.

You don't have to sing in a group. You don't even have to be able to carry a tune. The words are simple, the same Name over and over again;

you just sit down and sing to God. It's nice to give *kirtan* its own special time, but you can chant while you're doing the laundry or driving the car, and it will remind you of your other life in the heart, as a soul. This simple practice will open your soul horizon.

Krishna Das, whom Maharaj-ji sent to sing with the *kirtan wallahs* at Kainchi, says:

> *The words of these chants are called the divine names, and they come from a place in our hearts that's deeper than our thoughts, deeper than the mind. And so as we sing them they turn us toward ourselves, into ourselves. They bring us in, and as we offer ourselves into the experience, the experience changes us. These chants have no meaning other than the experience we have by doing them. They come from the Hindu tradition, but it's not about being a Hindu or having to believe anything in advance. It's just about doing it, and experiencing. Nothing to join, you just sit down and sing.[1]*

From the Indian spiritual perspective this time on earth is called the Kali Yuga, or Iron Age, about which the Tulsi Das *Ramayana* says:

> *In the age of Kali neither yoga (concentration of mind) nor the performance of sacrifices nor spiritual wisdom is of any avail; one's only hope lies in hymning Sri Rām's praises. . . . The power of the Name is thus manifest in the age of Kali.[2]*

Matter-nity

At one point Maharaj-ji said, "See everything as the Mother and you will know God." What was he talking about, seeing your mother in everything?

We Westerners have our share of relationship complexities with our mothers, with interpretations galore courtesy of Dr. Freud. The view of the mother in India is different. The country is called Mother India. A Western devotee once told Maharaj-ji he hated his mother, and nobody understood what he was saying. The concept didn't make it across the cultural barrier. In India the mother is so deeply respected and revered, there was no way that statement could be understood. There is an Indian saying that there may be bad children, but there are no bad mothers.

The Divine Mother, the Goddess, has many dimensions. In the broadest sense consciousness and energy, eternal spirit and matter are male and female (matter-nity). Out of the One in the first glimmer of duality comes *purusha,* the formless spirit, and *prakriti,* the cosmic energy that coalesces into form. As God and Goddess they are Shiva, who personifies pure absolute consciousness and the seed of procreation, and Shakti, who manifests infinite forms.

> Why does the God-lover find such pleasure in addressing the Deity as Mother? Because the child is more free with its mother, and consequently she is dearer to the child than anyone else.
>
> —*Ramakrishna*[3]

Seeing the world as the Mother, seeing everything as her manifestation, involves a shift in perception. The way you go about your daily life may be the same, eating, sleeping, defecating, reproducing, socializing, gratifying your senses, earning your livelihood, solving problems, contributing to society, relieving suffering. But you see it all as a child sheltered in the loving arms of your Mother, who is all creation. The blue sky is her mind, the green leaves pulse with her blood, the wind is her breath, the rain, her water of life. She is Gaia, the Earth Mother, but also subtler than that.

Close your eyes and imagine that all around you is a luminous mist, a substance finer even than the tiniest quantum of energy theorized by physicists. It permeates all forms—in fact all forms are patterns of this mist. That is the living spirit made manifest, the substance of the Mother creating our sensible world. Just think of it as another way of seeing.

The intense love between mother and child can apply to everyday experience as a way to bring you closer to the Beloved. Your attachments, desires, and impurities are also a manifestation of the Mother, and that makes it easier to deal with them. In your daily life as you work with all the ways you hold on to your own suffering, to your desires, you are reminded that the play of phenomena is all her play, including Maharaj-ji.

O Mother, make me mad with Thy love!
What need have I of knowledge or reason?
Make me drunk with Thy love's Wine;
O Thou who stealest Thy bhaktas' hearts,
Drown me deep in the Sea of Thy love!
Here in this world, this madhouse of Thine,
Some laugh, some weep, some dance for joy:
Jesus, Buddha, Moses, Gauranga,
All are drunk with the Wine of Thy love.
O Mother, when shall I be blessed
By joining their blissful company?

—Ramakrishna[4]

By telling us to see everything as the Mother, I think Maharaj-ji meant us to use every detail of life as grist for the mill of our spiritual development. Every experience is a mirror reflecting where we are in our consciousness and our work of the moment. In the compassionate embrace of the Mother the layers of old habits, preconceptions, and residues of past experience can dissolve in the ocean of maternal affection.

Love's Company

One way of remembering to stay in the heart is to hang out with other people who are on the same journey. *Satsang* is a community of seekers after truth. *Sat* means "truth," and *sangha* is a "meeting of the ways," a spiritual community. *Satsang* is the company or family of fellow travelers on this path of the heart. Each devotee feeds and inspires the others; "like a soaked cloth dampens a dry one, *satsang* drenches one heart and then another."[5]

At the most basic level, associating or surrounding yourself with friends who are working on themselves, who are on the path, creates a supportive atmosphere for your own *sadhana,* or spiritual work. Similarly, hanging out with people who are drinking beer and watching TV all the time is probably a distraction.

Being in a *satsang* doesn't mean you've gone to heaven or are full of love and light. If a *satsang* seems too pure, it probably is. If the people in your *satsang* aren't too busy pretending to be pure or spiritual and are truthful about where they are on the path, they'll help you to keep your perspective. If you sing and do service together, you will create a real heart space.

Satsang is a lot like family, albeit a spiritual one. There's always a crazy relative, and relationships have their ups and downs. Maharaj-ji's *satsang* is about as diverse as you could imagine. Without Maharaj-ji as our focus many of us would probably never have known each other. It's been said that Maharaj-ji took on the difficult and nearly hopeless cases. I used to call it the mark of madness.

At times Maharaj-ji seemed like a doctor in the back ward of a mental hospital. Many in the Western *satsang* are rascals—loving, but crazy. It's so intimate, because we've all known each other so long, and he's brought out all our stuff. We love each other, but we don't always like each other. Now I see us all as souls, and I love all of us.

Despite our differences, those of us who've stayed connected over the years have developed an inextricably deep bond of love through Maharaj-ji. We're a real family, in many ways closer than a blood family, one that crosses oceans and spans continents, cultures, and decades, with spats, jealousies, and forgiveness. *Satsang* provides a welcome embrace no matter how far apart we live or how infrequently we see each other and is by no means limited to those who were with Maharaj-ji when he was embodied. When we meet, we embrace not just each other, but him too.

Let Me Count the Ways

Love is the emotion of merging, of becoming one in the heart. In everyday life it is mixed in the natural riot of relationships, the biochemistry, emotions, desires, fantasies, and romantic illusions. *Bhakti yoga* cultivates the spiritual heart by turning those natural impulses into creepers that twine around the Beloved, converting them into a conduit to carry us toward ultimate merging. Every form of love, every loving relationship, can become that conduit: parent and child, lover and beloved, student and teacher, aspirant and religious guide, friend and friend, owner and pet too. Each has within it a seed of love that can grow into unconditional love. Any of them can become the road to the spiritual heart.

The *bhakti* traditions describe how these different ways of relating can develop and open into the relationship to the Beloved. The *bhavas,* the attitudes, moods, and emotional states you cultivate in *bhakti yoga,* use the analogy of our human relationships, like mother and infant, parent and child, lover and beloved, master and devoted servant, and true friends to create that space for divine love. Remember, this is really a relationship with your own deeper self, so see what works for you.

In India you might worship baby Krishna, Gopal, delighting in his divine pranks and cosmically childish ways. As he grows up and becomes Govinda, the sky blue cowherd, he plays his supremely seductive flute for his favorite, Radha, and the other cowherd girls, and you become one of them, a *gopi,* enthralled and pining for a Beloved who manifests ten thousand forms at once to satisfy every one of his myriad lovers.

> Hark . . . A flute? . . . Nay, I am dreaming! No earthly flute could contain such celestial music! . . . Could a flute carry so far? Ah, my heart will burst with joy! Truly I am dead, and in Indra's Heaven.
>
> —Heart of a Gopi[6]

The divine romance with Krishna, the *lila,* is sensual beyond the senses, and the very thought of him drives the love-intoxicated *gopis* into ecstasy. It's "like an upsurging ocean of nectar."[7] You fall in love, and you just keep falling until everything has fallen away.

Your glance, my love, intoxicates,
and all your form and face, is moonbeam-tender,
and when you walk, and move, beloved,
you move the hearts of all that is created,
they long for you.

You are so perfectly formed, beloved,
that all of love, and passion, swirls around you
making of you that perfection: an adept at love's game.
O my beloved, everything about you draws the eyes,
even your eyebrows are lines drawn to perfection.
Though you walk upon this earth formed,
O formless, you are the home and refuge of all.

—Jayadeva[8]

Then there is the Krishna of the *Bhagavad Gita*, Arjuna's loyal friend, charioteer, and guru, who raises him from battlefield despair to consider the infinite wisdom of the spirit in confronting his inner adversaries. This is a deeper kind of heart wisdom that engages the mind as well as the soul. The *Gita* is one of the great treasure troves of cosmic revelation and instruction on how to follow a spiritual path and yet live in the world. The subtle concept of working without attachment to the result through *karma yoga* is a revolutionary idea.

Karma yoga ties directly to another form of *bhakti*, *seva*, or selfless service. Hanuman, the monkey god who serves Rām and Sita in the great epic the *Ramayana*, incarnates selfless service and devotion. He dedicates his whole being to his Lord and master, Rām, and to the Mother, Sita. My guru, Maharaj-ji, is my model and inspiration for that Hanuman *bhava*. Hanuman combines the instinctive animal qualities of a monkey with the supernatural power and devotion of a great yogi and divine sage.

In the Tulsi Das *Ramayana*, Rām says to the wife of a sage, who has waited ages to see him:

"Listen, O good lady, to My words. I recognize no other kinship except that of Devotion. Despite caste, kinship, lineage, piety, reputation, wealth, physical strength, numerical strength of his family, accomplishments and ability, a man lacking in Devotion is of no more worth than a cloud without water. Now I tell you the nine forms of Devotion; please listen attentively and cherish them in your mind.

"The first in order is fellowship with the saints, and the second is marked by a fondness for My stories. Humble service of the lotus feet of one's preceptor is the third form of Devotion, while the fourth type of Devotion consists in singing My praises with a guileless purpose. Muttering My Name with unwavering faith constitutes the fifth form of adoration revealed in the

Vedas. The sixth variety consists in the practice of self-control and virtue, desisting from manifold activities and ever pursuing the course of conduct prescribed for saints. He who practices the seventh type sees the world full of Me without distinction and reckons the saints as even greater than Myself. He who cultivates the eighth type of Devotion remains contented with whatever he gets and never thinks of detecting others' faults. The ninth form of Devotion demands that one should be guileless and straight in one's dealings with everybody, and should in his heart cherish implicit faith in Me without either exultation or depression.

"Whoever possesses any one of these nine forms of Devotion, be he man or woman or any other creature—sentient or insentient—is most dear to Me, O good lady. As for yourself, you are blessed with unflinching devotion of all these types. The prize which is hardly won by the Yogis is within your easy reach today. The most incomparable fruit of seeing Me is that the soul attains its natural state.". . .

She gazed on the Lord's countenance and imprinted the image of His lotus feet on her heart; and casting her body in the fire of Yoga she entered Sri Hari's state wherefrom there is no return. "O men, abandon your varied activities, sins and diverse creeds, which all give birth to sorrow, and with genuine faith," says Tulsidasa, "be devoted to the feet of Sri Rama." [9]

Each one of these *bhavas*, or moods, is a way to approach unconditional love, to open yourself to divine love. In any of them you can use the ways of *bhakti yoga*—prayer, chanting, *puja* (ritual worship), repeating a *mantra*, or meditation—to create the mood of love. Ultimately there's no thinking about it; there's only doing it, becoming it, being in love.

Practice makes perfect. I can write and you can read, but if we really want that love, eventually we all have to actually tread on the path and do the practice.

There are complex traditions and lineages in India, gurus, teachers, and sects that teach and practice the *bhakti marg*, or path to love. Although the poetry and literature of *bhakti* traditions are inspiring even in translation, it can be difficult to transplant the actual practices from their cultural context. Centuries ago progenitors of those traditions in India, like Chaitanya Mahaprabhu, created vast revivals and spiritual movements that still attract adherents and pilgrims throughout India.

On a practical level, just as *bhakti* uses human relationships as an analogy for divine love, you can bring your own relationships with family and friends into your devotional practice. Try seeing your child, lover, spouse, or mentor as a divine manifestation.

Ocean of Devotion

Once you have drunk from the water of unconditional love, no other well can satisfy your thirst. The pangs of separation may become so intense that seeking the affection of the Beloved becomes an obsession. When we were with Maharaj-ji, we were intoxicated with his form, the colors of his blanket, the buttery softness of his skin, his tapering, almost simian fingers, the long eyelashes that so often hid his eyes, the red toenail on his big toe. As with any lover we, too, became fascinated and

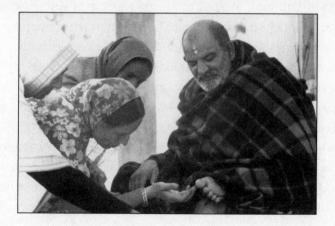

enamored of every detail, although these cues triggered spiritual bliss instead of physical desire.

In their way intoxication and addiction are analogies for devotion. Once you experience unconditional love, you really get hooked. The attraction is to that intimacy between the lover and the Beloved.

> Devotion to God
> is an addiction that
> lasts all the time.
>
> —Maharaj-ji

You are so drawn into the songs, stories, images, and constant remembrance of the Beloved that you may hold on to the form and not want to go on to the next stage. You are always thinking about it and tuning your being to stay in that intimate loving relationship with this person you love.

But the Beloved is not a person in the usual sense, and the form is just a costume for the play, the *lila*. Ultimately, this form is the one that takes you beyond form. What the Beloved, your guru, reveals to you is your own soul. Even so you may choose, like Hanuman, to remain in a kind of duality to serve and remain immersed in the ocean of devotion.

The devotional path isn't necessarily a straight line to enlightenment. There's a lot of back and forth, negotiation if you will, between the ego and the soul. You look around at all the aspects of suffering, and you watch your heart close in judgment. Then you practice opening it again and loving this too, as a manifestation of the Beloved, another way the Beloved is taking form. Again your love grows vast. In *bhakti,* as you contemplate, emulate, and take on the qualities of the Beloved, your heart keeps expanding until you see the whole universe as the Beloved, even the suffering.

As I have explored my own and others' journeys toward love, I've encountered different kinds of happiness. There's pleasure, there's happiness, and then there's joy. Addiction, even in the broad sense of just always wanting more of something, gives only pleasure. Pleasure is very earthbound when you're getting it from sensual interaction, and it always has its opposite; also, the need for satisfaction is never ending. Happiness is emotional, and emotions come and go. It may play into the complex of other emotional stuff that we all carry. But there is also spiritual happiness, which gets very close to joy.

As it becomes less personal, spiritual happiness becomes joy. Joy is being part of the One. It's spiritual, the joy-full universe, like trees are joyful. It's bliss, or *ananda*. It's all those things. The difference is that it comes from the soul.

Surrender

When I was first with Maharaj-ji, I experienced such bliss and love that all I wanted to do was just be around him and rub his feet. As time went on that love kept growing, but it became different, until I started to feel just as fulfilled being at a distance from him. I began to realize his love was not directed just at me.

It kept growing deeper and deeper until I really didn't care whether I was with his form. I stopped relating to him as "that man in India" and began to relate to the essence of guru. The dynamic kept changing as I understood more, as my heart continued opening and my surrender increased. He started to enter into me; his presence was with me wherever I was, until I realized there was nowhere I could go that he wasn't.

I still loved his form and I wanted to be with him, but I realized the form was just the doorway and I had to look through, I had to go beyond it. In a way, when he died that was the message, that we had to go beyond the form. Fortunately, I had that realization before he died, so the feeling of presence was the same.

In the West surrender implies giving up power. But surrendering to a guru or the Beloved doesn't mean giving power to another human being—it's letting go of the stuff that keeps you separate. Each time you

surrender, it leads you further in, deeper into yourself. You surrender to that place in yourself that takes you beyond form.

Renouncing the attachments and desires that are holding you back can be really difficult when you are trying to do it in an achievement-oriented, driven sort of way. On the other hand, giving things up is incredibly easy in the presence of love. They just dissolve. Those of you who have had a really powerful love relationship will recognize what it is like to care more about your beloved than yourself. Your favorite food is on the table, and your main concern is that your lover should have enough of it. You are fulfilled when your lover eats.

That's what you experience when you have a child. People say, "Aren't you self-effacing, aren't you sacrificing for your child?" But it isn't sacrifice—it's joy. Austerities done with a dry heart are heavy, but when they're done with love you're saying, "Let me give this up for my beloved. It will bring us closer!" When you really want to get close to your beloved, you can't give things up fast enough. Love lubricates the whole process. You just get more joyful.

Falling in love is a desire to merge with, to be completely immersed in love for, and be loved by the beloved. You want to know your beloved more and more intimately. That yearning has motivated human beings to give up everything, to renounce all forms of gratification, even life itself. Throughout history, people have undergone the greatest sacrifices to consummate their love. To love God or the guru is to let go of everything that separates you from the Beloved. This is the essence of devotional surrender and renunciation.

When they're misunderstood, the external acts that characterize surrender and renunciation can be motivated by a desire to imitate, by guilt, feelings of unworthiness, self-righteousness, a desire for security in structure, or masochism. But anyone who truly loves knows that to give up one's own happiness for the beloved is none of those things. It is the purest, most opening and flowing total ecstasy.

True, sometimes you have to prime the pump before your heart is open enough to love that deeply. You begin a process of purification based on how you think it could be. It's like diving into deep water—first you have to walk to the end of the diving board. You undergo purifications to get into a position to fall in love with God. You become disciplined not out of guilt, shame, or moral responsibility, but out of an incredible yearning to be pure enough to be with God. The actual moment of diving in is the inevitable culmination of your training and preparation.

There is no time off in this game, not because anybody's keeping score, but because you can't stand moving away from the light. The longing and despair of separation wake you up.

From Form to Formless Form

Maharaj-ji's methods were completely flexible, open to the fluidity of the moment. You couldn't point to something and say it was a teaching; it was just a momentary situation. It might touch your heart profoundly in that moment, or you might realize its import only years later.

"It is difficult to empty the mind," Maharaj-ji said, "but it is not necessary to go to the forest. You can do it anywhere.

"Worldly people go outward, but you must go inward like a tortoise, withdrawing the senses within your shell."

Was it a teaching? Or was it just life? Was it a miracle? Or had life itself taken on a miraculous tinge? Things happened so quickly on so many levels that it was breathtaking, and yet Maharaj-ji evinced a childlike simplicity that we all felt immersed in as well. From time to time he would say things like, "Is it? Isn't it? What to do?" The form of the teachings just flowed out of that loving quality of his being.

The transmission is just that flow of love. Maharaj-ji's love touches love in me, and I become that love. The forms that express that love are part of the existential situation. But the transmission is not the form; it's the love.

In this loving moment you begin to appreciate a new way of being. When you stop for a moment, when you dive into the presence of this moment, the drama goes on, but it's all just love. You just climb into the moment. It might just be a second. Being in the moment moves you out of time. It's the timeless moment. In the moment is eternity. In the moment is God. In this timeless moment is where Maharaj-ji's boundless love connects with my love. Then we can begin to look beyond the forms, into the formless, timeless *being* from which they emanate.

In this loving awareness of each moment there is also surrender, surrender to the guru, to the moment, to your soul. As Meher Baba said, "Being is dying by loving."

Then when you look at another being, you are looking at love. Sooner or later you are going to be in love with the whole universe. You'll be sitting in a place where it's all just one love. You are love, you are with love. You are in the state of love with all beings.

We learn how to love the universe just the way it is. We learn how to see the universe as the beauty of God's law made manifest. We learn how to take joy in the moment. We learn how to accept the responsibility that we are all one consciousness in many bodies. We are One Family.

Love with No Object

Although you may devote yourself to an aspect of the Beloved, like the guru or the deity as mother, child, or lover, you are in it for the love, not for the attainment, not for the object. It's one of those wonderful paradoxes you encounter on the path. You can't attain it; you have to become it. In the process subject and object, lover and Beloved, become one. You lose yourself and gain your Self. To go from the experiencer to the merger with the One requires grace.

> Know that when you learn to lose yourself, you will reach the beloved. There is no other secret to be learned, and more than this is not known to me.
>
> —Ansari of Herat[10]

To stay in love, or to serve as Hanuman serves Rām, the true devotee maintains a thread of connection to the self and pulls back from fully merging, or goes in and out.

The truth of this path of the heart is that there is no path. There is only the heart and the love that consumes the lover who becomes the Beloved. Love is a state of being, not a trip from here to there.

chapter four

darshan

ALL BEINGS are on an evolutionary journey, and not just a Darwinian one. There is an evolution of consciousness reaching toward perfection, oneness, and divinity. Hindus and Buddhists believe each individual goes through countless incarnations on this road to fulfillment.

A lot of people ask me, "How do you know about incarnations?" I haven't experienced my past incarnations, but from being with my guru, Maharaj-ji, who's farther up the mountain, I have an understanding of how it all works. He would speak of reincarnation as a reality, and I and the other people around him had a very deep relationship with him and each other that clearly had not come from our family backgrounds or upbringing in this life.

Our human forms are composed of and surrounded by an infinite myriad of forms, all in constant motion, from the subatomic to the cosmic in scale. This is the *lila*, the enchanted dance of existence, the divine interplay of consciousness and energy. Amid this divine play we seek fulfillment, perfection, flow, freedom, enlightenment, Oneness.

The dominant quality of form is change, because all forms are in time. That's another way of saying we don't know what will happen from one instant to the next. Or, as one of my guru brothers is fond of saying, "Don't be surprised to be surprised!" For instance, I didn't anticipate I'd be living in a wheelchair today. The way to live with change is to be completely present in the moment (remember, *Be Here Now*).

We cannot cling to forms or our experiences of them, because they decay and dissolve back again into their formless state. Attempting to hold on to anything in time is ultimately futile and a cause of much suffering. What is really there to hold on to? In reality there is nothing permanent, nothing solid, nothing constant except relativity and change themselves.

When we realize how finite are the limits of gratification or possible fulfillment within the play of forms, then despair arises. That despair is born of the world-weary understanding that nothing in form can provide ultimate meaning. It also forces and demands awakening and seeks transcendence of suffering.

If futile clinging to impermanence creates our suffering, letting go and making friends with change is joy, liberation. In youth our lifetime seems to stretch infinitely before us. As we age, the accumulation of our experiences seems to have occurred in the blink of an eye. Even now that I'm seventy-nine years old, I realize there's plenty of change to come before dying—change in the body, change in friends and family, change in memory. These experiences lead to deepening wisdom and freedom and to diving deep within to the realm beyond form.

Long before recorded history, human beings were awakening out of the illusion of form or separateness that the Indians call *maya*. A tiny fraction of humanity, but still many beings, finish their work and complete the process of realization, the integration of form and the formless. These awakened beings pass beyond the illusion of birth and death and attachments to this physical plane and every other plane. Their hearts fill with the bliss of that realization and with the infinite love that permeates the universe the way that dark matter permeates the space between stars. That love is the subtle texture of our material world, the unseen energy, the fullness of emptiness (*sunyata*).

> *Open your eyes of love, and see Him who pervades this world! Consider it*
> *   well, and know that this is your own country.*
> *When you meet the true Guru, He will awaken your heart;*
> *He will tell you the secret of love and detachment, and then you will know*
> *   indeed that He transcends this universe. . . .*
> *There the Eternal Fountain is playing its endless life-streams of birth*
> *   and death.*
> *They call Him Emptiness who is the Truth of truths, in Whom all truths*
> *   are stored!*
> *There within Him creation goes forward, which is beyond all philosophy;*
> *   for philosophy cannot attain to Him:*
> *There is an endless world, O my Brother! and there is the Nameless Being,*
> *   of whom naught can be said.*
> *Only he knows it who has reached that region: it is other than all that is*
> *   heard and said.*
> *No form, no body, no length, no breadth is seen there: how can I tell you*
> *   that which it is?*
> *He comes to the Path of the Infinite on whom the grace of the Lord descends:*
> *   he is freed from births and deaths who attains to Him.*
> *Kabir says: "It cannot be told by the words of the mouth, it cannot be*
> *   written on paper:*
> *It is like a dumb person who tastes a sweet thing—how shall it be*
> *   explained?"*
>
> —Kabir[1]

When they finally emerge from the illusion of separateness, these free beings can either merge back into that formless state or remain in form on one plane or another, or they can continue their evolution to the point where it makes no difference. They may or may not take birth again on the physical plane.

Sainthood

In the East, liberated beings are often referred to as saints. The term has different connotations in different cultures. In the Catholic Church a saint is someone who has been canonized by the church and is confirmed to have performed miracles. In the West, we also use the term metaphorically when we say, "She's a real saint," or "That was a saintly thing to do." We don't usually mean that they were canonized by the church, but that they are unusually good or loving or particularly self-sacrificing people.

In India someone might be called a saint who is a *sattvic* individual, someone who is pure and oriented toward the light, a good person connected to the spirit. A saint can also be a liberated being who continues to take birth to relieve the suffering of other beings, what Buddhists call a *bodhisattva*.

India also has an ancient tradition of yogis and *rishis,* or forest sages, who were the living sources of spiritual life and knowledge. These great souls, or *mahatmas,* laid the foundations of India's spiritual culture thousands of years ago as recorded in the Vedas. Some even entered the social and political arena, like the kings Dhruva and Shiva-ji and more recently Mahatma Gandhi.

There are also holy men and women who act as gurus, spiritual guides, and preceptors, a tradition much attenuated in modern urban society, but one that is still intertwined in Indian culture and persists to this day. Holy men are often called *baba,* a Hindi term meaning "father" or "grandfather" but used as an honorific, for example, Neem Karoli Baba. Beyond all classification is a rarefied class of great saints or yogis who have reached the pinnacle of consciousness, fully realized beings, the perfected ones, or *siddhas*. People revere and seek counsel from these great saints and go on pilgrimage to seek them out.

We in the West may lack this ingrained tradition of seeking out holy men and women, though doubtless they are present here too. I have met some: a car mechanic in Boston, a Taos artist, Native American elders, Zen Buddhists, Sufis, artists, chemists, musicians, healers, and poets. Some were wonderful teachers. Most still had *karma* (the results of past actions, the laws of cause and effect) they were working out. Each had some aspect of the One shining through, and all were beautiful human beings. This is not to say we Westerners are not truth seekers. Yet we are not a traditional culture like that of the Native Americans, whose deep reverence for their spiritual elders is similar to the way holy people are woven into the fabric of spiritual life in India.

This contrast was readily apparent to me when I traveled back and forth from Nainital in the Himalayan foothills to New York City. The people of Nainital, at least some of them, identify with their souls. In that part of India the world is still viewed from the vantage point of the soul. The Himalayan region is different from the plains and has been frequented by yogis and saints for millennia. The people seem simpler, hospitable, and loving, and their traditional culture keeps the stories of realized beings alive. They know they are souls.

Although the cities in India are largely Westernized, in the villages traditional people still realize they're on a spiritual journey. It's a long-term view, because they believe in reincarnation. It may take many births for a soul to become one with God, but they know that's where they're going. The villages of India have supported the traditions of *sadhus,* wandering monks and holy men, and of *siddhas,* realized beings, for millennia.

Jet travel makes the East–West difference more glaring. The minute the plane door opens in New York, it is ego, ego, ego—everyone identify-

ing with their roles. In the West who you are is defined by what you do. The view seen by the ego is bounded by this single incarnation, which ends in death. The fear of death is a very powerful motivator. The soul doesn't have that fear. If you make that shift of consciousness from the ego level to the soul level, the fear goes away.

I came back home from India and saw my dad and my future step-mother, Phyllis, at their house, and in my new perception they were indeed souls. They were both aging, and my dad had oriented himself toward death. Although he was on the board of trustees of the syna-gogue, his religious practice consisted solely of outer form, which left him with a lot of inner fear. The calm space I brought from being with Maharaj-ji must have been reassuring. I was in my soul and saw them as souls, which allowed them to begin to see their lives more spaciously. Over the next years there was a deep change in our relationship. We were together as souls.

Years before, we were sitting in deck chairs at my father's three-hole golf course on the family farm in Franklin, New Hampshire. It was a beautiful sunset, and I said, "Dad, isn't it beautiful!"

"Yes, look how beautifully it's cut," he replied. He had just mowed the grass and was proud of how the greens looked.

When he was about ninety-five and we were living down in Cohasset along the Massachusetts south shore, he was in bed, and I was holding his hand. We were looking out the window, and he said, "Look, Rich, what a beautiful sunset!" That was soul wonder—we had come full circle.

In Nainital people do the *dharma* of their social role, but at the same time they know their soul is separate from their role. A sweeper isn't necessarily just a sweeper, the king isn't necessarily just a king; they are doing their *dharma* for that incarnation, while the inner being is also there looking out. From that soul point of view, your *karma* is your *dharma*, what you do is part of your inner journey, and your role takes you into your soul. Then you get a chance to stand back and see what in your incarnation is helpful to you as a soul and to others on your trip to God.

A Meeting of the Minds, and Heart

In the West it's hard to even conceive of enlightened beings. We have much to learn about how to approach them, how to be with them, how to use them on our own journey into our heart. Cultures like that of India have customs and forms that, although perhaps not directly transferable, can show us how to be in the presence of a holy person.

As a teenager getting ready for a date, I would go to great lengths dressing, combing my hair, buying flowers, acquiring the money, planning the evening—there seemed to be no end to my preoccupation with the momentous trivia of going on a date. Only when everything was in order could I begin to open to the relationship. If my shoes were scuffed, I would spend a good part of the evening hiding them under an available chair or couch or being embarrassed or self-conscious about them. In its own way opening to the presence of a holy being, a lover for your soul, demands that same kind of psychological preparation.

When I first traveled around India and saw holy beings, I treated these meetings rather casually and just enjoyed being with whomever I happened to be with at whatever level we happened to meet. But as time went on, I began to appreciate receiving the presence of spiritual beings more deeply and having the opportunity to drink from the well of their experience. I came to understand that this transmission of living spirit involves preparation in order to be open to receive it. Slowing my mind down enough to be in the moment in "Indian time" was one part of that. Opening my heart to feel their love was another.

Imagine living in India twenty-five hundred years ago. You hear about an enlightened being walking the earth called Gautama Buddha. You set out to find him to receive his teachings.

Perhaps you go to Sarnath, where he delivered his first sermon in the Deer Park. You talk to the newly ordained *bikkhus,* or monks, gathered there and ask his whereabouts. They direct you to a town to the north. You travel on foot, in a horse-drawn wagon, or by oxcart. In each village you receive another report, making you feel you are getting closer. Your anticipation mounts day by day as you move from village to village, your mind fixed on the moment when you will meet this being, sit before him, and receive his teaching.

Weeks go by, and you begin to meet people who have just been with the Buddha. Their eyes are alight, their hearts open. They emanate a peace that speaks of the experience they've had. Finally you are within a day's travel of the Buddha. Your mind turns to how you will prepare yourself for this meeting. As you near your destination, you stop and bathe and wash your clothes, perhaps pick some flowers or fruit in one of the villages. As you get very close, you are so excited you are afraid that you will not be quiet enough to receive him. So you sit on a rock by a stream, collecting yourself.

Finally you approach the cave where the Buddha sits. You climb the hill to the door of the cave. It is dark inside. A small fire flickers, and in the firelight you see someone sitting in meditation. After some time, he becomes aware of your presence and motions you to enter. You enter, bow before him, and offer your fruit and flowers. You sit before him and finally raise your eyes to look into his. Time stops. Everything you have been anticipating is coming to fruition in this moment.

The universe disappears. Only his eyes exist. A flow of love, wisdom, consciousness passes between you. Perhaps a few words are said—words you take away and think upon again and again in the years to follow. Or perhaps he says nothing, and it is just his stillness, his presence, the incredible love that flows from him, the deep compassion you feel. You feel as if you were naked before his glance. He sees through you, he knows all—past, present, and future. He does not judge, but simply acknowledges how it all is. Even a moment of such compassion can be liberating.

Road Signs and Map Readers

There are no maps for this journey, but it's helpful to have some understanding of what realization or awakening is really about. In truth, the Great Way resonates in the heart for each of us. We each have our path. There are many routes up the mountain, but they all end at the peak. The grace and forbearing love of the great ones are there to guide our steps, if only we know to look for them.

O brother, my heart yearns for that true guru, who fills the cup of true love, and drinks of it himself, and offers it then to me.

He removes the veil from the eyes, and gives the true Vision of Brahma:
He reveals the worlds in Him, and makes me to hear the Unstruck Music:
He shows joy and sorrow to be one:
He fills all utterance with love.
Kabir says: "Verily he has no fear, who has such a guru to lead him to the
    shelter of safety!"

—Kabir[2]

Of course, things never happen as you expect. My primary motivation for being in India the first time was to find someone who could read the maps of consciousness that had unfolded for me when I first took psilocybin mushrooms on March 6, 1961. The maps of Western psychology were of no use with psychedelics. Those planes of consciousness were not explained by psychology. The *Tibetan Book of the Dead* was the best depiction I had up to that point.

I was convinced of that by an LSD trip I had on a Saturday night that was so completely ineffable I couldn't even talk about it. The next Tuesday I first saw the *Tibetan Book of the Dead,* which was given to us by Aldous Huxley. It was the old Evans-Wentz translation, and it led Tim Leary to meet with Evans-Wentz. In it I found an uncanny description of my LSD trip, and that was how our book, *The Psychedelic Experience,* came into being. We used the Tibetan *bardo* (the disembodied astral state between births) as a model for psychedelic trips. That was the "map" that inspired me to go to India.

My goal in India was to find someone who could read the maps of consciousness. But as I reflect back on the mind-blowing day I met Maharaj-ji, I thought I was merely a passenger in the car. My traveling companion, Bhagavan Das, said he needed to go see his guru about his visa. I had a Land Rover that my friend David Padwa had allowed me to use. I was responsible for it, and Bhagavan Das talked me into letting him drive it up to the mountains to see this guru. He knew I didn't like Hindus because

of all the calendar gods and statues and the loudspeakers at the temples. My anal-compulsive personality was more attracted to Buddhism.

As we headed up into the Himalayas, we spent the night at a house near Bareilly somewhere out in the country. In the middle of the night I had to go to the bathroom, which was an outhouse. The stars seemed very big and the heavens close. I thought of my mother, who had died about six months previously. She seemed very close too. I had to laugh at myself, because here I was, a Freudian, thinking about my mother on the way to the outhouse. Then I went back to bed. The next morning we continued another fifty miles or so, winding up the switchbacks into the Kumaon region, in the foothills of the Himalayas.

We finally arrived at a little roadside temple at a place called Bhumiadhar. A crowd surrounded the Land Rover. They were very warm toward Bhagavan Das, who spoke Hindi and was conversing easily with them. All I could do was listen. He told me, "They say my guru is up on the hill. So, if you don't mind, I'll go up there." He was so moved about seeing his guru that he was crying, and he loped up the hill. I stayed in the car. I was feeling tired and frustrated and eager to go back to America. I didn't know how long he was going to be gone. He didn't invite me to come because he knew I didn't like gurus.

I had no idea what was going on. There I was in this big fancy car. After he got out, I thought the crowd turned hostile toward me. I was very paranoid. I didn't speak Hindi, and I wasn't rushing up to see any guru. The people around the car were insistent that I go see him. They were yelling at me, because I wasn't following my friend up the hill to meet Maharaj-ji. Of course, they wanted me to have a chance to meet a saint, but I thought they wanted me to get out, so they could get the Land Rover. That's how paranoid I was. But finally my curiosity got the better of me, and I got out of the car and followed Bhagavan Das up the hill. But I kept looking back at the Land Rover, worrying that people were going to steal it.

Up on the hill a man in a blanket was sitting on the grass with ten or twelve people around him. I kept my distance. Maharaj-ji pointed to me and said something in Hindi. Someone was translating for me, who I later learned was K. K. Sah. The first thing Maharaj-ji asked me was "Did you come in a big car?" The next thing he said was "Will you give it to me?"

That immediately set off all my paranoia about gurus and made me angry. Bhagavan Das was flat on the ground in *dunda pranam,* a posture of deepest respect. He leaped to his feet and said, "Maharaj-ji, if you want it, you can have it."

That really fueled my paranoia, and my anger almost boiled over. Besides that, the Indians grouped around were all laughing at me. Of course, they knew Maharaj-ji would never ask for a car, but I didn't know that. He was playing with me like a cat with a mouse. I had no idea who he was or how he operated. Years later K.K. described me standing hunched with my hands in the pockets of my jeans looking angry and afraid. I just remember feeling very uptight. K.K. thought I was completely stuck in my ego. He was right.

What followed was the kind of opening that can only be performed by a true guru who knows the precise moment when the nut is ripe to be cracked open with a single sharp tap. Maharaj-ji began telling me things about my previous night under the stars and my mother's recent death that he couldn't possibly know. Then he said, "Spleen!" in plain English, which is what she died of, cancer of the spleen, and my unreleased emotions cascaded with the impossible fact that this *baba* in the Himalayas knew every detail about my mother. Something in me shattered, and I just began to sob. I was flooded with grief, and relief, and the immensity of traveling halfway around the world to find this loving old man in a blanket who *knew*. Still dazed and confused, I was sent to stay at K.K.'s house in Nainital that night. Maharaj-ji told him to feed me toast.

Becoming a Yogi: A Six-Month Short Course in Renunciation

From that first meeting with Maharaj-ji, I was totally in the moment. It was almost inconceivable that I was surrendering to him and that he was taking me over; it just didn't compute. I wasn't time binding; I wasn't relating it to the past. Maharaj-ji did that to me. His love made it okay.

I was planning to say good-bye to Bhagavan Das and go back to the States in two days. Instead, I found myself staying in an ashram in the Himalayas for six months, which seemed like Maharaj-ji's plan from the beginning. What always surprises me is that I had no resistance. Earlier that day I was so paranoid about the Land Rover and so averse to meeting a guru. Yet immediately afterward, I was perfectly willing to go and stay at K. K. Sah's on Maharaj-ji's instruction. It was like home to me.

That was a momentous shift. I still don't have words to define it, but it was a complete figure-ground shift in my perceptual vantage point. I went from being an assertive, decisive person to completely surrendering and allowing Maharaj-ji to run my life. And I didn't even think about it; I just shifted. I wasn't self-conscious about it; it just felt completely natural. I was suddenly on a completely different life path, and I hadn't made any kind of a conscious decision. The day before, Maharaj-ji and Hinduism had been anathema. But now they had just taken me over, and I felt as if I were home. That's the power of Maharaj-ji's love.

Because I had taken so many LSD trips, I was used to changing my consciousness in big leaps. Acid got me ready for Maharaj-ji. If it wasn't

for that, I never would have stopped long enough. I wouldn't have had the curiosity to open the door of the Land Rover. Before that, I was so busy making decisions about Bhagavan Das and all that melodrama. We were walking around Sarnath from temple to temple barefooted. It was hot and uncomfortable, and I had blisters. The Hindus were treating us like *sadhus,* wandering holy men. Poor pilgrims were leaving rupees in front of me as offerings. Meanwhile, I had traveler's checks in my pocket.

After that first meeting, when Maharaj-ji sent me to stay with K. K. Sah and his family, they were so gentle and kind to me. Here I was, an unknown foreigner disrupting their lives, and they just took me in. They treated me like a member of Maharaj-ji's family. K.K. is very much an instrument of Maharaj-ji. Maybe Maharaj-ji saw it all in advance, the role K.K. was going to play with the Westerners. After a day or two with K.K.'s family I saw Maharaj-ji again at Bhumiadhar. Then he sent me to the ashram at Kainchi to begin my *sadhana,* the inner work, including yoga with Hari Dass.

Darshan: *A Point of View*

In India there are simple rituals to prepare for *darshan,* to visit a saint, guru, or *siddha.* When you enter the temple, you pay your respects to the deities, which begins to open you to that heart space. You offer obeisance, or *pranams,* fruit or flowers, sweets or money to a holy person and touch their feet. It's not really giving or receiving on the material plane, but more like opening yourself to more spiritual energy, or *shakti.* Later as my heart opened, I came to appreciate how these simple ritual acts enriched my experience.

Of course, when I first met Maharaj-ji, I didn't do any of those rituals and it didn't matter. The real saints are beyond rituals, and gurus or *siddhas* are often unorthodox. They may acknowledge you or ignore you, send you away or feed you, maybe allow you to share their presence and enjoy their *darshan* for some moments or hours.

Darshan literally means "a view," sharing another's vantage point, a point of view that comes from that higher place of the spirit manifested through another being. It's a profound shift from the point of view of the ego to the point of view of the soul. It can make all your study and reading come to life in a moment. It can be an experience so profound as to change the direction of your life, return you to your spiritual roots, take you beyond all words and thoughts into the most profound depth of the heart. In that depth, the little soul begins to dissolve into the bigger Soul. That movement from the individual soul, the *jivatman*, to the greater soul, the *ātman*, is like dissolving into the ocean of love.

Although I was with Maharaj-ji in India, you don't need to sit in a saint's physical presence to have his or her *darshan*. *Darshan* can occur in a dream, through a picture, a statue, or a physical place or from hearing the voice or reading the words of a realized being. The true nature of *darshan* is not the meeting on the physical plane; it is the meeting on the soul plane. It is not words or pictures, pilgrimages or teachings. It is not the stuff of our senses or our thoughts. *Darshan* is the meeting of hearts, the merging of souls, sharing the moment with complete awareness, compassion, love, and energy.

Through words and pictures, we speak to one another about the unspeakable. We look to see the unseeable. We try to understand the unknowable. And all the time this process is going on—all that yearning, trying, listening, looking, thinking—on another level the moment is complete unto itself. In that complete moment the transmission, the transmitter, and the receiver of the transmission are one. It is a moment of pure love.

For the devotee, *darshan* extends far beyond the physical presence. Thinking about a saint, looking at a picture, remembering precious moments, recounting stories with other devotees all continue the *darshan*. Devotees are like bees drawn to flowers to make more honey. Devotees make *darshan* their focus, the way a compass needle points to magnetic north.

Around Nainital, in the foothills of the Himalayas, there is a long tradition of saints who have inhabited the area, and each family has its share of stories. We would often sit around the fire in the kitchen drinking *chai*, exchanging the intimate stories, the incidents of daily life with the beings that one or another of us had contact with. Individuals might be known for the way they recount a certain incident. As the stories are told again and again, they keep taking on new richness, enhancing the depth of the love. These incidents are not just stories or folklore, but the fabric of spiritual life and the foundation of faith. It's bliss to hear these stories, the *lilas* of the saints, described by the old devotees there. They make them come alive.

We would sit by the fire, Indian and Western devotees gathered together, sharing these loving stories of the saints. At the end someone would say, "But who can understand such beings?" Our minds could not expand enough to truly comprehend their consciousness, compassion, and wisdom. But these stories continue to take on meaning. Even the simplest acts of such beings reverberate on many planes through time.

We used to talk and talk. Bina, K.K.'s sister, would come in and ask if we would like tea again, thinking we would say no because we had had tea already. But we said yes, and she had to go and start up the wood fire

> He is like a flower turned into a nose to smell its fragrance, or a face enjoying the knowledge of its own identity which was already in existence but was due to its looking into a mirror. So the master and his disciple appear as two, the master alone enjoys himself under the guise of the two.
>
> —Jnaneshwar[3]

again, because there was no gas stove, as there is now. No one wanted to stop. The joy of that kind of devotion is hard to imagine for someone who has not been in that family atmosphere.

When I sat in the kitchens of that Himalayan town, at first I was only interested in stories about my own guru, Neem Karoli Baba. The other stories were of saints long gone from their bodies. But slowly I began to appreciate the profound teaching that came through each recollection. I began to listen for that kernel of light, the jewel of spiritual teaching in each incident, each commonplace miracle in the lives of these great beings. These gatherings are *satsang,* the community of seekers—a spiritual family that recognizes truth and shares the *bhava,* the mood, of devotion.

There are thousands of saints in India's history. A few like Sri Ramakrishna, Ramana Maharshi, and Shirdi Sai Baba are well known; books have been written about them. Some had thousands of devotees, and temples were built in their honor. Others are remembered through the poems and songs of God that poured forth from them, making up the folklore and music of India. So many others, local saints and jungle *sadhus,* yogis living in mountain caves or known only in a few villages, are no less pure, but their *dharma* didn't involve public recognition. Some are secretive or even intentionally put people off, like one *baba* who used to throw feces at passersby. Many of the most remarkable stories are about these beings.

Some of these stories tell of astonishing miracles far beyond the powers we attribute to human beings. Others are just about the daily trivia of life, each event reflecting in some way the living truth that comes through someone who is at One. Every act of a realized being is a teaching. The way they wash a dish conveys the wisdom of the ages. The way they walk down the street, the movement of a hand, a facial expression—it's all pure grace. A being who has merged with love, merged with truth, is grace itself. How many may walk among us we will never know.

Liberation

When I speak of a liberated being, I mean someone who is free from entrapment in any one plane of consciousness or relative reality. A rocket that can get out of the earth's orbit would be liberated from the pull of gravity. Each reality has its own gravitational field of desires and belief systems. A person who is liberated from this physical/psychological plane is someone who can break the identification with that which is born and dies, that which desires birth and believes in death.

Most of us are very attached to this physical plane of existence, and to become free of it, to enter into another plane, is in a sense liberation. However, you can be entrapped on other planes even though free of this plane, which is far from total perfection. The ability to get out is different from the ability to come back in, to integrate the planes. When someone breaks out of the earthly plane's psychic gravity, they may be so blown away by the presence of God that they don't want to come back. Sometimes they become what in India are called *masts,* the God-intoxicated, who may seem psychotic or disoriented, because they haven't reintegrated on the physical plane. Slowly they learn how to go in and out, to the extent there is still any inside or outside.

Some seekers may become so transfixed by the delights of astral planes that they linger there. There are many saints who are almost perfected, who work on one plane or another, but some of them have not dealt with the final stages. This doesn't mean they're not great teachers or saints, only that they haven't yet finished their work.

Perfected beings, or *siddhas,* hold to nothing, stand nowhere, and can go in and out of all planes. They do not really go in and out of planes, because they are in all planes simultaneously. Such beings are no longer bound by time and space and may manifest or not, keep a body or drop it. In that fluid state all is possible—to keep the body young or to leave it, to merge into God or stay in form for the liberation of all beings. Such beings are beyond all law and limitation. They are the *dharma,* the perfect harmony of God's will and the human mind. Every plane is flowing into every other plane, and God is flowing through them as instruments. It's just unbroken flow. Then it's nothing special, no difference, all One.

At this point it's not about the experience but about the *experiencer.* As the planes start to come together, you go to a place where you die as the experiencer into the experience. It doesn't have anything to do with you. It just *is,* and *you're* not doing it. Many beings have never taken that step, that immolation or dissolution of the individual. The separate self is alone, while the true Self is Unity, becoming One, the end of identifying as a separate being. (As in the joke, "What does the Buddhist say to the hot dog vendor?" "Make me One with Everything.")

The paradox of the One is that when the ego dissolves, there's an experience but no experiencer. The experience happens, but *you* the experiencer are different, you've gone beyond that small self. The outward experience may be the same. As Zen Buddhists say, "Before *satori* (enlightenment) you chop wood and carry water. After *satori* you chop wood and carry water." It's one of those "tree falling in the forest" things. But there's also the existential reality of that state, being in a physical body and at the same time in the void, the Absolute. The ultimate place is to be in form and not in form simultaneously, one foot in the world and one foot in the void, a physical reality completely continuous with perfect luminous emptiness. Emptiness is not an experience. Here words fall short. These are two different places of consciousness; human beings can function on two planes at once.

Nobody hOMe

The question of whether a being is fully realized or not depends on whether that being is really egoless or just appears to be so. If a person still identifies with thought forms or desires, the work is not complete. In perfection there's no clinging at all.

Perhaps now you begin to see the subtlety of the attachments that must be surrendered. The attachment to experiences, including the experience of God and the ecstasy and rapture of that union, even experiences of omniscience, of omnipresence, of infinite power, the *experience* of being the One (as opposed to just *being* One)—these are described in southern Buddhism as *jhanas,* or temporal absorption states. As long as there's a trace of an experiencer, there is still an element of self-consciousness, the ego of being the experiencer. If it's still an experience, it is not the ultimate reality. It's simple: if you're having an experience, you know you have to go beyond it. Isn't it beautiful?

For a perfect being, a Buddha, there's nobody home. They are completely *here* and nowhere and everywhere at once. A perfected being *is* fully in the flow of existence, so there's no place where they're not. The paradox of emptiness (*sunyata*) is that it is really fullness. Egolessness is not nonexistence, but an effulgence of *being.* Finally there is just function at every level. That's what Christ referred to when he said, "Had you but faith, you could move mountains."

I used to feel I was at the edge of a beautiful calm lake with the earth under my feet, and I would want to jump in, but I didn't have the courage. It was like trying to do a back dive

> The mind is a bundle of thoughts. The thoughts arise because there is the thinker. The thinker is the ego. The ego, if sought, will automatically vanish.
>
> Reality is simply the loss of the ego. Destroy the ego by seeking its identity. Because ego is no entity it will automatically vanish and reality will shine forth by itself. This is the direct method, whereas all other methods are done, only retaining the ego.
>
> —*Ramana Maharshi*[4]

when I was a kid. I would stand in position on the diving board for perhaps an hour, and I would know it would all be good, but I just couldn't do it.

Love is what lets you dive into the emptiness behind form. The jump from things to no-thing, to emptiness, just means it's empty of experience. It's like two planes: one is the plane of the soul; then you leave that behind and dissolve into the One, which is emptiness. You let love carry you into merging with the One. It's the devotion, *bhakti*, that takes you through to the wisdom, or *jnana*, the *satori* of Zen.

Love is what's melding the universe together. You love everybody and everything more and more until you love all things in the universe, and you identify with all things and become the One. When you dive into the One, you find emptiness, because there's no experiencer in the One. The love brings about that melding, that jump from being everything to being nothing, from being somebody to being nobody.

With Maharaj-ji there was nobody there; there was just love. I used to see him turn into a mountain, like Shiva, the pure absolute, but then I would feel this intense love. He is unconditional love, but it's impersonal. It wasn't him loving me; it was him being love. I turned it into something interpersonal, but it wasn't.

Love is the emotional color of the soul. Unconditional love is the color of enlightenment, unfettered by personal barriers or distinctions, devoid of ego, yet reflecting the highest Self. It's like sunlight unfiltered by clouds or the taste of water from the purest spring.

If thou desirest to be a Yogi,
Renounce the world.
Dye thy heart deep in His Love.
For real lovers drink the cup of Nothingness, and
Pass away into the Valley of Amazement, in remembrance of Him.

—Shah Latif (1689–1752)[5]

We can learn unconditional love from those who live in it, the saints and *siddhas,* from their *darshan,* their presence, their *satsang.* We may get a taste of it in an Indian family, absorbing the traditions and customs, the affection between grandparents and grandchildren. In any case, to feel it, we have to let go of our analytical minds and open ourselves to the moment and to those who have gone before.

chapter five

guides

As you meet beings along the path, you'll come to sense who are your teachers and who are *teachings* for you. Some teachers are obviously still working on themselves, and they feed you by sharing their experiences. Others serve as living examples of the detours and pitfalls along the way, which may help you reflect on how to get on with your own path. They become *teachings* for you, whatever the intention when you started out.

In Indian folklore there is a classic story of a guru and disciple. This guru is proud of his attainments, while the humble disciple takes the teachings to heart and deepens his practice. One day the guru is riding through the bazaar on a palanquin, and they meet. Knowing purity when he sees it, the guru bows at his disciple's feet, recognizing that the disciple achieved liberation, while all he himself achieved were recognition and material desires.

A pure-hearted devotee takes what he or she needs and leaves the rest. Even a great teacher's spiritual attainments ring hollow while the ego holds sway. If both teacher and disciple aren't getting free, they are just creating more *karma*.

When I was with Chogyam Trungpa Rinpoche, the Oxford-educated Tibetan *tulku* who founded Naropa Institute, he was drinking, gambling, and playing sexual games with his students, and it made me very uncomfortable. I saw that he was helping them run through their Western *karma*. My discomfort was that he was encouraging them to do things that trapped them further in worldly stuff, but I think from his standpoint (and, I hope, theirs) he was just taking them through it. He could see with the spiritual eye that they were ready for that teaching.

That is *tantra* in the classical sense, using desire to get free of desire. The trouble is it's hard to tell from the outside whether someone is getting more attached to a pattern of desire or whether that one experience will push someone over the edge into *vairagya*, the world-weariness that is the precursor to true detachment. If it is not an act of volition, what Gurdjieff used to call intentional suffering, but a teaching imposed from without, it's hard to see how it works.

Siddhi-*fied*

I met Swami Muktananda for the first time at Big Indian, the ashram of Rudi (Rudrananda, aka Albert Rudolph) in upstate New York. Rudi was also a devotee of Muktananda's guru, Nityananda. I was one of the musicians in the chanting circle on the stage with Muktananda. Muktananda's staff were encouraging me to travel with him and introduce him around the world. I had a vision of Maharaj-ji dancing in the middle of the circle, and he looked at me and said, "Help the man." When the music ended, I told Muktananda I would help him. I went on tour with him in the United States, and then on to Australia and Singapore, and finally back to India. Looking back, I wonder if that vision actually came from Maharaj-ji.

When I went back to India with Muktananda at the end of his world tour in 1970, he had me give a speech alongside him and a Supreme

Court justice at a football stadium in Bombay. The next day we drove up to his ashram in Ganeshpuri, a few hours north of Bombay. When we got to the ashram, there were fireworks and hundreds of people lining up to greet Muktananda. As is the custom they all brought offerings.

He had me sit on a lower throne next to his taller throne, and when they'd bring flowers he'd pass them on to me. When they gave him money, he'd put it under his cloth. I was inundated with about forty pounds of flowers. In the heat, the smell of marigolds was suffocating. That went on for two days. I sat under a lot of flowers, and he took in a lot of money.

Papa Trivedi, the president of Muktananda's ashram board of trustees, invited me to his home. I was a visiting yogi. He told me, "The doctor said that for my heart I have to take a little scotch every night." I said that I understood.

I went into his room expecting him to bring out a medicine glass, but he brought out an ice bucket and two glasses. I started remembering the days when I really loved scotch and soda. So he poured one and said, "Would you like some plain soda?"

I said, "No, I'll join you." I figured, "Tantra is for me!"

We staggered through dinner, and I could barely find the table. That was on one drink. Next evening we started a little earlier. He kept telling me to stay on and become part of the scene, because Muktananda was taking such an unusual interest in me.

While I was staying at the ashram in Ganeshpuri, Muktananda invited me to meditate in a "cave" in the basement where he had done his own meditation. He told me to stop meditating in the *satsang* hall where everybody sat together. At 3 A.M. I went down there. A *sadhu* with a large key opened the gate of the cave. The cave room was very dark and hot. I proceeded to take my clothes off and meditate. I immediately experienced *shakti* (energy) or *kundalini* (the "serpent power" latent in the spine) and entered a visionary state in which I was flying. In this vision I was kneeling in the air before Muktananda. Then I proceeded to shoot over his head, still flying.

When I finished the vision or whatever it was, I was so energized I wanted to leave the cave. I rattled the gate until the man with the key came. It was about 4 A.M. I raced for the outside courtyard, wanting to get some air. In the distance I saw Swami Muktananda and one of his devotees walking in the courtyard. I went running over to Muktananda, and he said, "Ram Dass, did you like flying?"

Later, as part of a *yatra,* or pilgrimage, that Muktananda led in his blue-pearl Mercedes, we traveled in a VW bus to a series of Shaivite temples in South India called *siddha peeths.* They were all power spots where great saints and yogis had lived. One night in a temple town called

Gokarn, Muktananda came and woke me about 3 A.M. He didn't speak any English, and I didn't speak Marathi, but he motioned me to follow him. We walked down a quiet street to a small temple on the top of a building. In this temple he gave me a *mantra* in an initiation. Right after that I fell asleep.

About 9 A.M. somebody came and woke me up and said, "Baba wants you."

When I got to the place he was staying at, I asked him, "What was that about?"

He said, "That mantra will give you vast wealth and power."

Being a self-righteous do-gooder, I said, "I will only accept it if you give me love and compassion too."

He looked at me with disgust. That was the Vaishnavite (me) meeting the Shaivite (Muktananda), the way of love meeting the way of power.

That experience of flying over Muktananda's head and all this special treatment from him were consistent with the effort of Muktananda's people to get me to become his lineage holder or heir apparent, whatever you call it. They kept saying things like, "Maharaj-ji was your *first* guru. Now you're ready for your *real* guru." But it meant nothing to me. That's how it is with your guru. My heart was so tuned to Maharaj-ji, it didn't even register.

Besides this manifestation of Muktananda's powers, or *siddhis,* there were several aspects of this experience that linked back to Maharaj-ji. First, when I met Maharaj-ji in 1966, he had said to me, "You really want to fly." I replied that I flew a plane—I had a pilot's license and I flew a Cessna.

After leaving Ganeshpuri I went back to the north to Vrindavan, where Maharaj-ji met us with cosmic precision. Afterward when we were sitting with him, he said to me out of the clear blue, "You know, it's good to meditate naked." He didn't say anything else about it.

One day later Maharaj-ji called me in and started talking about Hari Dass Baba. By this time Hari Dass was in America, surrounded by students who had heard about him through me. He was being taken care of by several very devoted women. The only thing is yogi renunciates are not supposed to hang out with women.

Maharaj-ji said, "He's with women!"

"Yes, I know, Maharaj-ji."

"What does he call them?"

"He calls them his mothers."

"Oh. How old are they?"

"One is twenty years old."

"Mothers?!"

He had taken me through this routine a dozen times before. Then he said, "You know what his mothers give him?"

"No, what?" I asked.

"They give him milk."

"That's wonderful. Mothers, milk, that's beautiful."

"Every night they give him milk."

"Oh, that's wonderful, Maharaj-ji."

Then Maharaj-ji leaned down really close to me and said, "You know what they put in the milk?"

"No, Maharaj-ji. What do they put in the milk?"

"Whiskey!" he said in a shocked tone.

"No!" I said.

He came even closer and he said, "Yes!"

He shook his finger at me, and we both knew whose drinking he was referring to.

It's tricky to tell these stories, because I was very much attracted to power, and Muktananda used his powers. My impression was that although these were truly *siddhis*, or yogic powers, his whole scene was power-oriented, third *chakra*, and although the power was spiritual, it was also being used to gain worldly stuff. I felt there was an element of personal desire and a misuse of power.

When I told Maharaj-ji, "Muktananda has a dining room table and chairs made of gold," Maharaj-ji said, "He holds on to too much." Of course, Maharaj-ji had also set me up to be with Muktananda. I believe he sent me to Muktananda to understand the distinction between love and power. Muktananda was a mirror in which I could see my own desire.

You may have many teachers and teachings along the way. A teaching may be a situation that reflects your desire back to you like a mirror and shows you where you're at, or where you're not, the way in Muktananda I could see mirrored my desire for power. An *upu-guru,* a kind of temporary guru, can be a teacher who points you to the path.

> Those who themselves have seen the Truth can be thy teachers of wisdom; ask from them, bow unto them, be thou a servant unto them.
>
> —*Bhagavad Gita 4:34*

Over the years as I've reflected on these experiences I realized that although Muktananda wasn't my guru, he was a guru for others, and he was a great teacher for me. The same person who is a guru for one person may be a teacher or a teaching for somebody else. Your true guru, or *sat guru,* on the other hand, is the true "remover of darkness" for you, beckoning to you from farther up the path and capable of taking you through to enlightenment.

Teachers may have much to offer, even though they may not be able to bring you to the final stage. Teachers who point the way as they work on themselves with an open heart may be very pure, or *sattvic.* They may have had that initial glimpse of divinity that turned their mind toward truth, and they are working toward realization. Pure teachers can give you the basic training in yoga and meditation to clear the mind, purification that gets you on your way.

Changing Planes

Every person has a guru, but only some have a guru on this plane. Some people contact Maharaj-ji by reading *Miracle of Love,* chanting with Krishna Das, or attending my talks, developing a heart connection to Maharaj-ji that many of us who were with him in the body do not have. We got distracted by his form. Those who meet Maharaj-ji in books, talks, or meditation have him as fully in their lives as those who saw him in the flesh.

Not all conscious beings have physical bodies. Some liberated beings exist primarily in other *lokas,* nonmaterial worlds or planes, in subtle or astral bodies. They work across planes, not only with beings on those planes, but also with us on the physical plane. You may have read about or experienced having a guardian angel, hearing an inner voice, or having an inner guide. Such astral presences are relatively real. They are real within that plane, the way a tiger is real in a dream until we awaken.

I was on the road lecturing in the United States, and I was scheduled to stay at a house of Buddhist practitioners. When I arrived, they said to me, "Before you go rest, there's a woman here who has been hospitalized several times. We've talked to her, but we can't do much with her. Would you see her?"

I went in and found a highly agitated woman sprawled on a bed. "What's the problem?" I asked.

"Well, I guess I'm crazy."

"Why do you think that?"

"Well, all this stuff happens to me. My mother thinks I'm crazy and put me in a hospital."

"What do the people in this house think?"

"Well, they say it's all in my mind."

That's what a Buddhist might say. "Well, what is it in your mind?" I asked.

"How does a pyramid with three stars grab you?"

"That's pretty nice. Do you see that?" I replied.

"How would you like to be driving down the street in your car, and suddenly there's an American Indian sitting next to you?"

Because I had worked with Hilda Charlton, a devotee of Swami Nityananda who used to call on Native American spirits in her classes at St. John the Divine in New York, I asked, "Does the Indian have a name?"

"Yeah, Blue Moon."

"Well, next time you see Blue Moon, tell him there's a tribe of Indians gathering on the astral plane to create a universal tribe of peace. If he would like to join that tribe, he should call into the ethers the name of Cochise, who will guide him to that group."

It blew her mind. I was obviously in control of my scene, and I thought her Indian was real. Then she told me about other beings and other experiences, and as far as I was concerned, it was all real. Now, she was at the beginning of her path, her third eye was opening, and that was part of her route. She was just frightened, and she had nobody to talk to. It didn't mean that this was the last thing she'd do before she got fully enlightened.

You can play with all this stuff, these different beings on all these different planes, and they're all incredible teachings. But it's not necessary to consciously pass through all the subtle planes, with the gods, or *devas*, and astral beings, to get to the One.

It's very paradoxical. There is nothing that you have to go through consciously, and yet there's nothing you don't go through. You might pass through incredible transformations that other people would experience as momentous personal turning points and never notice. You could go through tremendous changes in energy levels and never notice, because your path is the path of devotion, so energy experiences aren't relevant. You may be into Zen, for example, and never deal with them. The astral beings may be there, helping you, guiding you, but you don't deal with them. Your *karma* determines your path.

I was visiting with Dr. Venkataswamy, the founder of the Aravind Eye Hospital in Madurai, South India, which is named for his guru, the great Indian saint Sri Aurobindo. We went on pilgrimage with some friends to Aurobindo's ashram in Pondicherry. Dr. V., as he was affectionately known, wanted me to meditate in Sri Aurobindo's room. I started to meditate there, and as I began to go into a deep state of meditation, I heard somebody behind me. I opened my eyes, looked around, and saw a *sadhu* covered with ash sitting cross-legged on the floor. I watched him blessing me in some way or other. Then he disappeared. He dissolved like a cloud of water vapor in the sky.

The *sadhu* I had seen was an old, old *baba*. When I finished meditating, I went out and related this experience to Dr. V. and his friends. None of them seemed at all surprised.

The contemporary Brazilian healer Joao prefers to be known as Medium Joao, but is often called John of God in English. He came from humble origins and never received an education. When he was fifteen years old, St. Rita appeared to him and told him to go to a church where a crowd of people was waiting for him. He lost consciousness at the door. Only when he came out of the church did they tell him he was responsible for about a thousand people being healed. That was the beginning of his healing career. Later he came to understand that an astral being had taken him over.

Through Joao a "phalange" of incorporeal doctors provides amazing holistic healing and a taste of unconditional love to thousands of people every year from Brazil and abroad. Certainly the entities of John of God's astral medical college are real to him and to those who receive treatment at his center, the Casa. His consciousness can shift onto the plane where they exist and bring healing to those of us who cannot otherwise experience those other levels.

These astral beings can be loving and helpful guides. Their energy and wisdom can bring us to new levels in our *sadhana* and open us to higher vibratory planes. They can be a focus for developing our devotion, much as the Tibetans use visualizations and *mantras* to develop relations with celestial beings, gurus, and *dakinis* (tantric deities).

By acknowledging such immaterial beings and planes as equally real—but not more real—than this immediate reality, you start to free yourself of attachment to any one plane or level of reality. Thinking of them as more real than this physical reality, however, can create more attachment. The attraction to the energies and mysteries of other planes can be a tremendous distraction or side trip from one's path. Attachment is attachment on any plane. Recognizing the relative nature of reality allows you to go beyond the form to where Reality lies.

Astral planes and after-death states are connected; an example is near-death experiences in which people meet all their relatives and forebears. They're all there to help them to get through what the Tibetans call the *bardos,* which are disembodied astral states between births. The ego is frightened of death, because ego is part of the incarnation and ends with it. That's why we learn to identify with our soul, because that will reduce the fear of death, as the soul continues after death. For the soul, death is just another moment.

When we talk about these planes, we differentiate them as physical, astral, causal, and so forth. But the entire creation and every plane in it are one gestalt existing right here in the present moment. For pure beings who traverse these planes, what manifests is a function of the needs of the moment rather than their desires. In such cosmic existential moments Moses brought forth the Ten Commandments, Einstein a theory of relativity, and Mozart the *Requiem.* They each manifested an aspect of the infinite One in synch with their *karma* and their cultural milieu.

These are all just methods. Ultimately all methods are illusions, so in the end it doesn't really make a lot of difference. There are more illusions than you'll ever need to get enlightened. You just use the illusions you karmically need to get there. When you are fully realized, you will recognize the illusions for what they are—relative reality, symbolic reality. You recognize them and are part of them. And when it's happening to you, you see that it's universal, and the truth is the truth is the truth. This is what the Buddha discovered when he confronted the illusion of *maya* under the *bodhi* tree.

RE: Incarnations

Full realization is very, very rare. As they see it in the East, the perfection of consciousness does not come in one birth, but through thousands and thousands of incarnations. Sometimes we may see the culminating birth, the finishing touch, as in the case of Buddha. Otherwise most of the beings who are called "saints" in India or by the Catholic church are not perfected beings. We may be seeing them in very advanced births, where, as my teacher Hari Dass Baba used to say, there's only "a transparency left of the veil of illusion." For example, when Ramana Maharshi was seventeen years old, he lay down on the floor of his uncle's study and imagined his own death, finding in that experience the core of his true Self.

Imagine a mountain of solid rock six miles long, six miles wide, and six miles high. Once every hundred years a crow flies by with a silk scarf in its beak, just barely caressing the top of the mountain with it. The length of time it would take to wear away that mountain is how Buddha described the journey to enlightenment. That's the game of incarnations. In the vastness of time any one incarnation is like the blink of an eye in relation to a seventy-year life span. Every time you blink, that's like another incarnation. Every thought form is like a lifetime. A realized being is so completely in the present moment that every time a thought appears, there is creation, preservation, and destruction of the entire universe.

Of course, that's only a description from within our limited view of relative time. It goes from the smallest unit of thought, perhaps a billionth of a second in duration (called an *asta kalapa*), to a human life (perhaps seventy years), to an astral life of perhaps five hundred or a thousand years, to an entire cycle of the universe of form, four *yugas*, called a Day of Brahma, millions upon millions of years.

How you see this chain of incarnations is a function of where you are standing in relation to time. Its illusory nature (now you see it, now you don't) becomes more apparent when you reconsider your concept of time. Realization is beyond time and space, so at another level nothing is happening anyway. When there is no attachment to the past and no expectation of the future, there is only this moment—the eternal present, here and now.

Both Hindus and Buddhists say human birth is highly auspicious, because it has the elements for liberation. You have everything you need to work with in a human birth to become realized: consciousness or awareness, conceptual understanding, the emotional heart, joy and sorrow. When Buddhists talk about the preciousness of a human birth, it's the *awareness* associated with human birth that's the opportunity. We become aware to bring ourselves to higher consciousness. Suffering is part of it too; it's all grist for the mill of developing awareness. What's here in front of you is what you can be aware of; it's food for enlightenment. It's your part in the passing show of life.

All of this requires energy, effort, willpower. One way of looking at the possibility of our human birth is that it is the intersection of physical and spiritual energy, or *shakti*. Tibetan yogis up in the Himalayas generate body heat through yogic practices called *tumo*. They have contests in the snow where they wrap wet sheets around themselves to see who can dry them the fastest. In the Hindu tradition, *shakti* is described as *kundalini,* the "serpent power" that rises in the spine and progresses through the spiritual nerve centers, or *chakras,* until it reaches the crown *chakra,* opening the yogi to cosmic consciousness.

We can also see how our human feelings and emotions can be stepping-stones to enter into divine emotion, the deep longing and love for God. The *gopis,* the milkmaids and cowherd girls, of Vrindavan cry for their playful lover Krishna, the cosmic cowherd. Responding to their intense pangs of separation, Krishna comes, and they are intoxicated by his presence, lost in divine love. For true devotees, or *bhaktas,* that unsurpassed love shines out through every pore as they dissolve themselves into it.

We can use our intellect, too, in its capacity to conceive what is beyond perception. Rationality, the power of deductive reasoning, gives us a matrix, so we can act in time and space; it takes us beyond simple survival. The power of thought leads us to wonder about the ultimate and to search for it in both our perceptual universe and our inner being. This is called *jnana yoga,* the yoga of intellect. *Bhakti,* devotion, combines with *jnana* in the heart-mind, the core of individual identity or individual soul, the *jivatman,* which merges back into the One, the *ātman,* where it originated.

From the cosmic perspective an incarnation is like the blink of an eye. For us in our human condition, it's like a full dress rehearsal with an audience. That's the witness perspective that you get if your *jivatman,* or heart-mind, is your reality. The *jivatman* is the same as the individual soul, and *jivatmans* know each other across incarnations.

On this plane you identify with who you think you are, your ego, which is the "I" thought in the thinking mind. On the soul plane you can have an individual soul, but no ego. That shift of your identification from ego to soul moves between two distinct perceptual vantage points. When you identify with the individual soul, the *jivatman,* with

some help from the guru, you go deep within and begin to merge with the collective soul, the *ātman*. The *jivatman* takes you to the *ātman*. The *jivatman* is the individual soul. The *ātman* is the One . . . nobody home.

To us Maharaj-ji often repeated, *"Sub ek!"* "It's all One!" He had a gesture in which he would hold up his index finger, almost in admonition, as if to say, "Can't you see, it's all One?" Buddha, Christ, Moses, and Krishna are all just different aspects of the same being.

I think when I die I will go to where Maharaj-ji is. That's one of the guru's jobs, to show up when you travel between incarnations. I guess it's an astral plane or a *bardo*. Then he will guide me to the One.

Once Maharaj-ji put one of his close devotees, Guru Datt Sharma, into *samadhi* with a pat on the head. Guru Datt went rigid and stopped breathing. While he was in *samadhi*, Maharaj-ji explained, "We have been together for many incarnations." That's why Maharaj-ji could affect him so quickly.

Entering the Stream

Beings who have understood how it all is, who have realized their identity with the *ātman,* are stream-enterers; they have tasted the flow of the nectar of liberation. They are a breed apart from other people in the world. They know something others do not know. Every part of their life is colored by that merging. They touch us not only through what they can share, but also through what they cannot share, what they themselves have become. We can only begin to imagine or intuitively absorb those states from our limited vantage point.

These individuals have embraced higher awareness in this life and, though realized, they are still finishing off their *karma* accrued from past lives. Perhaps their awakening is sufficient so that no new *karma* is being created and their acts are free from personal attachment. Yet they must still complete the *karma* of the body and the personality originated in previous lives or former acts in this life. The soul, the *jivatman,* carries the accumulated *sanskaras,* or tendencies, from birth to birth until the full realization of the greater *ātman.* When the soul merges in the One, there is no more separation.

> *I have stilled my restless mind, and my heart is radiant: for in Thatness*
> *I have seen beyond Thatness, in company I have seen the Comrade*
> *Himself.*
> *Living in bondage, I have set myself free: I have broken away from the*
> *clutch of all narrowness.*
> *Kabir says: "I have attained the unattainable, and my heart is colored*
> *with the color of love."*
>
> —Kabir[1]

A free being no longer identifies with the body or personality, with a personal past or future. The body, the packaging, still has its *karma* running off and the *skandhas*, the mental aggregates, continue, but with nobody in them. A saint's body may be growing old, getting sick, and so forth—that's the *karma* of the body. These beings may have the power to change their bodies or personalities, but the only reason they would do so would be for the benefit of other beings. There is no personal desire to stay on this earth. They're not going to make their bodies healthy, because it's no big deal. They might do so if it were useful to somebody else.

As the body *karma* runs off, so too does the *karma* of the personality, because no one is identified with it. Saints all have distinct personalities and qualities, their own unique *karma*. But the reason a being who no longer identifies with the body, personality, or thinking mind stays incarnated is not out of personal desire, but for the collective *karma*, the needs of other beings.

There are many beings who have attained different degrees of perfection, who have entered into different states of *samadhi*, or absorption, whose devotion and love have brought them to merging, but not quite all the way. Beings may become enamored of many subtle planes along the way. There are states, like *nirvikalpa samadhi* (*samadhi* without form), that are so deep there is no body consciousness. But even these states pass. Finally form and formless are a continuum, interpenetrating and all-pervasive, a constant tension of being and nothingness held together by the supreme attractive force of unconditional love.

Swami Vivekananda describes cosmic consciousness and *nirvikalpa samadhi*:

> "Can it be," he said, "that the water pot is God, that the drinking vessel is God, that everything we see and all of us are God?". . .
>
> At the marvelous touch of the Master, my mind underwent a complete revolution. I was aghast to realize that there really was nothing whatever

in the entire universe but God. I remained silent, wondering how long this state of mind would continue. It didn't pass off all day. I got back home, and I felt just the same there; everything I saw was God. I sat down to eat, and I saw that everything—the plate, the food, my mother who was serving it, and I myself—everything was God and nothing else but God. I swallowed a couple of mouthfuls and then sat still without speaking.[2]

One day in the Cossipore Garden, I expressed my prayer [for nirvikalpa samadhi] to Sri Ramakrishna with great earnestness. Then in the evening, at the hour of meditation, I lost consciousness of the body and felt that it was absolutely nonexistent. I felt that the sun, moon, space, time, ether, and all had been reduced to a homogeneous mass and then melted far away into the unknown. Body-consciousness almost vanished and I nearly merged in the Supreme. But I had just a trace of feeling of ego, so I could again return to the world of relativity from samadhi. In this state of samadhi all differences between "I" and "Brahman" go away, everything is reduced to unity, like the water of the Infinite Ocean— water everywhere, nothing else exists. Language and thought, all fail there. Then only is the state "beyond mind and speech" realized in its actuality. Otherwise, as long as the religious aspirant thinks or says, "I am Brahman"—"I" and "Brahman," these two entities persist—there is the involved semblance of duality. After that experience, even after trying repeatedly, I failed to bring back the state of samadhi. On informing Sri Ramakrishna about it, he said, "If you remain day and night in that state, the work of the Divine Mother will not be accomplished. Therefore you won't be able to induce that state again. When your work is finished it will come again."[3]

Perfection: The Siddha

Beyond all distinctions is a class of saints who have finished their spiritual work in every sense, who have completed their *sadhana* and are fully realized. There is no identification with a personal self, no attachment to personal *karma*. Everything they do in form is empty of personal need. The fullness of the One permeates their every moment.

When in the role of a guide such a being is a *sat guru*, a true guru who beckons from the destination farther up the mountain. The living presence of such gurus, the example of their being, shines like a light on the path. They *are* a statement of the spiritually possible. Their unconditional love is the color of the One. They are pure mirrors on which there is no dust. As saints, they may be referred to as *siddhas*, perfected beings. They call from the realm of the supreme state, enlightenment, which in terms of *samadhi*, or the state of absorption, is sometimes called *sahaja stithya* (easy or relaxed, fixed on God) *samadhi*. I remember Maharaj-ji's state being called that. He acts on this plane and is in *samadhi* at the same time; in that state there's no difference.

A perfected being lives in harmony with the universe with no clinging whatsoever. In Buddhism that state may be called "nothing special," "crazy wisdom," or the *arahat*. Taoists call it *wei wu wei*. Hindus may refer to such beings as *avadhoot*, without body consciousness, or *siddha purusha*, merged in the cosmos, or, again, as *sat guru*, gurus who bestow ultimate truth.

Perfected beings rest in emptiness, in presence, in nonconceptual, nondifferentiated awareness of every moment. Out of them comes the optimum response to any life situation. They may not think about saying it or doing it, or even know they have. It's not on that level. There's no ego.

When we were with my guru, Maharaj-ji, at times he seemed like an *avadhoot*, beyond form, like Shiva lost in meditation on a mountain peak above the clouds. On the other hand, much of the time with him was spent in seemingly trivial conversation, though that often felt like a cover for the deeper work occurring within. The talk was often laden with meaning, though we might not catch the meaning unless it was meant individually for us. Maharaj-ji's fingers were often moving as he constantly mouthed *Rām Rām Rām*, the name of God. In and out, form and no-form, past, present, and future—it was all there in every moment. There was no discontinuity between form and formless, no boundaries, no edge to his being.

It is true that at the moment of entering beyond all planes into the void, *brahman,* a being seems to have an option of merging completely or of entering the One and returning, which was mentioned in the previous chapter. Such a being is liberated in the sense of being free from all forms. At that point there is a kind of choiceless choice, a bounding condition that Buddhists call the *bodhisattva* vow, a voluntary postponement of ultimate merging to stay in form and continue to reincarnate to relieve the suffering of all beings, the ultimate act of compassion. From where we stand, the *bodhisattva* vow sounds like a heavy load, but it's actually light, because there's no self to take seriously.

In the *bhakti,* or devotional, version, it isn't even a choice. It's a surrender; it's God staying in form to extend the *lila,* the divine play. The *bhakta,* the devotee, is God's dance partner in the divine *lila.* Hanuman, the monkey god, the supreme devotee, chooses to stay separate from Rām in order to serve, to remain immersed in love for Rām and to play in the *lila.* When Rām says, "Come up here and sit with me," Hanuman refuses. He stays separate to serve Rām. He won't come up no matter how Rām attempts to persuade him. Going against God is *hard*! It's turning away from Grace to stay in the love.

Hanuman knows just how far he can push, because Rām understands perfectly. It's all part of the *lila.* Otherwise there would be no Rām and no Hanuman. And Hanuman is the one who stays incarnate for us.

That's the boon that Rām gave Hanuman, that he will always be present on earth as long as the *Ramayana* story is told.

As we pass through these seemingly endless incarnations, our predicament is that a veil of unknowing surrounds us so that we don't know who we are. Enveloped in this subjective illusion (*maya*), we think we are who we think we are. We forget we are one with God or that we've had other incarnations. As we evolve spiritually the veil of *maya* gets thinner and thinner. Perfected beings, *siddhas,* have ultimate knowledge of who they are on every plane—all their incarnations, this incarnation, and their identity with the Absolute.

> You are the guardian of Rām's door, none may enter without your leave.
>
> —*Hanuman Chalisa, v. 21*

That kind of knowing is not knowledge of a mental sort; it's wisdom or being. Perfected beings have merged with God, have become One, have gone beyond all form, beyond all polarities, merged into truth, into love, into wisdom. Perfected beings don't know those qualities—they *are* those qualities incarnate.

Every act that comes from such beings is optimum in all dimensions. It can't be anything else. The only reason they're in form is to alleviate suffering. Their acts, no matter how heartless or immoral they may seem from the outside, cannot deviate an iota from God's will, God's love. It's the nature of their being. That's who they are, a statement of that perfection. If there's no clinging, there's no way they can go against the will of God. They are the will of God.

To think of a *siddha* as experiencing you as *other* is a projection. For the *siddha* there is only One, though there may be many in that One. Your impurities are part of the terrain of existence, the texture of the One. Because perfected beings are pure awareness, their perception of the world is in no way colored by individuality or by any desire or clinging, so they see with perfect discrimination. They see it all just as it is,

> The only thing a man must renounce if he wishes to attain the Supreme Truth is the notion of individuality. Nothing else.
>
> —*Swami Ramdas*[4]

the unfolding of *karma*, the interplay of darkness and light, good and evil, life and death.

I said to Maharaj-ji, "I can't go back to the West and teach. I'm too impure."

He had me stand up and turn around, and then he said, "I don't see any imperfection."

That complete clarity of being, *is*-ness, is the origin of true compassion. It's not exactly seeing another's suffering; it is *being* it. Realized beings don't have sympathy or empathy for someone else's pain; they experience it as their own within that pure awareness. Within that greater identity there's no difference between self and other.

The Form of the Formless

All planes exist within the One. Paradoxically, the One is also a plane of consciousness. But from within the One there's no subjective experiencer, because the One can only experience itSelf. And so it creates all the other planes to experience itSelf. That's the paradox, the mystery of existence that creates the play of forms, the dance, or *lila*. A perfected being is no longer an actor in the play moving in and out of planes, going up or coming down. The subjective self has disappeared in the merging of subject and object, the One.

> Once a salt doll went to measure the depth of the ocean. . . . It wanted to tell others how deep the water was. But this it could never do, for no sooner did it get into the water than it melted. Now who was there to report the ocean's depth?
>
> —*Sri Ramakrishna*[5]

Realized beings are so vast in every dimension you can only get a glimpse of their full being, you can only approach that vastness in terms of something finite. Our limited view falls so short, it's like seeing only a mountaintop above the clouds and not the immensity of its slopes spreading beneath. As you approach the vast being-ness of this mountain, your individuality pales in comparison with that immensity, until finally you begin to dissolve into that infinite God-being. Then you, too, become one.

The guru's form is a door leading to the formless guru, to God. You love the guru's form and slowly that love transforms itself into an oceanic love. It's the lover dissolving into the Beloved.

Hanuman

In the *Ramayana*, Hanuman takes incarnation as a monkey to serve God in the form of Rām. By the grace of the Divine Mother, Sita, and his love for Rām, Hanuman possesses all powers, or *siddhis*, and he soars through the universe doing Rām's work, now merging into oneness, now coming back into separateness to embody service and devotion. He dances playfully on the edge of form. He blesses Rām's devotees and acts as a powerful model for totally devoted service to God.

Maharaj-ji's temples are Hanuman temples. In one sense Maharaj-ji is an incarnation of Hanuman. In another, Hanuman is his *ishta deva*, his personal deity, the form through which he gets to God. In that way Maharaj-ji worshiped Hanuman-ji. In another way they're the same.

A story is told about Maharaj-ji's earlier days when he used to meditate and do *tapasya*, austerities, in an underground cave. An old woman brought milk every day for Maharaj-ji to offer to Hanuman. Then Maharaj-ji would drink what was left of Hanuman's *prasad*. In this way Hanuman became his *ishta deva*, his form for the deity. One day the milk didn't come. Maharaj-ji threatened Hanuman with a stick, berating him for the lack of sustenance, because Hanuman was supposed to be taking care of Maharaj-ji.

One of our elder guru brothers in the *satsang* family, Dada Mukerjee, told numerous stories about Maharaj-ji turning into Hanuman. One night monkey paw prints appeared on the wall in Maharaj-ji's locked room at Dada's house. Another time Maharaj-ji's feet became red and hairy like Hanuman's.

Sometimes when Maharaj-ji would talk, we would realize we were talking to the Shiva or Hanuman aspect. Because from within, these are all facets of Maharaj-ji's identity, and he floats in and out of these planes like a balloon floating through various layers of the atmosphere. To speak from those planes, to form words from those spaces, to carry on a conversation when your consciousness is shifting planes, is an incredible feat. I can only compare it to being on LSD and carrying on a conversation while my consciousness was completely changing.

With Maharaj-ji the result was sometimes a hilarious juxtaposition of the childlike and the cosmic. Sometimes Maharaj-ji would complain about the way the temple was being run or be irascible and temperamental. Sometimes he would be just a cosmic giggle rolling on the bed, and sometimes he'd become like Shiva, the perfect yogi, seated on his *tukhat* as if it were Mount Kai-

At a reading of the *Ramayana*, when the reader asked what section he should recite, Maharaj-ji said, "Recite the part where I am talking with Vibhishan." (It was, of course, Hanuman who spoke with Vibhishan.)[6]

lash. Sometimes he would just be shimmering light, and sometimes, though the body was there, he would be gone, merged, absorbed into Rām.

One time I hid on the second floor overlooking the front of the temple and saw Maharaj-ji, who had just been telling us never to get angry at anyone, apparently blow up at one of the temple workers who had let some potatoes rot in the storeroom. I thought I was well hidden.

Later in the day, Dada came up to me and asked me whether I saw Maharaj-ji get angry, and I said, "Yes," though I was feeling completely bewildered.

Then Dada said, "You will understand."

The next afternoon a Western couple in our *satsang,* Radha and Mohan, complained to Maharaj-ji that they were having an argument and couldn't get advice from Ram Dass, because there was a sign on his door that said he was meditating. At that point, Maharaj-ji said, "You can get angry at someone as long as you don't throw them out of your heart." And then he pointed at me.

It's impossible to fully comprehend beings like Maharaj-ji. In their highest manifestation they aren't really *in* the incarnation; they are the universal One. Then they come down to experience the play within God's will, of which an incarnation is the dense form. Spiritually, this is where the rubber meets the road. They may enter still more deeply into other forms and experience separateness, though they never forget for a moment the Oneness. At the same time they are fully human, warts and all, and the *lila,* the divine play of forms, continues moment to moment. For a fully conscious being there's no discontinuity, never a flicker of forgetfulness of God. Maharaj-ji would be carrying on a conversation while at the same time doing *japa,* touching the joints of his fingers, doing *Rām Rām Rām Rām Rām Rām Rām Rām Rām Rām Rām Rām Rām Rām Rām Rām Rām Rām Rām Rām Rām Rām Rām Rām Rām Rām Rām Rām Rām.*

remover of darkness

MY PATH OF THE HEART comes from my guru, Maharaj-ji. It's called *guru kripa,* the guru's grace. I ended up in India, but the trip is not Eastern; it's an inner journey. In that sense it's individual. You don't have to go anywhere. I can't do it the way other people have done it, and you can't do it as I have, although in a way I think I took a lot of others along on the India trip through talks, *Be Here Now,* and so forth.

As a Westerner you're just as likely to find it in Manhattan as in India. That's not to put down India. The atmosphere and the culture of India provided fertile soil for souls like the saints in this book to flower. But realized beings aren't limited by time and space; they're just *here*. So you don't have to go there to find them.

This book shows you something of the consciousness of saints and gurus and the power of their love, so that you can bring them into your life too. How you do it is up to you and your own path. Now that Maharaj-ji has died, left his body, he's not limited to that form. The guru doesn't need to work from a body. The guru can be an astral being. An image of a deity or a Tibetan *thangka* or a photo of a saint can connect you to the guru. These are real beings, and at the same time they are doorways to the inner guru that is your true Self.

You can contact these beings, this Being, by lighting a candle and incense and surrounding yourself with Ramakrishna, Ramana Maharshi, and the wisdom of the Tao, the Kabbala, the Egyptian Gnostics, and the Bible. You hang out with them. That's who I hang out with. Those are my buddies; they're on my *puja* table. Wherever I go, I set up a little portable *puja* table, or altar. I put out the Buddha, Christ, Ramakrishna, and my guru, maybe Teilhard de Chardin, and I sit down and here we are. Home again. You create that heart space right where you are, in your own room, in a tent, next to your bed. It can be purely Western; it doesn't have to be Eastern at all.

If you want to use something to center yourself, to open yourself to the guru, *mantras* and prayers work well. You can use any *mantra* that holds the possibility of faith for you. It doesn't have to be a secret *mantra*. A name of God is a word that signifies the boundary between the form and the formless; it can act as a bridge. You might try *Rām*. My guru used only *Rām;* I use *Rām* most of the time. You can use the Tibetan *mantra* for Guru Rinpoche, *Om ah hum vajra guru padme siddhi hum,* or the Jewel in the Lotus, *Om mane padme hum*. There are many mantras that can help you center yourself to connect with the guru.

Kirtan (chanting the names of God) or *bhajan* (devotional songs) are other ways to open your heart to the guru. You chant a simple phrase or name over and over, entering the spiritual heart through sound, while putting your mind to rest in a place behind ego. *Kirtan* or *bhajan* isn't necessarily meant to sound beautiful. It can be extraordinarily beautiful, but its purpose is not aesthetic. You do it for what happens inside. The name of God is like a boat to cross the inner ocean to the deeper Self. When you sing to the guru, you're singing to God, you're singing to your own heart, to your own true Self. When you sing with enough love, you merge into that love, where lover and Beloved become One. That's *bhakti yoga,* that's how it works. It's not a marathon; there's no pressure. Chanting goes on as long as it goes and then it stops. After it stops, there's silence.

Now, just close your eyes and get into your *jivatman,* your soul, your spiritual heart, and there will be your guru. Imagine that radiant being of infinite compassion and caring. Just rest in the purity of your soul. You have to be in your soul to get the guru.

It's all available to you; there's no cause to panic. You don't have to hold on to anything. Let it all pass through and watch it with love, compassion, and awe. There's no coming, no going, no gain, no loss. There's no drama. Just watch it all.

You don't have to demand or cajole. You don't have to ask for anything from the guru. Don't try to tell the guru what to do; just let him or her in. As your attachments arise, offer them into the fire of that love.

The outer world becomes the inner journey. If you know what you're looking for, the messages are all around. If a situation seems full of cosmic irony, that's probably your guru. If your life seems to be running on crazy coincidences and synchronicity, that's the guru too. The guru's a rascal, always playing with you, always showing you where you're not.

> When you understand that form is the form of the formless, your coming and going takes place nowhere else but where you are. When you understand that thought is the thought of the thoughtless, your singing and dancing is no other than the voice of the Dharma.
>
> —*Hakuin*[1]

Your work is to practice contentment and surrender. That's how you allow the guru to work on you. Even when bad times or painful things come up, let yourself be with them as fierce grace. It's just the guru helping you to see your attachments and your suffering from the vantage point of the soul. You surrender to the deeper will. Not my, but Thy Will.

You begin to see your life and your work on yourself as a dialog with the guru. There is less and less difference between you and the guru, between lover and Beloved. More and more it's just *being* in Love. The guru and your inner Self are one.

The true relationship between the guru and devotee is like the one between Krishna and Arjuna in the *Bhagavad Gita*. The *Bhagavad Gita,* meaning "Song of God," is a relatively short piece of the giant *Mahabharata* epic. It's a conversation between a warrior prince, Arjuna, and his charioteer, Krishna, who happens to be God incarnate, and takes place in the middle of a battlefield just before a major battle. As Krishna is the charioteer, the driver, and a divine friend and counselor to Arjuna on the battlefield, so the guru guides us through the battlefields of life to higher consciousness.

Through all these *lilas* of divine "play" the guru keeps reminding us that he or she isn't the human form, but the divine One. At the same time there's intimacy with a being who knows our hearts from inside. In the eleventh chapter of the *Gita,* Arjuna asks to see who this God really is, and Krishna reveals his universal form as the whole cosmos. Arjuna is overwhelmed, and begs Krishna to resume his human form, so he can keep relating to him as his friend.

What's a Guru?

Guru literally means "remover of darkness," one who can en*light*en you. We usually take it to mean a guide or teacher, and certainly the term has infiltrated pop culture, for example, fashion gurus or sex gurus. A real guru is different from a teacher. If you think of the spiritual path as the road home to your true Self, a teacher is someone standing next to you, pointing and giving directions, while the guru is up the road ahead, beckoning to you from your destination. He or she is someone who has already made the journey and knows the lay of the land. In fact, the guru knows it's all One, that the journey is an illusion and that it's all right here, and your being is just another face of the One. The guru's job is to get you to know that too.

The guru may be called by many names. In the West people might receive messages from their guru, whom they think of as an angel, astral being, or ascended master.

In the Vedas, the ancient sources of Hinduism, there are three ways to acquire spiritual knowledge. The highest is direct personal experience. Next is hearing it directly from someone who *knows,* which is the transmission from the guru. Last and least is reading or studying about it, which is what you're doing now.

Once we catch a glimpse, a *darshan,* of everything as One, the possibility of becoming One ourselves leads us to seek further on the path. That's where a guru can help, providing grace to reunite us with the Beloved, to take us into the One. The guru is the model. The guru's been there, done that. He or she *is* there. The guru is someone to hang out with on the inner journey, like an imaginary friend in your mind, not quite as close as your own Self, but not distant either. This friend and you are going on a journey within, which is your spiritual life, and your friend just happens to have total compassion, wisdom, peace, love, and joy. It's completely intimate. Your friend may seem to be coming from outside, yet he or she manifests inside.

I could see that my guru had this power, this peace, wisdom, and love, but it was hard for me to see them in myself. My neurotic ego didn't allow me to think so positively about myself. But once I began to see myself through the guru's eyes, with his grace the weight of all those negative habits of thought began to drop away, enough to allow me to go on with the journey.

That's a little of what the guru does. Who he *is*, is bliss, presence, love, compassion. The joy of being in his presence is an ambience, the field of his consciousness. When we were with Maharaj-ji, most of us interpreted his physical form as the source or generator of that field, but it was really his being attracting our souls. It's a feeling that you get only when you're contacting your deeper self, your soul. He invites us into a soul plane, he's a soul connection. It's a different plane of consciousness. It's being in love, really *being* in it, being bathed by love until it suffuses your being.

Someone asked Maharaj-ji, "How do I know if someone is my guru?"

Maharaj-ji said, "Do you feel he can fulfill you in every way spiritually? Do you feel he can free you from all desires and attachments? Do you feel he can lead you to final liberation?"

Maharaj-ji said, "The guru is not external. It is not necessary for you to meet your guru on the physical plane."

It's like having intense love for Jesus as a human being. Initially there's dualism. Then as your love for Jesus grows, you start to meet the Christ. Then as you love the Christ more and more, you keep merging into that love. When you've merged fully into the Christ, there is only One. That's the route of devotion to the guru. You feel the presence of the inner guru and then keep merging into that presence.

Each of us has our way of tuning into that place where the guru dwells inside, the telltale sign of that presence. For me, it's as if I'm in a dark room and there's someone else in the room, the presence of another being whom my external senses don't register. It's like a faint fragrance that permeates the air and evokes a deep memory.

If I'm really tuning into Maharaj-ji, there's a sense of joy, of truth. It feels right-on, it resonates, and I can't get away from it. It takes me over. I associate a feeling of deep harmony with him.

He comes to me in different ways, in different voices, in different people, and yet there's something about his presence that's the same. It's ecstatic. For you it might be a feeling or a remembrance that comes from looking at the infinity of the night sky, or meditating, or listening to certain music, or reading a poem with an intimation of divine love that stirs your heart.

Being with Maharaj-ji is an eternal moment. When I was first in India, I was blown away by how the six months I was there seemed like one timeless moment. If we are just present in the moment, it expands into infinity. That's where we can view ourselves as timeless souls in evolution. That's Maharaj-ji time; that's where he lives. His being draws us into that no-time zone. Once we get free of time and space, everything is just consciousness and energy. Every moment is *The Moment*.

Maharaj-ji was so monumental and so loving. He climbed inside us. He turned most of our lives around. We were pretty worldly, and he turned us toward God. Once you've seen what you can be, there's no turning back, even if it takes lifetimes. After a meeting like that there's nothing, no pleasure, no worldly happiness that compares. All we can do is be close to him the rest of our lives. There is such joy in touching the feet of such a being.

When Maharaj-ji left his body, I was surrounded by people crying. I was in the States. I wanted to cry too, because it's the usual thing. But wasn't he still here? In India he would tell me to go away, *"Jao, jao,"* push me away, so I wasn't so caught up in the body part of it. Death was really nothing special. He was just changing form. When he was in India, I used to think that I could get away from him. Now I know I can't get away from him, because he's wherever I am.

My relation to Maharaj-ji has gone way beyond any psychological relationship or any feeling of specialness or personal need. We share a space of presence together that is very soft and liquid. It's not interpersonal;

it's more like the merging of my consciousness with his. It's just a loving presence together.

Searching for the Guru

Westerners who come to India on a spiritual quest often have a shopping list of places to visit. They have heard about teachers, ashrams, or scenes in India from friends. They may have taken a Buddhist meditation course, a basic discipline to deepen their meditative space. Such courses are often gathering places for sharing information about other spiritual scenes.

From there many Westerners set out alone or in small groups—on foot, by train, bus, or rickshaw—to places where they hope to find reputed saints. Some find real teachers, perhaps only to have *darshan* or to sit for a while, or to live in a temple or ashram and receive teachings. If the karmic chemistry is just right, they may find their guru.

Every seeker dreams of making that contact—the one that will end their search. But most of us aren't ready for that kind of opening. We may meet but not recognize our guru. We may meet a being for whom we feel love, but not be ready to surrender.

The guru allows us to come and go, knowing that sooner or later in this life or another we will meet when the moment for transformation is ripe. In a brief moment the guru may plant a potent seed that will take root and sprout only years later, when the surface soil has been weeded and cultivated, and light and moisture have begun to penetrate.

Finding a guru is really an oxymoron. It doesn't matter whether you know your guru. Your guru knows you. There is no way that you can determine through your intellect who your guru is. You don't choose the guru; the guru chooses you. The relationship between guru and devotee is not the same as other human relationships.

By his mere glance,
Bondage becomes liberation,
And the knower becomes the known.

—Jnaneshwar[2]

In the early morning hours the Buddha would look out over all the Buddha-fields to see who was ready for enlightenment. In similar fashion, the guru sees that he can do something to further the *dharma* by bringing someone closer to the One. He sees the whole progression of incarnations, past and future, and where the point of leverage is that will move a being along the path.

The guru doesn't waste time touching people before they're ready. You've probably walked right by your guru. She may have stopped you and given you a traffic ticket. You probably didn't even give him a quarter when he was asking for a handout. What do you know? Do you think the guru's going to be someone with light streaming out, wearing a sandwich-board sign that says, "I AM YOUR GURU"? When you're ready to see, you'll see your guru.

Hundreds of people would come to see Maharaj-ji. They would come up to him, one after another, and touch his feet. Some people he'd ignore; he'd just go right on talking about the weather, politics, or whatever. These people would be given food, and then they'd leave. Others, who by my standards were people you would just ignore, who didn't fill the bill at all, drew Maharaj-ji's attention, and he would do a whole thing with them. I finally realized how unfathomable it is, what the guru is doing with whom and why. I think that he must have been seeing the whole parade of other births and subtle karmic causal factors, or *sanskaras,* and responding to certain ones.

A friend of mine who was a Canadian professor visited the ashram, and I wanted to show off Maharaj-ji's powers. Maharaj-ji asked him, "You are from the United States?"

"No, I came from Canada," the man answered.

Then Maharaj-ji asked, "You have four brothers and sisters?"

"No, I'm an only child, Maharaj-ji" the professor said.

After a few more of these exchanges the professor looked puzzled, and I was cringing. As he got ready to leave, the professor said to me, "You have a *very* nice guru."

After he left, Maharaj-ji recited a completely accurate dossier about him to those who remained.

The guru manifests when the devotee is ready. The manifestation matches the capacity of the devotee as to the level of surrender and their karmic ripeness. One person is ready for enlightenment. Another is ready just to know the guru exists, that there is a possibility of realization. Those are different stages. The guru sees the inner longing of the devotee. If you are a pure seeker, your guru knows you.

In 1949 Maharaj-ji was in Kashipur in Nainital District. He went walking along a dusty road to a lonely area outside the town. A caravan of clay potters passed by going the opposite direction, the donkeys laden with earthen pots. In the last cart a young potter of about eighteen was puffing on a pipe.

Maharaj-ji called out to him, "Who are you?"

The potter replied insolently, "Who are you?"

Maharaj-ji repeated the question more loudly, and so did the potter.

Then Maharaj-ji changed his question and asked, "What caste are you?"

The potter repeated the question back to him.

Maharaj-ji immediately replied, "I am a sweeper, and you?"

This time the potter said proudly, "I am a potter."

Maharaj-ji humbly asked him, "Will you give me a smoke from your *chillum*?"

The potter offered the clay pipe to Maharaj-ji, who puffed it a couple times (when you meet a guru you make an offering).

Maharaj-ji put his hand on the potter's head. In that instant the young potter became completely detached from the world. Leaving his donkeys with his companions, he went with Maharaj-ji to the nearby garden of a devotee. On Maharaj-ji's instruction he took a bath using the well water and had his head shaved. Maharaj-ji gave him a *mala,* or rosary, got him robes, and initiated him into *sanyas,* renunciation. He made arrangements for his food and lodging in the garden. He instructed the boy to go to Badrinath from there, and then left.[3]

That boy was ready for *sanyas;* maybe he was even praying for it. He caught Maharaj-ji's attention. Your purity brings the guru. If you can open to the space where you exist in love, then when the guru calls you may hear, or when you call he or she may hear you.

Your attachment to how the guru will manifest is just your projection. Instead of judging and pushing and pulling, allow yourself to be here without clinging. You *will* let go of concepts and attachments sooner or later, and nobody's in any rush except you, because the beings who *know* aren't in time. You're the only one who's in time, and suffering. You have to let go of your self-pity, feelings of unworthiness, feelings of inadequacy, and the desires that increase your separateness and push the universe away.

The Great Way is not difficult
for those not attached to preferences.
When neither love nor hate arises,
all is clear and undisguised.
Separate by the smallest amount, however,
and you are as far from it as heaven is from earth.

—Seng-ts'an, Third Patriarch of Zen[4]

Lightening

A true guru, whether on the physical plane or not, can show you the possibility of enlightenment. That *darshan,* that flash of reality, gives you a perspective on the spiritual state and your psychological stuff. As you see with clarity what's holding you back, you start trying to figure out how to release the attachments. You gravitate more toward identifying with the soul.

As we begin to observe the roadblocks that impede our way, we see how we need to clean up our mental clutter and clear away the distractions. We may need some measure of quiet and clarity to plumb the depths of our spirit, to become whole.

Clearing the mind is a process of becoming simple, but it's not a simple process. There's plenty of room for excursions into more delusion (*maya*). We have all encountered, whether in ourselves or others, the tendency to substitute piety for purity, ritual for personal experience, or concepts for consciousness. These are ways we pretend to be spiritual while maintaining the fiction that we are the center of the universe. These delusions are not good or bad, but the ego can be very subtle and convincing at "being spiritual" too. "I'm a spiritual person"—how many lifetimes will we spend on that one? Eventually those fictions may lead us to real spiritual work anyway.

The guru acts as a mirror for your soul and at the same time reflects your impurities and attachments back to you. As you surrender more and more to the guru, those attachments begin to fall away. It's a natural process of seeing what keeps you separate from love and letting it go. They just start to fall away.

Of course, not everyone has a guru in a body to reflect their attachments back to them and show them where they are stuck. Some gurus were once in form on the physical plane and now remain in subtle form on other planes. This may be a being like Christ, Ramakrishna, Ramana Maharshi, Muhammad, or Padmasambhava. The seeker is guided by the guru from that higher plane, though when faith is weak, it's hard to really know that. Many people are guided by Maharaj-ji from the subtle plane, though they never met him in the body.

Without somebody on the physical plane, it is easy to preserve your subtle ego defenses, in effect to stand in your own way. With a guru on a subtle plane you can too easily interpret his or her teaching to maintain your ego. I imagine I hear Maharaj-ji, and I interpret it. It's the interpretation that gets me in trouble! Is it Maharaj-ji, or is it my ego? I have to listen *very* carefully.

When a new experience presents itself, I ask, "Does it fit? Is it a teaching from the guru? Does it feel right?" Your intuition, the quality of the heart that connects you to the guru, is how you validate and integrate the teachings. There is an intuitive stamp of approval. That intuition is based in the *ātman,* so you're using the spiritual heart as your radar. It's not like using the intellect to judge.

For instance, I received direct teachings from Swami Muktananda and others. Some of them fit with my path of devotion; others I rejected because they did not. Over time you develop that discrimination of the heart. You take what you can use and leave the rest. Later you may realize that even what you rejected was from the guru too.

As long as we perceive ourselves as separate entities, this relationship with the guru helps us to witness our incarnation. Everything we do, everything we think, everything we feel is seen from the perspective of that being, the guru, who witnesses with absolute wisdom and compassion. It keeps us seeing our life as *lila,* as a spiritual play.

All the world's a stage,
And all the men and women merely players;
They have their exits and their entrances,
And one man in his time plays many parts.

—Shakespeare[5]

This world is like a stage, where men perform many parts under
various disguises. They do not like to take off the mask, unless
they have played for some time. Let them play for a while, and
they will leave off the mask of their own accord.

—Sri Ramakrishna[6]

The guru is such a perceptive playmate. He or she allows you to take life's dramas lightly or, as one of my Buddhist teachers, Munindra-ji, put it, to see it all as "passing show."

Under the umbrella of that relationship every experience becomes a teaching from your guru. Over time you begin to amass wisdom and compassion for your own life from the guru's perspective. You begin to assimilate the body of your guru's teachings, and you are starting to become it. From the point of view of the guru, your traveling companion, you are a soul coming to God.

God = Guru = Self

Ramana Maharshi said that God, guru, and Self are the same. The guru, the true guide, awakens our own deeper being, or *ātman,* which is God itself. Ramana Maharshi realized that Self directly. His view from the Arunachala mountain, his *darshan,* his teaching, pointed directly at the *ātman,* at Self-realization. That unity of God, guru, and Self is the higher truth, and if your veil of attachment is very thin, you may be able, like Ramana, to penetrate directly to that essence in the heart.

But most of us, to get through our busy human incarnation and the profusion of forms we find in our lives, need guidance and help. Seeing the guru as separate from oneself is a way to approach it in steps of lesser truths. It's a first step toward becoming One. The reality of the guru or guide as separate from oneself is a method or vehicle for coming to God.

It's using a relationship with a separate entity, dualism, to get to the One, to the reality that the guru is identical with your inmost being.

The guru and the devotee are already related, not only in that higher realm where they are One, but because they have been together for many lifetimes. At some point the seeker is called to the guru or an inner realization reveals the guru, however he or she manifests. Wherever they are in their incarnations, the devotee is pulled to the guru by those associations like a moth to the flame.

Love, Merge, Surrender

At first when you're pulled into the gravitational field of the guru's consciousness, there's a degree of awe. There may be some fear of the ego losing control, of the surrender, but it disappears in merging into the depth of the love. As the fear diminishes, the guru may more openly manifest the true form behind the form, as Krishna reveals to Arjuna his universal form in the eleventh chapter of the *Bhagavad Gita*:

> *If the light of a thousand suns suddenly arose in the sky,*
> *That splendor might be compared to the radiance of the Supreme Spirit.*
> *And Arjuna saw in that radiance the whole universe in its variety,*
> *standing in a vast unity in the body of the God of gods.*
> *Trembling with awe and wonder, Arjuna bowed his head,*
> *joining his hands in adoration. . . . (12–14)*

And later:

> *Krishna said, Thou hast seen now face to face my form divine so hard to see:*
> *Only by love can men see me, and know me, and come unto me.*
> *He who works for me, who loves me, whose End Supreme I am,*

free from attachment to all things, and with love for all creation,
he in truth comes unto me. (53–55)

As mentioned earlier, Arjuna gets freaked by this overwhelming cosmic revelation and begs Krishna to resume his familiar human form. But it is still a crucial opening, a preview for Arjuna. In similar fashion the fear and awe of God referred to in the Bible are steps on the path. As the attachments of the mind begin to disappear, even the awe is transcended as the separation begins to dissolve between the guru and the devotee. Form after form of the guru is acknowledged, honored, and released, as the seeker sinks deeper and deeper into the guru, into the Self, as the space between them decreases. It is like two intimate friends sitting together on the bank of the Ganges, and after a while there is only the river.

Finally comes the mystic union of seeker and God, lover and Beloved. The grace of the guru is the catalyst for that merging. After fulfilling the function of midwife or arranger of the marriage, the guru disappears as a separate entity, and the journey is complete.

Although the Guru and disciple appear to be two,
It is the Guru alone who masquerades as both.

When you look in a mirror and see your own face,
You know that both are only yourself.

If one could see his own eye without a mirror,
There would be no need of this sport of the Guru.

Therefore he nourishes this intimate relationship
Without causing duality or disturbing the Unity.

—Jnaneshwar[7]

For me the path to merging is just hanging out with my guru. On the dashboard of my car, next to my bed, in my *puja* room, and in the kitchen by the refrigerator are pictures of my guru. They're constant reminders of the relationship. He keeps butting into my thoughts and conversations; I hear his voice in my head. If I find myself in situations or with emotions that take me away, missing his presence reminds me how far I have gotten from him.

That nearness to Maharaj-ji has become so natural that when I am removed from it, when I get captivated by pain in my leg or some other situation, I suddenly think, "What am I doing caught in this place? This is a terrible place to be." Then I remember him again and somehow pull myself back to his force field, his presence. If out in the world I find myself becoming paranoid or lost in the material stuff of the marketplace, eventually the discomfort leads me back to him. That suffering reminds me that I've lost my connection to Maharaj-ji.

I immediately start a mechanism of reorienting or centering, of coming back into the moment, of opening the flow of love again. I know my heart has closed, and I know it feels wrong. So I start working to get out of it. I start a *mantra* like *I am loving awareness* or another *mantra* or start attending to my breath. I make an intention to love everything again.

The ways to hang out with him are as various as the situations in my day. Every *mantra* or prayer that I say is taking me into him. Intervals of silence open into his being. Thoughts of him arise many times a day. I may be sitting with someone, looking into their eyes, and they turn into my guru over and over again. Just hanging out with this incredible being of consciousness and love and light is a way of opening oneself, a process of surrendering.

Whether or not on the physical plane, the guru transmutes your *karma* in a way that speeds up your awakening. But you have to quiet your mind enough to allow it to happen.

MAHARAJ-JI: *It is difficult to sacrifice thought. The mind, in a blink of an eye, goes many miles.*

RAM DASS: *How does one sacrifice thought?*

MAHARAJ-JI: *It comes through grace and blessings.*

RAM DASS: *Whose grace?*

MAHARAJ-JI: *The blessings of Christ. Then the mind will be empty. Concentrate on one thing.*

RAM DASS: *Which center should we concentrate on?*

MAHARAJ-JI: *Don't speak, see, or hear evil. Christ didn't. Purify and wait for grace. The worldly people go outward, but we must go inward like a tortoise withdrawing within his shell (senses). It's difficult to empty the mind. It's not necessary to go to the forest. One can do it anywhere, with any point.*

You begin to focus more on the internal quest than external stimuli. As the *karma* lightens, your faith gets stronger and you become more attuned to the feeling of that presence or guidance, even though you can't know it through your senses or your thinking mind. That faith allows you to come into a deeper intimacy with your guru.

Curiosity Killed the Cat

How did I get to my guru? As I said earlier, I was curious. When I arrived with Bhagavan Das at the Bhumiadhar temple and he went up the hill to see Maharaj-ji, I thought I would just wait in the car. Finally, I got curious about what was going on up there, so I got out and went up the path.

Then, up there, the whole thing happened with the car. I was still about twenty feet away from Maharaj-ji when he asked if I came in a big car. "Will you give it to me?" Everybody laughed, because they knew he would never ask for anything, but I thought he wanted the Land Rover, which I was responsible for.

Maharaj-ji saw my soul in that moment, and he also saw how caught I was in my ego. My paranoia about the car took my fragile ego closer to the edge. Everything about the situation—my paranoia, people laughing at me, my cultural disorientation—conspired to make me more and more uptight.

Maharaj-ji sent us down to the temple to have some food. A few minutes later when I again sat before him, he spoke to me in the most loving way about my thoughts of my mother from the night before. When I looked up into his eyes, there was only this deep unconditional love and compassion that has remained with me ever since. Looking back, I see how this barrage of feelings and events—first fear, then confusion, then nourishment, my feelings about my mother, and the intimate revelation that he knew my inmost thoughts and emotions—caused my ego to collapse into his heart space.

At first I saw the miracles, and I didn't even see his love. Maybe because I was a psychologist and my thing was the mind, his reading my mind seemed like the big thing. We didn't know how to do that in cognitive psychology! I kept thinking that was it, but in truth the mind reading just softened me up. The real thing was unconditional love. For years I talked about the power of his *siddhis* as if the love was nothing special, just taken for granted.

It took ten years before I realized the real miracle was the unconditional love that pulled me in and opened my heart. When I looked up at him all those years ago, he was looking at me from about a foot away with such love and I was just hiding. But that's the moment I cracked open. And for all that intervening time I thought it was the psychic or spiritual power and put the love aside.

A being like Maharaj-ji is *antaryamin,* which means the in-dweller or ruler within, the knower of all hearts. He knows past, present, and future. There are other mind readers in India, but there's a difference between someone who reads thoughts and someone who knows the heart.

Dada Mukerjee first had Maharaj-ji's *darshan* when he was a teenager in Calcutta visiting the Dakshineshwar temple, where Sri Ramakrishna had lived. Dada had no idea about Maharaj-ji. He thought he was just a wandering *sadhu.* Maharaj-ji gave him a *mantra,* which he continued to repeat. Dada didn't see him again until thirty or forty years later, when his wife brought him to see a saint at a neighbor's home in Allahabad in a different part of India. When he arrived, Maharaj-ji stood up and said, "Now I'm coming to your house." Later he reminded Dada about the *mantra.* The seed planted many years before had grown and ripened.

Second Darshan

Things happened pretty fast for me after that first meeting. I had this surreal feeling that it was all just happening, and I wasn't doing any of it. After Bhagavan Das brought me to Maharaj-ji, I stayed the night at K.K.'s house in Nainital, a beautiful "hill station" town around a lake.

The next day K.K. brought me to Maharaj-ji's temple in Kainchi about ten miles away. When K.K. and I arrived at Kainchi, Bhagavan Das was there with the Land Rover. We drove from there to Bhumiadhar, the temple where I'd met Maharaj-ji the day before. Maharaj-ji was sitting on a wall, on the parapet at the side of the road. He motioned to me to come up, and he asked, "Do you know Gandhi?"

"No, but I know of him," I said.

"Be like Gandhi," he said.

Later I went to Nainital and purchased some glasses, of the kind Gandhi wore. That was my wise-guy way of following his instructions. I knew I wasn't going to start spinning thread to make my own clothes or get into politics like Gandhi. Years later I read that when Gandhi was leaving once on a train, a newspaper reporter asked him for a message for his readers. Gandhi tore off a piece of a brown paper bag and handed the reporter a scrap that read, "My life is my message." What Maharaj-ji meant finally clicked in.

The Acid Test

The whole reason I was in India was to find a map reader, a guide to these planes of consciousness we had opened ourselves up to with drugs. But I didn't in any way identify Maharaj-ji with that. There in front of me sat the reader of the maps, if not their creator, but I was so overcome by the experience that it was the last thing on my mind. It was too far out for my Western scientific mind, although, of course, that's why I was looking for a guide in the first place.

I think Bhagavan Das must have told Maharaj-ji about the "Western medicine." He touched his head and asked, "You have medicine for the head?" I thought he had a headache. I didn't even think of LSD. I said, "I'm sorry I don't have any aspirin. I'll look in my medicine bag and see if I have something else." I brought the medicine bag. Again he said, "Medicine for my head." I looked through the bag. Somebody said, "I think he means the LSD."

They'd all been discussing it behind my back. I found three pills. They were each about 100 micrograms, a solid dose. Owsley Stanley, the underground chemist, had made these especially for me, and they were very pure.

I extended my hand with the pills. "Will it make me crazy?" he asked. Then he took one. I was sitting to his right. Then he took another, and another. He tossed them deliberately one at a time into his mouth. Or maybe over his shoulder, I couldn't tell from where I was sitting. Afterward, for the two years I was in the West, my doubting mind kept replaying that instant. Did he really take the acid?

Nothing happened. Psychedelics, my route to opening my consciousness up to that point, appeared to have no effect on Maharaj-ji at all. From my Western point of view this was the strongest thing I had, and he was saying, "These pills aren't much. My medicine is more powerful than your medicine." His medicine was love, and his taking the LSD brought the two together for me, consciousness and love.

Later he took care of my doubts. After I returned to India in 1971 Maharaj-ji said, "Did you give me some medicine last time you were here?" I said, "Yes." Then he said, "Did I take it?" And I said, "Well, I think so." Then he said, "Do you have any more?" I had four pills, the same dose as before. I held out my hand, and he carefully took them one by one and with studied intention he put each one of them onto his tongue and into his mouth so that I could see the whole process. He acted like they were especially good and he liked them.

The previous time I had been acting like a scientist. This time I felt guilty. My heart started beating faster. He didn't know how strong they were. I shouldn't let an old man take such a big dose! He put his blanket up over his head. When he lowered the blanket, he looked like he was going crazy. But it was all just a put-on. He laughed and went back to talking to people. Nothing happened, nothing at all. I was watching like a hawk.

Later he said about psychedelics that similar herbs were used a long time ago in the Kulu Valley by yogis who would first do *hatha* yoga, but that the knowledge had been lost. They should be taken in a cold place when you're alone. He said they allow you to have *darshan* of Christ for two hours but then you have to come back.

The day after that second *darshan* my yoga training began, and I spent the rest of the fall and winter of 1966–67 in seclusion at the ashram. Before I met Maharaj-ji, I had been planning to leave India in two days. I stayed another six months. Every person I saw during that period at Kainchi was Maharaj-ji's. They were all acting on his direct instruction.

On the third visit to see Maharaj-ji at Bhumiadhar, a local mathematics teacher, Bhagawati Prasad Pande, was sitting next to me at Maharaj-ji's feet. He was massaging Maharaj-ji's foot. In India the feet of the guru are venerated as a source of great *shakti,* or spiritual energy. I longed to rub Maharaj-ji's feet too. Two days before, that would've been complete anathema to me. For the first time I wanted to do that. The teacher moved aside, and I thought, "Well, I'll give it a try."

As soon as I touched Maharaj-ji's foot, he withdrew it under the blanket and kept it there. Feelings of unworthiness flooded over me. I felt as if I had done it the wrong way. Maybe I did it with my mind, or *I* was still *doing* it. I thought I had too much ego. Maybe I wanted to do it for me more than for him. Maybe I wasn't ready. Or I was too impure. I was filled with self-doubt. He was always fanning my self-doubt, always leaving me enough rope to hang myself up. It's amazing how these tiny incidents take on enormous significance when you're with the guru. It's like that first rush of being in love, but this is a lover for your soul.

A man had published an article about Maharaj-ji, and Maharaj-ji was upset with him for writing about him. The man was very apologetic. It turns out he was the State Governor of Uttar Pradesh, K. M. Munshi. Maharaj-ji shunned publicity. Other people had gotten in trouble for writing about him too.

At that *darshan,* a crazy man who had speared a bird came to Maharaj-ji. The small bird with a stick through it looked quite dead. Maharaj-ji kind of cupped the bird in close to his heart and did something. Then he just opened up his hand, and the bird flew away. The crazy man continued raving, talking gibberish. I saw it happen, but I was confused; I wasn't sure what I had seen. Did he really bring that bird back to life? No one else seemed to notice. There was a lot going on.

I brought oranges or tangerines for Maharaj-ji, and he ate eight or ten of them. Somebody told me that was unusual, that he was taking on my *karma.* In fact, I can't remember ever seeing that happen again. He usually gave away all the fruit that came. That's about the last time I remember him actually noticing me for a long time.

Immersion

After that, on Maharaj-ji's instruction, I was installed at the Kainchi ashram, which at that time of year was practically empty. Maharaj-ji was away most of the time. I was left in this freezing cold place with only a charcoal brazier for heat. With charcoal you have to keep a window open for ventilation to prevent carbon monoxide poisoning, which kind of defeats the purpose. Most of the time there were only four of us there, the cook, the *pujari* who performed the daily rituals for the deities, and a crazy sweeper. None of them spoke English. Bhagavan Das came from time to time in the Land Rover, but never stayed for long. It was very unpleasantly cold. This wasn't the luxury resort. I'd make oatmeal and tea, and the cook made spicy potato *subji* and *khichri,* rice and *dal* (lentils) cooked together.

A month or two months passed without my seeing Maharaj-ji. During those times I felt as though I was in cold storage. And it was cold! Despite his physical absence during the winter of 1966–67 I was completely immersed in Maharaj-ji. The temple and the people were like a cocoon of his love, taking me into myself. What previously would have been great hardships were now part of my daily life. I slept on a reed mat on the cement floor in front of my *puja* table, getting up at 4 A.M. to meditate. I took my bath by carrying a small pot of hot water from the kitchen back to my room or bathed directly in the cold river. After I woke up I would take my bath and make my tea. Then I would meditate cross-legged or lie in front of my *puja* table and read the Vedas, the Upanishads, or accounts of saints like the ones in this book. Later, if it wasn't too cold, I would go visit the deities, the *murtis* of Hanuman, Laxmi-Narayan, and Shiva. It was there I came to love Hanuman.

I felt lighter than ever before in my life. Caring for my body was no longer the big deal I once had made of it. There was nothing to do except meditate and read holy books. I didn't really sleep that much; the straw

mat on the concrete floor wasn't very soft. I was meditating in the dark a lot. I didn't have any room for dreams or my normal fantasy life. I would practice *asanas* (yoga postures) and read books. As I kept going inward, the pull kept getting stronger and stronger, and the external world kept growing more and more distant. Very slowly I quieted down, meditating and watching the sun come and go over the hills.

Kainchi is down in a valley, and in the winter there are only about four hours of sun. One day I sat with K.K.'s elder brother-in-law, I. L. Sah, watching the chill shadows grow as the sun set in the early afternoon.

I said, "Every day I sit and watch that shadow move up the hill."

He turned to me and said, "It's all shadows."

I made my tea. I didn't know why I was there or what was going on, yet my trust in Maharaj-ji was complete. I was no longer a scientist with a model. I didn't know why I was doing things. All I knew was that I was home, and I trusted this being. It was the first time I had really known that depth of trust. This was where I wanted to be. I had dropped out of Western time; I was just being there. I was under a spell, Maharaj-ji's spell. Everybody was very kind to the new yogi, though this new being they were caring for was still unfamiliar to me.

I wasn't even wearing my own clothes. They bought me a white woolen robe called an *ulfi*. Just being seen by people in this robe was a trip. The feeling of wearing that robe and being out in the snow barefoot was very different. I was being transformed, but I was just doing what I was told.

At the time I never considered what I was being taken through. I didn't think about what was going on. I was just trying to go deeper. I was reading the *Bhagavad Gita* and the *Ramayana,* finding new worlds that resonated in my soul. Bhagavan Das would come, play music, and talk to me about where he had been, and it was as if I was watching. I was a spectator, but I was also completely present, more present than I had ever felt before. Later I learned to call this state "the witness."

K. K. Sah, Bhagavan Das, and Hari Dass Baba, whom Maharaj-ji assigned as my teacher, treated me as though I was a different being than the person I remembered. They treated me as if I was already Maharaj-ji's. The first time I saw him, Maharaj-ji told K.K. to give me double *roti,* or toast, because I was a Westerner. But a day later it was *chapatis* all the time. Nobody asked me what I wanted. They just assumed I was a *sadhu* after that, because that must've been Maharaj-ji's instruction.

K.K. walked over the hills in the snow every few days from Nainital to bring me biscuits. I didn't know why he was doing it. At first I thought he wanted something. But Maharaj-ji had told him to take care of me, and he was following his guru's instructions. He was so pure and loving. Little did either of us know we would become lifelong friends and brothers in Maharaj-ji's family. He brought me things he had written out for me, stories and *pujas* that helped me understand the rich tapestry of culture and tradition surrounding me.

Over the years many saints had lived around Kainchi, and there was a spiritual ambience about the whole area. K.K.'s mind, his spiritual awareness of all those saints from his upbringing, affected me. He started to tell me about some of the *siddhas* who had inhabited the Kumaon, the hill area where Kainchi is. It was a supernatural world I could barely imagine, but it gave me a context for what was happening for me with Maharaj-ji.

I had almost no desire or nostalgia for my old life, just lingering thoughts. In the afternoon when it started to get dark, I'd watch for the last bus. When I saw the bus, I'd take out my airline tickets and think how easy it would be to get on the bus and go to Nainital, then take it to Delhi and get a plane to America. But it was only then that I'd have nostalgia. That's all I remember of missing my old life.

I was two people. I was the guy holding the tickets, scheming to get away. The tickets were precious remnants of my other life. I'd fantasize about escaping, going home to San Francisco and dancing to the Grateful Dead or the Jefferson Airplane at the Fillmore. But it was a ridiculous fantasy. What would I be escaping? There weren't any chains or locks. Nothing was keeping me at Kainchi but Maharaj-ji's love.

The other part of me had settled in. Maharaj-ji wanted me there. It was like a conspiracy, everybody was being so nice to me. I was just satisfied with my lot. I was content. K.K. and Hari Dass would just say this is what Maharaj-ji wants. I guess I was surrendered to Maharaj-ji; it just kind of snuck up on me. I wasn't choosing to surrender—I was surrendered. My will was gone. I was submerged in love.

Each morning around 11:30 Hari Dass Baba would come from Hanuman Garh sixteen kilometers away to give me lessons in yoga, *asanas* and *pranayama,* for about twenty minutes. Other than K.K., Hari Dass was my principle contact. He was very loving and very demanding. He told me Hindu stories like those in the *Ramayana.* He kept silence, so he would write on a chalkboard, things like, "Desire is the creator, desire is the destroyer, desire is the universe." He made traditional renunciate things for me like a rope belt of seven strands. He was training me to become an ascetic, although I never really became one. He was doing it because Maharaj-ji had told him to, though I'm not sure he held out much hope.

"Conversing" with Hari Dass just about wiped out my linguistic abilities, my discursive thought process. I had questions, but because he kept silence, or *mouna,* his cryptic responses to my questions appeared on his small chalkboard. I started keeping *mouna* myself about a week after I got there. He brought me a chalkboard to hang around my neck. It was all by Maharaj-ji's instruction. He was giving me all these practices, and

I was changing, changing; these things were changing me. I was just doing what I was told, but you can imagine how radical the change was, going from a Harvard professor to a *sadhu* in silence with a chalkboard. Maharaj-ji was controlling the game, the whole thing. Only in retrospect do I realize how drastic that change was.

Even with all the writings from K.K. and the intense yoga instruction from Hari Dass, I was still thinking like the old me. When I got there, I thought I had just been an accidental passenger in a car, and an unwilling passenger at that! It finally dawned on me that something was happening. I felt as though Maharaj-ji was preparing me for something. Up to that point there was something unreal about it all. I was in and out of being immersed in *sadhana* or just being along for the ride.

I had no one to talk to. I kept silence and "conversed" with Hari Dass only via the slate. Later I heard people say that the ashram is the body of the guru, and I realized Kainchi was a warm home (not physically warm) where I was supposed to be doing something.

One day a guy came to see me who spoke only Hindi. He wanted something. He kept asking and told me a long story, which I couldn't understand. Then he waited for an answer. I said to myself, "Maharaj-ji, this one's on you." I answered affirmatively but didn't know what I was saying yes to. It could have been to murdering his wife for all I knew.

Maharaj-ji left me completely alone there for weeks on end, and I thought maybe he'd forgotten me. It was a long time in between. Every now and then we'd hear that Maharaj-ji was at Bhumiadhar, and I'd go over there with Bhagavan Das or K.K. We would walk over on the road from Kainchi to Bhumiadhar, which took a couple of hours. I remember the crowd of devotees. He also went to the plains, and I remember long periods of time when he was traveling.

On one of those visits to Bhumiadhar Maharaj-ji called me up and said, "There's a woman who has come to India looking for you."

I said, "Oh no, Maharaj-ji, there's no woman."

Before I left for India I was living with Caroline (later Rukmini) Forrest in New York. Caroline and I met dancing at a Grateful Dead concert; Owsley stuffed acid in our mouths. Caroline and I lived together in California, then in a school bus at Lama. We lived on East 72nd Street in New York before she came to Millbrook. I hadn't heard from her in months. Later I found out she had indeed come to India. She had studied Indian architecture and temples. She hadn't wanted to crowd me. She was there, and I didn't know. At the time my old life seemed distant and dreamlike. When Maharaj-ji said she'd come, I thought he was crazy.

Bhagavan Das had brought me to Maharaj-ji. After those first days at Kainchi, I was so completely submerged in Maharaj-ji's love I forgot all about Bhagavan Das. He kept going off into the world. It's strange how little I remember of him. He was coming and going quite a lot, while I stayed at Kainchi through that fall and winter. I bought him a sitar, and he was playing beautifully in the next room while I was meditating. I felt sorry for him. I had this wonderful quiet space inside. I had come out of all the busyness, and it was so refreshing. I wasn't comparing it to anything; it was just what was happening. He said I was like a little child, because I was so new to the whole game. I had become so simple.

He'd come and tell me where he'd been. He took the Land Rover back to Harish Johari, who was a friend of David Padwa's, the guy I had traveled to India with. Then he got Harish to give him the Land Rover again. It was parked at Kainchi as if it were Maharaj-ji's. After all my earlier paranoia about the car being taken, I didn't even notice it was there! By then I didn't care what happened to it. That was the beginning of detachment.

When I was leaving India for the second time in 1972, I saw the Land Rover in New Delhi in the impound lot of the Government Excise Tax Department. It was sitting right next to the Volkswagen van I had bought from some devotees of Hari Dass in 1970. Out of all the cars in India, there were both of my car-mic attachments right next to each other!

One day the Land Rover pulled up to the gate at Kainchi with Bhagavan Das driving and Maharaj-ji in the front seat. We took a trip up into the hills to a devotee's apple orchard. This was a strange and unusual occurrence, since I hardly ever went anyplace during that time. Maharaj-ji sat in the front with Bhagavan Das, and I sat in the back with K.K., Guru Datt Sharma, and some of the Ma's, the women who often accompanied and took care of Maharaj-ji. At the orchard we just had fun and ate apples. Then Maharaj-ji said, *"Chalo.* Let's go!" and we drove on and stopped at a Forest Guest House, a government rest house with a big room up in the mountains.

Guru Datt went inside with Maharaj-ji, while the rest of us stayed outside and sat on the grass. Guru Datt appeared in the doorway, and said, "Ram Dass, Maharaj-ji wants to see you."

Inside, as I approached Maharaj-ji, he said, "You like to feed children."

I said, "I guess so."

What went through my mind was how I disliked children, because they always were stealing the attention when I'd speak at gatherings.

Maharaj-ji motioned me over. He got up from the *tukhat* and tapped on my third eye with his fourth finger three times. Then he went on talking to Guru Datt. When I came outside, people said I was radiant, my face was red as a beet, and I wasn't communicating.

I felt dazed. I had no idea if it was an initiation or what. I was in some other space. Thoughts were going through my head. What does he mean about feeding children? What kind of a thing was that? But at another level I was just silent and peaceful and loving. That was the first time I felt any sense of specialness. And then Maharaj-ji got up, and we all went back home to Kainchi. It was completely weird. It was as if we went up there just to do this one thing.

I felt Maharaj-ji constantly. He was a presence in my room. It was as if he was watching me, as if there was someone else in the room. From the standpoint of my old life the whole thing was crazy. I was taking baths in an icy river in the middle of winter and living in an unheated room with the snow outside and only a charcoal brazier for heat. I started talking to the marble images of the temple deities, Hanuman and Laxmi and Vishnu and Shiva, but they didn't have much to say in return.

Maharaj-ji pulled me in with love. There I was, completely in his control. I had left the drug world and all the stuff and busyness of the West. I was living in a state of simplicity I had never imagined. I was plumbing my depths. They bought me clothes, because Maharaj-ji told them to buy me clothes. Maharaj-ji was taking care of me. K.K. brought foods he knew I would like, biscuits and samosas and dried fruit. I wasn't doing anything!

Every two weeks or so I would walk into town to K.K.'s to have a meal and visit. We walked out to another of Maharaj-ji's temples at Hanuman Garh outside Nainital and sat on the cold floor in front of the twelve-foot orange Hanuman. I wondered what my colleagues at Harvard would think of me now, worshiping a cement monkey. But it was in Nainital that I first felt how people identified with their souls and not with their incarnations or roles. It was such an eye-opener. The culture of India taught me it's possible to identify with the soul.

They let me go to Delhi to get my visa renewed. I was so surprised they would let me go out on my own! In six months I had become a re-clusive *sadhu*. I went on the bus. K.K. and others gave me a loving send-off just like a family member. I was kind of scared. I was very yogi-ish. People gave me special treatment because of the *ulfi*. At the Foreign Reg-istration Office in Delhi, they were deferential. I felt strange standing in line at American Express in the *ulfi* waiting to get my mail. To celebrate getting my visa, I went out for lunch at the Shudh ("Pure") Vegetarian Restaurant, where they gave me a special booth. At the end of the meal they brought me a sweet with some biscuits in it. It wasn't something a real *sadhu* would eat, but a Jewish boy from Boston couldn't pass it up. I distracted the other diners who were observing me, and I snuck the biscuits into my bag for later. When I arrived back at Kainchi and saw Maharaj-ji, he said, "How did you like the biscuits?"

I got some mail too. I got letters from Sara and David Winter at Wes-leyan and from Bucks County Seminar House asking me to speak. I got a letter from Allen Ginsberg. He'd been at an antiwar demonstration in Chicago and was beaten by the police. I remember thinking that he was on the front lines, but I was on the front lines too. He was being public, but I was going inside, exploring inner space.

I would sing in my room. I was doing *puja* with Hanuman and Anandamayi Ma on my altar. I lit incense. Hari Dass was teaching me to be a renunciate, eating what renunciates ate, sleeping on the floor, bathing in the river. They were all very impressed, and I was proud of myself too. It was like an "Inward Bound" course with Maharaj-ji as the leader. But he'd never talk to me about it. I'd always get it from Hari Dass, "He said to tell you . . ."

Maharaj-ji came back in the spring. He said I should go back to the States and stay for two years. He said I shouldn't tell anybody about him. I was very happy to go. What an idiot I was! I gave up my renunciate life for the dazzle of the West. But my *karma* was pulling me.

Before I left, Hari Dass gave me the message that Maharaj-ji had given his *ashirvad,* his blessing, for my book. I said, "What book?" I had no idea what he was talking about.

Reentry

Going back to the States was the midterm exam. We would see how much had sunk in, and if I had learned enough to keep my head above water in the West. I figured I would go back to America and write the book, whatever it was, check in with my home base, and see how these Hindu teachings fit into the life of a Western explorer of consciousness.

I landed at Logan Airport in Boston, where my father, George, met me. I was wearing my white *ulfi* robe and *mala* beads and had a long beard. It was winter, and I was barefoot. He was in a gray suit, had his cigar, and was driving his gray Cadillac. I thought he'd be glad to see me, open arms, but none of that, not a word asking about anything I did. He took one look and said, "Get in the car quick before somebody sees you!" I knew I was back in the West.

I stayed with Dad in Boston for a little while. Then I moved to an unheated cabin at the family summer place in New Hampshire. I arrived at Franklin in my father's Cadillac with Massachusetts license plates and stopped at the grocery store for supplies. When I came out, three teenagers were draped over the car. They were expecting their drug connection from Boston and wanted to score. I told them I wasn't that kind of connection and said, "I'll tell you something that will take your mind higher than you ever expected." I talked to the kids, and they seemed interested, so I invited them to come by later. After a long discussion on the first occasion, one of them asked if he could bring his mother to hear me. They and their mothers and their minister were my first audience after India.

I cooked my *khichri* every day. I did my yoga and *pranayama*. I wrote a manuscript about my travels in India, but no publisher was interested. I figured the publishers were Maharaj-ji too. I wondered what happened to his blessing for my book.

When it got cold, I moved into an attic bedroom in the main house that was the servants' quarters (after all, "Dass" means "servant"). I did my best to re-create India. I meditated, I slept on a mat, and they

all left me alone. I was having *darshan* from Maharaj-ji's picture and his presence.

Maharaj-ji's Mouthpiece

While in India I had received a couple of speaking invitations that I responded to now. The first was from Wesleyan University in Connecticut, where I had done graduate work. The talk went on far into the night and the next morning. Maharaj-ji was completely present. I think I was as much blown away as the audience. Then there was one at Bucks County Seminar House in Pennsylvania, and a series of talks at a sculpture studio on the Upper East Side of Manhattan in the winter of 1968–69.

It was all sort of doing his service, his *seva*. The powerful things that happened to people, like that night at Wesleyan, all felt a little surreal, because he was doing it—it wasn't me. Coming from the silence of the temple at Kainchi, all I knew was that I had a jewel and I wanted to share it. I had that *darshan,* that glimpse of perfection from Maharaj-ji. I wanted to share it, because nobody I knew was aware of that reality.

During the summers of 1968 and 1969 there were impromptu yoga summer camps at the farm in New Hampshire. A motley group would show up on the weekends for talks under the trees; some put up tents and stayed. Everyone helped out, and my father good-naturedly put up with it all. Something was attracting people like bees to nectar. As the power of this information spread by word of mouth, the audiences grew bigger. Cars were lined up, and people were coming from Boston, New Haven, and New York.

When I started traveling and lecturing, it was all Maharaj-ji. I was like Charlie McCarthy; I was Maharaj-ji's ventriloquist dummy. It was as if Maharaj-ji were a precious jewel in my hand. People came to my lectures because of Harvard and drugs, but I was dealing a different kind of high.

I was thrilled. I was the explorer of consciousness back from the East with maps, and I wanted to show them around. The trouble was the maps could only be interpreted in the heart; words were really of no use. And when my ego got in the way, I saw clearly that it didn't work.

Occasionally, I would remember Maharaj-ji had said not to talk about him, but I couldn't help it. Inside I felt Maharaj-ji's blessing and that is was okay to share. It felt like my *dharma*. I was feeding something in people, as he said I would, but it wasn't me doing it. This was feeding children in the realm of consciousness, reminding us all that we are children of a higher consciousness.

Be Here Now, *Later*

A chain of apparently coincidental events that began in New York and extended to Esalen in California and the Lama Foundation in New Mexico led to the publication of *Be Here Now*. A lovely woman named Lillian North, whose day job was as a public stenographer, was deeply affected by the sculpture studio talks. She transcribed them and handed me a pile of typescripts, saying, "These are your words." I didn't want to carry the whole pile and asked her to put them in the trunk of my car. I drove out to California. When I was at Esalen in Big Sur, a writer, John Bleibtreu, saw it and asked, "What's that? Can I read it?" Afterward he said, "You've got a great book here." His selections became the core text of *Be Here Now*.

From California I drove to the Lama Foundation commune up on a mountainside outside Taos, New Mexico. I had been part of its conception before going to India. A group of creative artists were living there, Dwarka Bonner, Francis von Briesen, and Tenney Kimmel, and, of course, Steve and Barbara Durkee, who were the founders. Steve was the head honcho of Lama. He also noticed the manuscript in the trunk of my car. He said the same thing as John, "What's that?"

Steve read it, and sitting around at dinner we all came up with the idea for the artwork and publishing it in a twelve-by-twelve corrugated box that was the original *Be Here Now*. The box was called *From Bindu to Ojas*, which signified the evolution of consciousness up through the *chakras* to liberation in the crown of the head. The core text with the art was printed on brown paper and bound with string, and there was a *HisStory* section about Maharaj-ji, a part about practice called *A Spiritual Cookbook*, pictures, and a book list called *Painted Cakes*. It also had an LP record with *kirtan* chanting, which sounds pretty homemade now.

We produced a thousand boxes paid for with contributions from my lectures. Anyone who sent in a postcard requesting it received one for free in the mail. They were all sent out, and more people wanted them. When I went back to India, Steve put together a distribution deal with Bruce Harris, who worked for Crown Publishers, and the box became a book. The royalties went to the Lama Foundation, and later half went to the Hanuman Foundation. Bruce later became editor-in-chief at Crown and eventually at Random House.

In early 1971 I received preliminary copies of the book in India. When it was read to Maharaj-ji, he told me to change some of the parts about Hari Dass Baba, who had been my *sadhana* tutor while I lived at Kainchi that first year. I had written that Hari Dass had gone into the forest when he was very young, at something like twelve, and became a *sadhu*. Maharaj-ji called a man up before him, and said, "Do you know Hari Dass?" He said, "Yes, Maharaj-ji. He was my clerk in the Forestry Department office for a long time." Instead of living in the forest, he had been a tenant in a house owned by K.K.'s family. I had mixed up Hari Dass and Maharaj-ji when I heard the story from Hari Dass. Maharaj-ji was the one who had left home as a boy.

While I was in America, Hari Dass had a parting of the ways from Maharaj-ji. Hari Dass became ill with a life-threatening intestinal blockage that required surgery. Maharaj-ji arranged for his medical care and subsequent recuperation, and after that Hari Dass was no longer involved in the intense physical work and management of the Nainital temples. He had a group of his own followers, including some Westerners who had heard about him through me, and he was living in Haridwar when I came back to India in 1970. I didn't see him. Maharaj-ji asked me to help Hari Dass get a U.S. visa and send him to America, so I did that and paid for his ticket.

By the time these changes to the *Be Here Now* text came up, Hari Dass had arrived in America and was teaching at the Lama Foundation. They all loved Hari Dass, and they didn't know Maharaj-ji from a hole in the ground. And here I was calling Lama from India and telling them to take out the part about Hari Dass, while he was right there at Lama—a cosmic irony that was typical of the many dimensions of being with Maharaj-ji.

Maharaj-ji said, "If you don't know, it's all right. But if you know the truth and you don't print it, it's bad *karma*." I was at the ashram at Kainchi, so I hitched a ride on an army truck over twelve miles of twisting mountain roads to get to Nainital, to telegraph Steve Durkee. Steve's return telegram said the book was already being printed. It was going to be hard to stop it, and it was going to cost a lot of money. We would have to throw out the whole first printing. Steve drove down the mountain from Lama three hours to the book printer in Albuquerque, the same printer that produced the box originally.

I showed Steve's telegram to Maharaj-ji, telling him that the first printing was already under way. I said it would cost a lot of rupees, and he said, "Money and truth have nothing to do with one another."

The next day I got another telegram from Steve. When he arrived in Albuquerque, he found that the printer had it all on the press ready to go, but at the last minute they discovered that one page was missing. It was also missing from the file, so they couldn't reproduce it. The printing had been held up and had not gone forward. That page had a picture of Maharaj-ji on it. Steve was nonplussed.

Gift of Gab

As time went on, I began to see that the talks and lectures I was giving were part of my *sadhana,* my path, my relationship with Maharaj-ji. Using myself as an example of the twists and turns of the path kept me honest, and the more I kept my ego out of the way, the purer the message I transmitted. I painted with words, but as long as I stayed in my heart, the message came across. People would come up to me from the audience and say the evening had opened their spiritual heart.

Although I use my path as a vehicle for others in my lectures and writing, my journey toward enlightenment is just *my* journey toward enlightenment. That's all it is. I'm just another soul trying to find my way home. Whether or not it manifests in a public role is a function of the cultural needs of the moment, and what I hear Maharaj-ji telling me is my *dharma.*

I use my personal explorations of consciousness as a teaching tool, as examples of how to tread the path and avoid its pitfalls. I think I do this with more wisdom and compassion as I go along. I'm still here, being a test model for the boomer generation. We all have a ways to go!

Since I stopped traveling after my stroke, my inner work has become more reflective. I've taken up contentment as a theme. Contentment is a good model for an aging person like myself. Bringing a soul perspective to aging is one thing that I can contribute now.

As I identify more with my soul, I feel more detached from the drama of my incarnation. As I become more aware as a soul, I am less an actor in the drama. The soul is awareness.

The shift from the ego to the soul happens through love. You realize that love comes from your soul and the other emotions come from your ego. When Maharaj-ji said, "Love everybody," that's a way into the soul, where soul awareness and love come together.

That's also the place where *karma yoga,* selfless service, and surrender and devotion come together. According to *karma yoga,* it's not even *my* incarnation; it's just another incarnation to be offered to the Beloved. I don't know how the incarnation comes out—that, too, is up to him. He's writing the script.

The ultimate nexus of full consciousness and compassionate presence is Maharaj-ji's state, *sahaja samadhi,* all planes simultaneously, one foot in the world and one in the void, the divine absorption of *samadhi* and the ocean of human compassion constantly converging in the moment.

Talking with My Dead Guru

I feel Maharaj-ji's presence constantly now, and I use my imagination to talk with him. A while ago someone asked me if I talked to my dead guru, and I said yes. The person said in a put-down kind of way, "Well, that's just your imagination."

I thought about it and, of course, it's true. But Maharaj-ji is also in control of my imagination, which is another level of being with the guru. And it's not just talking. We keep getting caught in words, but he communicates to us through the heart. When I'm doing something that's dharmic, tuning to the place that's God or the guru in myself, my heart feels that harmony. I'm flooded with love, even for myself. The guru comes closer to me, the more my actions come from love.

Maharaj-ji said things to me like, "Ram Dass, tell the truth," and "Love everybody." Of course, those were just words. It's the attunement in the heart that's important. If I'm coming from the right place and doing the right thing, it feels spiritually in tune, in harmony with my soul's work for this incarnation. Often when I'm giving a talk and I'm unsure of something I'm talking about, I'll stop if I feel disconnected. Then I'll get a story going and feel Maharaj-ji's presence; then I'm in it and I can feel the audience in it too.

There's also this quality of synchronicity that I associate with Maharaj-ji. It's like a monkey paw in the karmic stew, everything fitting together in this inexplicably coincidental way. It's the manifestation of grace. Synchronicity is a wake-up call, an intrusion of another plane into the everyday existential mess, a momentary reminder of perfection, a signal that everything is inextricably connected in the One.

I use these feelings as a kind of radar or a homing device. When I'm working with someone, I go through a sequence inside in which I say, "Maharaj-ji, are you here?" And then I feel, whether it's my imagination or not, a presence that fills the space. That's his *ashirvad,* the umbrella, the blessing. When I'm in that presence, I can go down into my imagination, where Maharaj-ji speaks to me. I would call it the *ātman* conversing with the *jivatman,* the universal soul with the individual soul. It's not a thought process. I don't notice it at all if my mind is too busy.

Enlightenment Just Now Coming

In India when you ask how long your food will take in a restaurant or when the train will arrive, the response is often, "Oh, it's just now coming." That can mean anything from a few minutes to a few days. I don't know how long enlightenment takes. I feel as though I've known Maharaj-ji for many lifetimes, and I don't think this is my final lifetime.

It's as if Maharaj-ji has been my father or mother forever, and the *satsang,* the circle of devotees, is a family of the heart that keeps coming and going, having reunions and going away, but over many lifetimes. We all have different guises and costumes and appear on stage in different scenes playing different characters. We're all parts of the jigsaw puzzle of each other's *karma.*

I sometimes look around and wonder how this crazy troupe came together. But that's my ego, because as an ego I look at them as egos. This is Maharaj-ji's show. Maharaj-ji is like the director of the play. He's not one of the actors or puppets. He's the only one who has the whole script. And we're too involved in the play itself to remember it's just a play. The only thing that turns out to be real is his relationship to us as souls. Then that, too, goes and there's only One.

The script for this play of getting enlightened is already written. It's not in time anyway. And the moment you project a future, you're trapped in your mind again. You say, "Well, I'll get enlightened by next December." Then that changes everything you do until December, when you're going to have to give it up anyway. It's like when people say the end of the world is coming on a certain date. Then the end of the world doesn't come, and they're confronted with the fact that they got caught in their own minds.

You can only go at the rate you can go, and when you're done, you're done. The only thing you can ask is that you keep awakening at the fastest rate at which you're capable. You can't go any faster than that, and whether you think you're going to make it in this lifetime or not doesn't really make that much difference, as long as you keep going. Speculating just creates more thought forms. I try to just think about what I can do immediately to clean up my game. That's about all I do. I'm not preoccupied with the future.

chapter seven

the way of grace

M Y RELATIONSHIP WITH MAHARAJ-JI is one of faith, faith that what comes to me from him is grace. When I have faith, I feel grace coming from the guru. If I have faith, then there is no event in my life and no place where that grace isn't.

When I live in faith that I am under his umbrella, then there's no fear. He gives whatever is needed to deal with whatever comes along. Without faith, the existential fears that we all have dominate. Faith, no fear. No faith, fear.

When I had the stroke in 1997, a lot of suffering came with it. A stroke isn't something you plan for, and it was a surprise. In the first days after the stroke I couldn't feel Maharaj-ji. I asked him, "Were you out to lunch?" I really lost faith, which put me into a depression. I had to learn how to ask for faith again at that time. The Brazilian healer John of God, whom I talked about earlier, helped heal my heart. As I began to recover my faith, I accepted the stroke as the hand that Maharaj-ji had dealt me, and I began to call the stroke "fierce grace."

But when Siddhi Ma, the Mother in India who maintains Maharaj-ji's scene, saw Mickey Lemle's documentary about this time, called *Fierce Grace,* she sent me a message that Maharaj-ji would *never* give me a stroke. I took that in and realized finally that his grace was not the stroke, which was my own *karma.* His grace lay in helping me deal with the effects of the stroke, which included paralysis, aphasia, and dependence on others. Dealing with the suffering from the stroke in my mind changed my life. I wouldn't wish it on anybody, but it had its positive side. And over time it has tempered and deepened my faith.

A few years after the stroke I wrote to K.K. saying I didn't think it would be possible for me to return to India. K.K. wrote back with some simple words that Maharaj-ji had said to him about me: "I will do something for him." Like Hanuman, he thought I needed to be reminded of the power of my faith so I could get it together. As I recollect and reconnect to him, I realize Maharaj-ji has done, has been doing, is doing something for me. I did go back to India in 2004 and I experienced a resurgence of the deep faith I have in him, in that Oneness in which we exist together. Just that remembrance deepens my faith.

His presence helped me see it as a "passing show" of body phenomena, while my soul

A disciple, having firm faith in the infinite power of his Guru, walked over a river even by pronouncing his name. The Guru, seeing this, thought within himself, "Well, is there such a power even in my name? Then, I must be very great and powerful, no doubt!" The next day he also tried to walk over the river pronouncing "I, I, I," but no sooner had he stepped into the waters than he sank and drowned. Faith can achieve miracles while vanity or egoism is the death of man.

—*Sri Ramakrishna*[1]

remains enveloped in his love. I'm quieter now inside, and I've learned from my own silence, which increased when I couldn't talk after the stroke. From being the driver of my own car I became a passenger in a body that now needs help from others. From someone who had written a book called *How Can I Help?* with Paul Gorman, now I needed to write one called *How Can You Help Me?* It's been deeply humbling for my ego.

As I questioned my own faith, I began to ask, "Faith in what?" I found that my faith is in the One, not faith in a person, but in the One. Faith is a way in which you are connected to the universal truth. Faith and love are intimately connected. As it says in the Ramayana, without devotion there is no faith; without faith there is no devotion. In a way it's the guru's own incredible relation to God that's the transmission of living faith, the fact that he or she is living in the light of God. That connection is love.

A book doesn't give a living transmission. It's the light coming through the guru, the remover of darkness. Faith really comes from within you, and the guru is awakening it. Faith comes through grace. You can cultivate it by opening your spiritual heart and quieting your mind until you feel the validity of your identity with your deeper Self. The qualities of that Self are peace, joy, compassion, wisdom, and love.

Faith is not a belief. Faith is what is left when your beliefs have all been blown to hell. Faith is in the heart, while beliefs are in the head. Experiences, even spiritual experiences, come and go. As long as you base your faith on experience, your faith is going to be constantly flickering, because your experiences keep changing. The moment you recognize that faith lies behind experience, that it's just *being,* not the experience of being but just *being,* then it's just "Ah, so."

For the unified mind in accord with the way
All self-centered striving ceases.
Doubts and irresolutions vanish

And life in true faith is possible.
With a single stroke we are
Freed from bondage;
Nothing clings to us and we hold to nothing.
All is empty, clear, self-illuminating,
With no exertion of the mind's power.
Here thought, feeling, knowledge, and imagination
Are of no value.
In this world of suchness
There is neither self nor other-than-self.

—Seng-ts'an, Third Patriarch of Zen [2]

Working Guru

The guru intensifies experiences. Right there in your consciousness all the time is this being who is completely free, loving you totally and with the deepest compassion for your situation. The absurdity of your attachments in relation to this incredibly wonderful being drives you to deal with your petty stuff and to get it out of the way. In a sense the guru uses your attachment to daily situations to show you your own delusional system.

The guru is constantly showing you where you're not, your most secret places where you're holding on to your stash of attachments. For people who are still intensely attached to their senses and to their thinking minds, the guru manifests the teachings on the physical plane. The true guru is also beyond form, even though he or she may take on a body in order to do this work.

As the intimacy between you and your guru increases, the desire to merge intensifies too. It's a bit like going downhill on a runaway train. There's a point where the velocity becomes so great you can no longer jump off without it being fatal (to the ego), and at the same moment you realize the ride itself may be fatal too.

I experience it as if my body is in big surf, being buffeted and mashed into pulp on rocks and coral by the force of the ocean. When you're in the surf you can feel its power. You're in the power of the ocean and you just get pummeled again and again until you practically become part of the foam. You just dissolve into the ocean. It's just this oceanic process, and every part of you that's separate just gets beaten and pulverized until it becomes part of the ocean.

There are moments when you come up for air, but that only makes you more desperate. There's a maximum rate at which you can go in spiritual work without breaking. If you try too hard or get pushed too hard, you get tossed out and land on the beach. And then you may be stuck, sort of rotting in the sand, until the next big tide comes, picks you up again, and takes you back out to pulverize you some more. The tide, and the ocean, is God—it's the Ocean of Bliss! Pain and pleasure come together at that point, because it can be painful, but the bliss of getting free is very great too. We're used to pain not being productive, but when it's that blissful, it's delicious.

You're giving up stuff that is so connected to the root of your worldly identity that it's like a death. You go through some of the same things people go through when they are physically dying—denial, anger, resentment—"Why is it happening to me?" or "Can I bargain my way out of it?" First come depression and despair, then surrendering to the situation, and finally the lightness of a new state of being.

The image of the ocean and the rocks is one way of thinking about it. Fire is a good metaphor too. You are in the fire knowing the only part of you that won't be burned by this fire is the part that is in God. Everything else will go. You realize how much you are attached to everything, your thoughts, your senses—those have to go too. Remember that mantra? *I am a point of sacrificial fire, held within the fiery will of God.*

At first I kept a diary of my experiences at Kainchi, but after a while I stopped making entries. What do you do with these experiences? Do you just collect them, file them, and plug them into your model, your same old worldview? Or do you work with each experience, squeezing it like a lemon, and then discard it and let it go? If you keep letting go, then you notice it's all new every moment.

When Balaram Das, one of the Westerners with Maharaj-ji, used to be sent away by Maharaj-ji, he'd walk around the back of the temple and come in the other door. Each time Maharaj-ji treated him as if he was just coming in. I thought, "Maharaj-ji's being conned!" But it was also a beautiful example of letting go, letting go and starting fresh.

Balaram is a good teaching in that sense. I wish I had his total one-pointed chutzpah. I am too smart for my own good. I'm too clever, not simple enough. He's simple in his devotion, in his love, in the intensity of his desire. That can get you a long way, that kind of devotion.

Everything a guru does in relation to other souls is part of that process of liberation. You might not even notice a guru in the street, unless it is

helpful to your spiritual growth. Even when you're sitting in the back row or seeming to be ignored, that is the optimum thing for you at that moment. The full consciousness of the guru is with you from the moment you turn to him or her.

You crave to be in as pure a relationship to the guru as the guru is to God. There's a moment, like an initiation or an opening, when the guru shows you who they are. Maharaj-ji opens his eyes, and in an instant you see the universe. Then he closes his eyes, and you're back. Or Krishna showing Arjuna his universal form. It's like taking acid. As Maharaj-ji said of LSD, "It allows you to have the *darshan* of Christ." It's that first thing that compelled all of us to go on. But then you have to come back, do your work, and go become it. The only way you can get that purity is to let go of your impurities. It's a two-stage thing: first the guru shows you who he or she is (really, who you are reflected in the guru), and then the guru sends you back to finish your work.

Guru's Grease: The Path of Grace

You can't integrate the guru in your mind. You can't *understand* a perfected being; you can only use that being for your own perfection and, eventually, become that place, that state of consciousness, yourself. If you want to come to God, the guru becomes the perfect instrument for getting you there. Gurus have no other motivation. That's the only reason they are even in our field of view. That's the only reason any of us are graced to have relationships with these beings. How fast, how consistently, and how totally we use them depends on the intensity of our desire to come to God.

The way these beings help us is to accelerate our journey back to God. That's the quality of grace, or *guru kripa*. If you're aimed away from God, they won't interfere, but the moment your despair is great enough and you turn toward God, they are called forth by your prayer, by your cry for help, by your seeking for God. Then they shower upon you the grace of their presence and their love, and that higher vibratory rate speeds up your journey incredibly.

Grace lubricates your way, smoothes it out and makes it easy, speeds it up. It's like having ball bearings instead of wagon wheels. It's like having the wind fill your sails or walking downhill. It's like perfumed air, the subtle smell of spring. Obstacles are reduced to a manageable scale. The way to God is grace-full. Grace has humor too, making things lighter, so we don't take them so seriously. You're aware of the spiritual meaning and perspective on your life, but it's a light touch; it's not heavy. Grace makes it lighthearted, the heart full of light.

> For by grace are ye saved through faith; and that not of yourselves: it is the gift of God: not of works, lest any man should boast.
>
> —St. Paul, Ephesians 2:8

This process of thousands and thousands of incarnations now becomes a geometric curve under the intense light, love, and compassion of this grace. The guru doesn't go against the will of God, but since the will of God has no time in it, since God is beyond time, the guru can speed up the process.

A being like that is only in form for other people. There is no desire in him. That's why he is such a pure mirror. He keeps showing you where you're not.

Karma *or Grace?*

People are drawn to a guru by their own good *karma,* the result of past actions, the laws of cause and effect. As I sat in the temple with Maharaj-ji day after day, experiencing the incredible grace of his presence, I would think and talk with my guru brothers and sisters about our good *karma* to be in such a situation. These discussions led to some confusion, for grace seemed to be something freely bestowed at the whim of a higher being. *Karma* seemed to be something irrevocably bound up with the laws of cause and effect, and it was hard for me to understand how these two things went together.

If Maharaj-ji's presence was my good *karma,* it was lawfully demanded, including the way in which he was manifesting. Where, then, was the space for the free play of grace? If, on the other hand, this was the grace of God, bestowed freely outside law, how could one understand the cause-and-effect nature of *karma* over time?

So at one of the group afternoon *darshans* sitting before Maharaj-ji, I asked him, "Aren't *karma* and grace the same thing?"

Maharaj-ji's answer through a translator was, "This is a matter that cannot be discussed in public."

He never said anything more about it, although later he sent a message through Dada, "Ram Dass understands me perfectly." I'm still working on it.

> And he said unto me, My grace is sufficient for thee: for my strength is made perfect in weakness. Most gladly therefore will I glory in my infirmities, that the power of Christ may rest upon me.
>
> —St. Paul, Corinthians 12:9

For a long time, I concluded that I had been right—that *karma* and grace are the same thing. Later I came to appreciate that it was my *karma* to reach out for teachings, but it was Maharaj-ji's oceanic compassion that opened my path, through a grace that was indeed free of karmic law. The guru's grace is beyond the realm of *karma,* but grace is not necessarily part of everyone's *karma.* Maharaj-ji's grace is a constant flow, whether or not we are aware of it. He said, "You may forget me but I never forget you."

When asked how to get enlightenment, Maharaj-ji said, "Bring your mind to one point, and wait for grace." Bringing the mind to one

point entails working through the thought forms that are the result of *karma.* The end of *karma* is a quiet mind completely concentrated on God, and what takes you beyond that is truly grace. At that point, where the reaching up toward God meets the rain of grace, they're both the same.

At the level of the nondual, in the One, they are the same. But between the devotee and God, as long as there's separation, you need to make an effort to get to one-pointedness and wait for grace. At the level of *karma,* or action, there's something to do. For the devotee it's not productive to sit around waiting for it to happen. From where we sit, *karma* and grace are not the same thing, although from the unitary consciousness where Maharaj-ji sits they are the same. Siddhi Ma said, "From the place of Oneness (*sub ek*) it is true that *karma* and grace are one. But it's best for the devotee to act as if they are separate to do the spiritual work." For Maharaj-ji there's nothing to do. He always said, "God does everything." Things just happened gracefully around him. The simple focus of attention by a *siddha,* a mere thought, brings things into being. Grace remains free, a river of blessing.

My understanding of this keeps evolving. That's how a teaching keeps feeding you until finally it clicks into place and ceases to exist as a teaching at all. It becomes part of your being. Maharaj-ji functions within the laws of *karma,* except when he doesn't.

One day Maharaj-ji asked to be driven from the plains to the distant mountain town of Bhimtal. He went straight to a devotee's house and told the people there to go to the old pilgrims' rest house at the Shiva temple and bring back whoever was staying there. For centuries no one had stayed in the dilapidated rest house, so the devotees thought it was very unusual when they found one of the doors locked from within. They knocked and shouted, but no one answered. Then they returned and reported to Maharaj-ji.

Maharaj-ji left the house and went to see another devotee. He again sent people to the rest house with instructions not to return without its occupants. They caused a great commotion at the door, until finally an old man opened the window. He tried to send them away, but they persisted, until finally he and his wife were taken to Maharaj-ji.

Immediately Maharaj-ji started shouting, "Do you think you can threaten God by starving yourselves? He won't let his devotees die so easily. Take *prasad!*" He called for *puris* and sweets, but the man refused them. Maharaj-ji insisted, until finally they ate.

The couple had come from South India on a pilgrimage to Badrinath and other holy places. Coming from a very rich family, they'd decided to leave home and family behind to devote their remaining years to prayer. They had resolved to always pay their own way and never beg. As they were returning from Badrinath, all their money and possessions had been stolen. They had only enough money for bus fare to Bhimtal, where they found the rest house deserted.

They resolved to stay there and die, since that seemed to be God's will. They had been locked inside without food for three days before Maharaj-ji forced them out.

Maharaj-ji insisted that they accept money for their trip back to Madras. They said that they would not beg. But Maharaj-ji said that they were not begging, and they could mail the repayment when they reached home. They accepted the money and were sent off.

The Perfect Mirror

The guru is an example of what's possible for us as human beings. You experience a peace around the guru that's his or her vibrational field. It shows you a possibility, creates a yearning in you to be in the space that the guru's in. As you look into a still pool and see your reflection, so the guru reflects back to you your soul and its *karma*. If there are no desires clouding your view, you see the pure reflection of your soul.

> Everyone is a reflection of my face.
> —*Maharaj-ji*

A free being can be a perfect mirror for you, because he or she is not attached to being anybody or to any particular reality. A person who has no clinging is an exquisite mirror, and the beauty of a mirror is that the moment you change, the mirror changes too. It doesn't reach out and demand you stay who you were a minute ago.

When you let go of any models of how you think the universe is supposed to be, you can see the true reality. You see the guru is none other than God, none other than your Self, none other than Truth.

Looking into that mirror of the soul allows you to see the way you're creating the universe and helps you perceive your own attachments. When you're around somebody who doesn't want anything, your own desires start to stick out like a sore thumb. It allows you to grow and to see where you're not. You begin to see how your desire system keeps creating your reality.

None of us knew Maharaj-ji; we just knew our own projections. But the relation with the guru is not totally our projection, nor is it entirely created for us by the guru. It's an interaction in the circumstances of the moment. Your needs as a soul determine the form of manifestation of the guru. Of course, how the guru manifests may not agree with your values or concept of a guru.

Maharaj-ji was fat. His great belly contradicted my idea that conscious people are thin and ascetic. And the foods he favored were so counter to my ideas of what constituted nutritious food. The basic diet at Kainchi was *puris,* potatoes, and sweets: fat, starch, and sugar. But it didn't matter, because it was all blessed food; it was *prasad.* Then when I heard that Maharaj-ji steered away from important politicians and wealthy people, it knocked the whole value system that I'd grown up with for a loop. He was the exact opposite of my father, who always cultivated wealthy and important people.

> The saint is a mirror, everybody can look into it; it is our face that is distorted, not the mirror.
>
> —*Paltu Sahib*[3]

A guru is perceived differently by all the beings around him, depending on their karmic predicament. One person may have known Maharaj-ji in a deep meditative space, another as somebody who got upset about potatoes that were allowed to rot. If you got ten people talking about him, everyone would describe Maharaj-ji in a different way.

It's like the blind men and the elephant. One touches the tail, one the leg, another the side, and another the trunk. They can't agree what the thing is. One blind man says, "An elephant is very like a tree," another says, "No, he's like a snake," and another says, "No, he's like a wall." And they get into a fight, because each of them has touched a different part of the elephant. Each person is describing what he has touched, and each touches what he is capable of reaching, but no one gets the whole thing. Maharaj-ji is interacting with everyone from their own viewpoint. The guru keeps all of these relationships going on all levels at once, and at the same time doing work on other planes with many other beings. Everyone gets what they need.

A perfected being sees exactly where individuals are in their karmic evolution in the same way you might see an automobile at a particular stage in its assembly. To see the entire assembly line is to know we are all One, that we are all God. It's seeing beyond time, seeing that it's all perfect.

Swami Muktananda comes from the Shaivite (Shiva) side of Hinduism, which emphasizes *shakti,* or power, as distinct from the followers of Vishnu (Vaishnavs), who tend more to the *bhakti,* the loving or devotional side. Muktananda meditates on his guru, Nityananda, as a powerful way to shift his identity to the enlightened state. This meditation is a way to bring the qualities of the guru—wisdom, compassion, peace, and love—into yourself. In his autobiography, Muktananda describes how he came to this meditation.

This is Muktananda's method for merging with the guru. As you keep doing it, you get to a point where you start to fully identify with the guru and you flip your whole consciousness around until you are the guru. As a child identifies with a parent, you just start to absorb this whole other being. Muktananda would get so flipped out, he wasn't sure who he was most of the time during this *sadhana.*

Hide and Seek

Maharaj-ji is a mirror of our highest Self. Each of us has within us many levels of consciousness, though most of the time we don't experience them. We never got to play with Maharaj-ji at his highest level, because we could only play at our highest level.

The last time I saw Maharaj-ji, I looked back when I was leaving the temple. I saw him sitting looking at the hills, and it was just like Shiva sitting in the Himalayas. He seemed to embody that quality of absolute stillness, at one with pure consciousness. He was like part of the mountain, the same as the universe around him.

I wanted to be able to share that with him. I could feel that vibration from him, but I couldn't live there yet myself. I didn't have the key to that level of consciousness. Each person has the ability to resonate with that state, like a sympathetic string on an instrument. The more conscious being, the higher vibration, always sets the tone. Slipping in and out of those higher states is seductive.

That's what *darshan* is, seeing or getting a glimpse of that place. It makes you yearn for it. The guru creates that aspiration just by being here. There's a vibrational field around Maharaj-ji; we all know it. It's like an aura. The higher vibration brings you up as far as you can go, even though he's still beyond it all.

The difference between a guru and us is that he inhabits those planes always, with no discontinuity. He lives in the *ātman,* the One. We experience our consciousness as separate, but through the guru's love we begin to experience it as shared in common, because love dissolves boundaries, love is universal. Maharaj-ji brings us as far as we can go into that state of merging into love before our individuality kicks in and we hold back out of fear of letting go. That's the crux of the whole matter.

For the close devotees around Maharaj-ji the approach to those higher states has been the *bhakti* path: love, service, *kirtan,* devotion. Dada Mukerjee asked for nothing; he was just there, serving, serving, serving. That's what Siddhi Ma has done, continued serving Maharaj-ji until she has become absorbed into him. Those old devotees around Maharaj-ji; they're just serving him. They have no other motive except love.

Dada (an affectionate term for "elder brother") was a professor, the head of the Economics Department of Allahabad University. His devotion was a model for me of this form of guru yoga. He pursued total surrender to Maharaj-ji. He was a highly intelligent man who in his own right was the editor of the leading economic journal in India. In the latter part of his life he did everything solely in relation to Maharaj-ji. He kept his job because Maharaj-ji told him to. When serving Maharaj-ji, he became like an extension. It was like looking at your hand. When you go to make a fist, do you notice how your fingers come together? Each finger doesn't think for itself. Your brain sends a message, and the fingers come together. Dada was like a finger on Maharaj-ji's hand. There was nothing in him that was wondering, "Should I do it, or shouldn't I?" or, "But you said . . ." or anything like that. He was just a perfect extension, like Hanuman is for Rama.

One day we were sitting in the courtyard at Kainchi. Dada was passing in front of us on his way somewhere, when Maharaj-ji called to him to do something. But we saw that Dada actually started turning toward Maharaj-ji a split second before Maharaj-ji called him. That was the level of attunement.

That's the Hanuman mode, serving through love, opening and opening until you become the Beloved or the Beloved becomes you. You're absorbed into that consciousness, and the Beloved's being permeates yours. Then the ego perception shifts to the soul perception, the whole world is radiant, and the grocery store is your temple, full of souls. Sometimes when I'm speaking to an audience, if I drop into that place, Maharaj-ji's presence enters the room and then there's only one of us. We are all touching the *ātman*.

Once, Dada had been missing Maharaj-ji very much, and he was sitting at night correcting examinations from his economics class at the university. Finally, after locking the house, he went to bed. In the morning nothing had been disturbed, but across the whole page of the top examination paper was written, "Rām Rām Rām Rām Rām Rām Rām," in Maharaj-ji's handwriting.

On another occasion, Didi, Dada's wife, said to Dada, "I hear something in the next room." Their bedroom was near the room they kept for Maharaj-ji, although he wasn't there at the time. When they went in there, as they opened the door, they heard something. There were tracks all up to the ceiling on the wall. Maharaj-ji's footprints were all over the walls.

Hanuman said, "O Rama, sometimes I find that You are the whole and I a part, sometimes that you are the Master and I Your servant; but O Rama, when I have the knowledge of Reality, I see that You are I and I am You."

—*Sri Ramakrishna*[4]

Once while Maharaj-ji was away, Didi made *kheer,* a sweet dish of rice and milk and put it right under the picture of Maharaj-ji. One of the young children came running out of the room, excited. They all went in, and the *kheer* was dripping down from his picture. Maharaj-ji had taken it.

In similar fashion Maharaj-ji scolded a *pujari* for not having remembered to put milk out for the *murti* of Hanuman before he locked up the temple for the night. So the man went and did it. When he unlocked it the next morning, the milk was all gone.

Dada experienced Maharaj-ji turning into Hanuman:

We were walking around and Babaji caught hold of my hand. When he did that I would sometimes experience such a heavy pressure that I felt my hand would break. He was leaning so heavily on me, I was afraid that if I fell down, he would also. It was early afternoon and we came before the mandir *when many people were sitting. Babaji sat before the Shiva temple, my hand locked in his. He said, "Baitho, baitho." ["Sit, sit."] I wanted to extricate myself, but could not.*

I was feeling as if I were suffocating, as if my breathing were coming to an end. My hand was so tight in his grip that there was no question of getting free. Then I saw, not Babaji, but a huge monkey sitting there, long golden hair over the whole body, the face black, the tail tucked under the legs. I saw it clearly. I closed my eyes, but still I saw it. After that, I don't know what happened.

At ten o'clock that night, I found myself sitting alone down by the farm. Purnanand, from the tea shop, came and said, "Dada, here you are. We have been searching for you all evening." He took me back to the ashram.

Babaji had not gone inside his room yet; he was sitting on a cot and many devotees were around him. As soon as we came across the bridge and near the temple, somebody said, "Baba, Dada has come." He just said, "Accha, thik hai." ["Very good."] There was nothing to take notice

*of, nothing to be excited about. I was feeling very depressed. I didn't want
to talk; I just wanted to be alone and go to bed.*

*The next day Guru Datt Sharma and Siddhi Didi and others kept
asking me what had happened. They told me we had been sitting there in
front of the Shiva temple, surrounded by many people, when suddenly we
were both missing. Then Baba and I were seen walking on top of the hill.
An hour or two later, Baba returned alone. I knew what I had seen—that
it was actually Hanuman. It was not a dream, not a mistake. How the
time passed, I do not have any recollection.*[5]

That's another aspect of Maharaj-ji, of course, in which he is very intimately related with Rām and Hanuman. Just how intimately related
was a source of some mystery to those of us around him. Other people
also reported seeing him turn into Hanuman. Every time one man came
near Maharaj-ji, he would take one look and pass out cold. When they
revived him, all he could say is "All I saw was a huge monkey." Perhaps
on another plane, Maharaj-ji is Hanuman, he is Hanuman manifest at
this time. But even that is only a game, because a being who is nobody is
everybody, and he may be taking that form, because that aspect of God
is connected with that particular situation. I think it is limiting to call
him anything at all.

In a way a being like that is everywhere you think of him. He is, and
in a funny way there's nothing you can say he isn't. He has been known
to show up in many places simultaneously, to appear and disappear.
Whenever possible, he denied everything, always leaving you with your
doubts. If you tried to test him, you'd always come away thinking he was
just an old man in a blanket. Only those who say, "Forget testing, I'm
going!" begin to experience his grace.

Maharaj-ji can be in thousands and thousands of places. Many people
have visions of Maharaj-ji, dream about him, have visits from him, see

him, or remember him in a way that's very vivid—and in each case he *is* with them. Or an aspect of him is there, and the aspects can be as many as there are thoughts. A realized being can send out his or her thought form, which is an aspect of that being, and that thought form takes on reality. It becomes manifest somewhere and is truly seen by the person having *darshan* in a vision, dream, or even ordinary waking consciousness.

The quieter your mind is, the more open you are to that meeting with the guru in the heart. Your thought brings the guru to you the moment that thought is pure enough, intent enough, single-minded enough.

The guru only exists to serve the devotees; that's the only reason for the guru's existence. And seeing the guru in the physical form is only another part of the dance, another part of the illusion.

Dada once said to me, "I'm closer to Maharaj-ji when I'm away from him than when I'm with him. Because when I'm with him, my senses get in the way. I get lost in enjoying being with him."

When Dada says, "He's just Baba," that really says it all. Dada was totally blown away; he was full of awe. Dada was as close as you could get to knowing Maharaj-ji, and yet his awe kept him from becoming Maharaj-ji, from doing the final thing that would have let him merge. It's like the *bhakta* Hanuman, who tells Rām he'd rather remain a loving servant than sit with him.

Maharaj-ji had devotees at many different levels of attachment to him. Some were attached to his body and saw him as a grandfatherly figure. Many Indian families were like this with him. He had many devotees who were villagers, very simple people. They each had different *karma* that created a certain kind of relationship with Maharaj-ji. For one he was like a grandfather, for another a friend, for another a teacher, for others Hanuman, and for others he was God beyond any concept.

When he was in the body there were few big gatherings, except a few festivals at the temples, but no great big public things. His simplicity and humility were awesome. He wore a blanket, a *dhoti* (a cloth wound around the lower portion of the body), and a T-shirt, and he sat on a wooden bed, or *tukhat*. When you entered a room he was staying in, you were struck by the absence of everything you would associate with somebody's lived-in bedroom. There was no reading lamp, no books, no evidence that a human being was living there. He would just walk in, sit down on this wooden bed, and there he is and that's his universe. And he was fulfilled. There are many pictures of him just sitting by the side of a road. That was enough for him.

Some devotees simply saw Maharaj-ji as God Incarnate. They were very humble before him; they asked for nothing. They just served him in any way they possibly could. They felt blessed just to have a being like that in form. He never had any big ashrams, and compared to the well-known saints like Sai Baba and Anandamayi Ma, his scene was very small. Most of the time he would send people away soon after they came. He would let them stay five minutes and tell them to leave. You couldn't collect him, you couldn't hold on to him. You couldn't just hang out however you liked.

> In this "not two" nothing is separate, nothing is excluded. No matter when or where, enlightenment means entering this truth.
>
> —Seng-ts'an,
> Third Patriarch of Zen[6]

If you've touched that higher place, you know where you're going. Talking or reading about Oneness is not being in the One. As I understand it, when you become One, the objective universe ceases to be. There's no knower, only knowing. Subject and object become one. In truth Maharaj-ji and I are one. But *I* can't stand it; my ego can't exist there. So I will just keep serving Rām and Maharaj-ji until there's no difference between us.

O servant, where dost thou seek Me?
Lo! I am beside thee,
I am neither in temple nor in mosque; I am neither in Kaaba nor
    in Kailash:
Neither am I in rites and ceremonies, nor in Yoga and renunciation.
If thou art a true seeker, thou shalt at once see Me: thou shalt meet
    Me in a moment of time.
Kabir says, "O Sadhu! God is the breath of all breath."

—Kabir[7]

Maharaj-ji is not bound by time and space. Time and space are within him. In that sense, these incarnations we are in are *maya,* or illusion; they're not real. From where he sits it's all simultaneous. The planes of consciousness, past, present, and future coexist at the same time like dreams one within another. It's a continuum. It's all One, or as he used to say in Hindi, *"Sub ek."*

Maharaj-ji usually wore a blanket. Dada Mukerjee comments:

People asked me so often, "Why does Babaji go on covering himself with a blanket?" Not only would he wear a blanket in the winter when it was cold, but also in the hottest summer months. I used to say that there were two blankets: one blanket covered his physical body, that we all knew. It was not indispensable; it could be thrown off. Some miracles were no doubt done through it: he would be taking something out from under it, sometimes the blanket would be very heavy, sometimes it would be light, and there was the

People gave Maharaj-ji blankets. When he finished with a blanket, it suddenly became much smaller, and he said, "Why are you giving me these blankets that are too small?"

smell of a baby in it. But there was another blanket that was inside. He was covering all his sadhana, all his siddhis, all his achievements, all his plans and programs. Why was he hiding all this? Perhaps it was for our protection, perhaps to save himself from crowds of followers. We cannot know.[8]

The blood in us all is one. The arms, the legs, the hearts are all one. The same blood flows through us all. God is one.

Everyone is God; see God in everyone.

It is deception to teach according to individual differences in *karma*—all are one, you should love everyone, see all the same.

—*Maharaj-ji*

Being with Maharaj-ji not only expanded my conceptual horizon—he certainly blew my mind—he also filled my heart. At the same time there was no clinging in him. That quality of detachment and emptiness was combined with such intense love, an oceanic love that pervaded every being around him. He said that attachment grows both ways, but he also said, "Saints and birds don't collect. Saints give away what they have." He often quoted favorite lines from Kabir's poems like, "I am passing through the marketplace, but I am not a purchaser."

At first I was awed by a presence so powerful that I felt purified just by being near him. Even now, bringing him into my heart does the same thing. I never learned much Hindi, but to me it didn't matter. Words were only the surface of that relationship.

At the time we got to him Maharaj-ji appeared to us as a revered saint or guru who stayed in various temples or ashrams in northern India that were built for him. He would appear in one, stay for a little while, and then, just when everyone was settling down to hang on to him forever, he would be gone. In the middle of the night he'd get someone with a car to take him off, and he would disappear. Then he'd turn up somewhere else, staying here and there with this or that devotee, traveling as the wind of God moved him. Only after he left his body did we discover that was only one aspect of his life and that he had a family.

When I was with him when he was in the body, I experienced his being at many levels. Personally he could be playful and funny, frustrating and repetitive, sweetly childlike, stubborn, like an old man or a little child, very concerned or totally indifferent. We experienced that person because that was our desire, our need for a loving guide. But what we perceived as a personality was in reality more like the changing of the weather, because he had so little attachment to it. We saw the cloud of Maharaj-ji's *maya*, the illusion, though behind it was the sun of the *ātman*.

Simultaneous with this seemingly personal relationship was the palpable power of his presence. There was awe and respect on the part of the devotees too. It was like standing next to a mountain with its upper reaches vanishing in the clouds. When I was in his presence, I experienced an ecstasy and a depth of love—a drunken kind of love where I would often find myself dissolving into tears. When I started going into that, he would interrupt with small talk about others, "How much money does Stephen make?" or something like that, to bring me back. He kept me firmly down on the physical plane to do my work. He didn't allow me to just float around in bliss very much.

On a deeper level, when he asked me why I returned to India, I told him I had come to purify myself more. He said, "I am always in communion with you." Now I understand that to be the case. He is with me always. Sometimes people's reactions are not to me, but to him. At times I don't even feel his presence; he's just coming through me.

The rest of the time I just feel as though I am constantly hanging out with him and he is drawing me in toward himself, toward that place in myself, just pulling me ever so gently. There's no rest. The process is continuous. Everything that happens to me is part of his teaching, if I can remember. If I get uptight about something, I hear him saying to me, "Well, you're still caught, aren't you? Too bad . . ." I talk with him all the time at that level.

As I look back over the times I was with him when he was in the body, when I was able to be at his feet, from the beginning the figure and ground were slowly shifting. Initially there was a fascination with having all this love and attention from Maharaj-ji, K.K., and Hari Dass Baba. Having a guru, having this man whom everybody worshiped giving so much love to me, and feeling completely at home in this strange culture—I was completely hooked.

At first all that fed my ego. I came with a big ego, a great sense of specialness. After all, I was a Harvard professor who had come thousands of miles from America! But then I began to see that however lovingly he treated me, it was no different from the way he treated anyone else, including the sweeper. My self-importance got no confirmation, and I was the only one who even noticed. And after a while my need to feel special began to dissolve in the ocean of his love. Simply opening myself to that love was more blissful than any ego gratification.

That was back in 1966–67. After that I was away from him in the States, and I had to make a new kind of connection. When I returned in 1970 I wasn't as fascinated by the body form as the Westerners who had just arrived. Although he could always pull me into it, I began to feel less involved with the day-to-day drama of being with him. It became more like theater, an entertainment to distract us from the intense transformation going on inside. There was a point where I saw that he was everywhere and in everything.

One day he called me over and asked, "What do you do about your mail?"

"I answer it," I said.

"Don't save your letters," he said.

He had just received two letters. He put one on top of his head, and the other he threw into the wind unread. A cow started eating it. I got very upset.

Another time I got a letter at the post office in Nainital and then got on the bus to go to the temple. I walked into the temple, and Maharaj-ji asked, "What's in the letter?" I started to tell him, and he kept adding things I had missed. I knew that if he knew there was a letter, he knew what was in the letter. So why was he asking?

I began to see how empty all these forms were. I'd look at him, and I'd know he knew I knew he knew, and it just kept going deeper and deeper. It's like a joke where you laugh, and then you laugh again at another level, and then you laugh again at a third level.

> In a Buddha there has never been
> anything that could be said to be there
> Just as a conjurer
> Tries not to get caught up in his illusions
> And therefore by his superior knowledge
> Is not attached to magic forms,
> So also the wise in Perfect Enlightenment
> Know the three worlds to be like a magic show.
> Liberation is merely the end of error.

—Gampopa[9]

The Little Things

Maharaj-ji's devotees depended on him for more than their spiritual welfare. They also looked to him for the mundane details of life. Because he lightened their burdens and anxieties, it also gave them faith to pursue their inner lives. The way Maharaj-ji took care of his devotees, how he looked after them, responded to their needs, and just showered his love on them, deeply endeared his followers to him. He spent most of his time helping people and advising them on the details of their personal lives, families, businesses, jobs, health problems, marriages, emotional worries, school exams, financial stresses, and politics. Dealing with the minutiae of so many hundreds of lives would have quickly overwhelmed a normal person, but his generosity of spirit and loving-kindness buoyed many who were adrift on the sea of existence, so they could then turn their attention toward God. As I watched people from all walks of life coming to him with their problems, I saw directly how his compassion led him to spend all this time listening and helping, and how focused his life was on the needs of others.

> Maharaj-ji said, "I don't want anything. I exist only to serve others."

He didn't teach highfalutin philosophy. But he showed me that the spirit can be transferred into people's hearts by the simple acts of loving them, feeding them, and remembering God. He said Westerners had been denied food. He must have meant spiritual food—none of us lacked for basic sustenance.

He felt each devotee's every need, because he was one with everyone, and yet there was also a level of detachment that comes from seeing how it all is. He protected people from danger and comforted them in times of grief or anxiety. Often they had only to remember him, and he would appear. At times he stood by as people died or endured some suffering, because he recognized their *karma*. Even then he helped to lighten the load of grief or pain or helped them extract the needed wisdom from the situation.

This photograph of the Sah family sitting with Maharaj-ji hints at the subtlety of this mosaic. Each individual here is being fed by his presence. and each is receiving what their karma allows. The elder just to the right

of Maharaj-ji is a devotional scholar who is reinforcing his ideas about God. The child is experiencing the closeness of family, the paternal love of a grandfather. The wife is simply drinking of the ambrosia, the bliss of being in the presence of God. On the right, the brother has a quiet and deep devotion, a simple faith. The cousin on the left is going in and out, merging in the love.

All these experiences add up to a transmission, a deepening of the moment, into the very heart of Being, the eternal moment of God. This is a moment shared on many planes, a silent pause in a moving sea of love.

We enter into each other when we are in each other's presence. If you're not threatened, you can relax your separateness, let it fall, and enter into a kind of liquid merging with other beings. Sitting with Maharaj-ji is total contentment. Nothing may be happening, the conversation may be completely trivial, yet there is a richness of presence, of emptiness, of a unity that transcends blood family to become spiritual family.

When I returned to India in 1970, Maharaj-ji had gone from the temple in the hills, and I couldn't find him. Other Westerners were in the same boat. We finally found him, or he found us, in Allahabad. Then he sent us on our way, saying, "See me in Vrindavan." So I went to Delhi, and then went on several weeks of pilgrimage with Swami Muktananda.

When we finally returned from our pilgrimage in March, it was the time of year he would be up in the mountains. I didn't want to stop in Vrindavan, because I knew he wouldn't be there. But the group insisted, and so we went there. We arrived at the temple at about 8:30 A.M., and the place was deserted. I was so disappointed. It was the second time I had gone to that temple and he wasn't there. And he had said he would see me in Vrindavan. The *pujari* said, "Oh, Maharaj-ji is in the mountains. Go see him in Kainchi."

So I said, "Well, let's not waste any time here. Let's go to the mountains."

So we went out and got in the car, and just as we were putting the key in the ignition, a little Fiat drove up, and who was sitting in the front seat next to the driver but Maharaj-ji. He got out looking utterly bored and walked into the temple.

We ran to the driver and asked, "What is he doing here?"

The driver said Maharaj-ji got him up at 2 A.M., saying, "Come on, we have to go to Vrindavan right away!"

Then when they got to Agra he said, "We still have an hour to wait." So they went and visited a judge.

Then he said, "Come on, let's go," and they drove up just at that moment. That's timing. That's cosmic show biz. Maharaj-ji fulfilled his promise to meet us in Vrindavan, so we wouldn't be disappointed. He performed this deeply caring act as if it were totally ordinary. As he walked past us into the temple, there was no outer demonstration at all.

In a collection of devotee stories titled *Divine Reality* there is a story about Maharaj-ji coming to visit one of his devotees, the civil surgeon in the city of Jhansi. It was during World War II. The man made a bed for Maharaj-ji and slept on the floor next to him in case he should need anything during the night. About 1 A.M. he heard Maharaj-ji tossing and turning and asked him why he was restless. Maharaj-ji gave him his blanket and asked him to go and throw it in the water. It was a dark night and the lake was some distance, but Maharaj-ji insisted on his going right away. When he returned before dawn, Maharaj-ji told him that his son, an army officer, had been in a German attack, jumped off a ridge, and gotten stuck in a marsh. Germans had fired on him from above, and taking him for dead, they left. Maharaj-ji said, "All those bullets got stuck in my blanket, and their heat made me uneasy. When you threw the blanket into the lake, I was relieved of my discomfort."

The blanket was new, and there were no holes in it. The surgeon didn't understand what was going on, but was comforted to know his son was safe. Some days after Maharaj-ji left, the man's wife received a letter from their son relating the same circumstance described by Maharaj-ji and expressing his surprise that an unknown power had saved him from a rain of bullets.[10]

"Never disturb anyone's heart. Even if a person hurts you, give him love."

"I can't get angry with you, even in a dream."

"If you can't love each other, you can't achieve your goal."

From stories that have been passed on to us by the close Indian devotees who traveled with Maharaj-ji and spent time with him at places like Kainchi and his "winter camp" in Allahabad, there was a great sense of intimacy and playfulness as their lives revolved around him. At Dada's house in Allahabad they slept on mattresses on the floor and ate together. Maharaj-ji would sit on the end of their beds and joke with them. Dada's mother and auntie would sit preparing vegetables and cooking. While Maharaj-ji was in his room, the others would be exchanging intimate stories about him. When he emerged he would tease them about reciting lies behind his back. Everyone's habits and failings, like Dada's smoking, would come in for some discussion, all done in an atmosphere of affection and humor.

With such close devotees he was informal, intimate, and colorful in his language. Because of our lack of knowledge of Hindi and our unfamiliarity with the culture, we sometimes missed the delicious details. Once at Kainchi one of the Western women who was living outside the ashram reported that her rented room had been broken into and some of her things had been stolen. Maharaj-ji launched into a lengthy and heated response that was translated as, "Maharaj-ji says you should keep your door locked." Some of the Westerners who had learned a fair amount of Hindi heard what he actually said, which was, "Those stupid sister-fuckers, they leave their doors open for any passing thief!"

He was sometimes called "Latrine Baba," partly because he put in the first flush toilets in Kainchi, but probably also because he used foul language. It always seemed affectionate. I guess the Indians were embarrassed, because they wouldn't translate it for us.

We were the junior members of this family, but even so he lovingly kidded us and occasionally included us in the much sought after honor of being abused—teased or lovingly insulted—by him. Within weeks we felt fully welcomed under the shade of his umbrella and began to get at least some sense of the delights that the Indian devotees had enjoyed for so many years.

One time Maharaj-ji was nudging those of us who enjoyed an occasional toke of *ganja* or *charas,* marijuana or hashish, to cease indulging. He was rarely moralizing or alarmist about such habits, pointing more toward how they distracted one from the pursuit of God. To buttress his case Maharaj-ji brought in Purnanand Tewari, a longtime devotee and a farmer and owner of the *chai wallah* (tea stall) outside Kainchi. Berating Purnanand at length for wasting his time smoking *charas* and thus spending the money that was to feed his family, Maharaj-ji excoriated him for his weak moral fiber. Through it all Purnanand sat looking humble and guilt-ridden, the picture of contrition, confessing to each of Maharaj-ji's accusations, "Yes, Maharaj-ji, yes, Maharaj-ji!" Though we took his point, most of us saw this as an affectionate charade.

Even our receiving the news in America that he had left the body occurred in a compassionate and graceful way. His death was part of the fabric of how he lived in us. Rameshwar Das had come to visit me in Franklin. Soon after his arrival a telegram was delivered to my father saying that "Maharaj-ji has dropped his bojay" (telegraphic mangling of "body"). As the news spread quickly, others came to join us. Being part of his spiritual family gave us all solace and support as we worked to come to terms with this cataclysm in our firmament. I was surprised to find myself not really grieving. There was really no change in my relationship with him.

I felt a curious emptiness. It was scary, because I had really only wanted to get away from him for a little while, until I was ready to go back to the rigors of *sadhana*, and now he had gotten away from me. The power had been taken out of my hands. I could, in truth, have gone back to India before that if I'd wanted to. But I didn't want to. I was enjoying "name and fame" too much and rationalizing it all perfectly.

But all the time Maharaj-ji was there in my consciousness. When I felt his presence, I thought maybe I was creating it, and when I denied his presence, I felt I was pushing away something that was in fact true. So he was both there and not there. Either way, he was still here.

How to describe the degree of caring and solicitude Maharaj-ji manifests for those who remember him? To compare him to a parent or a doctor, lover or spouse vastly understates the case. His level of compassion is based on being it all. He actually feels the fear, anxiety, and pain of his devotees, because he *is* them. And at the same time he is beyond it all. His compassion comes from the deep wisdom of how things are, not just from sympathy with our temporal misery. His true focus is on the soul.

There were women who took care of Maharaj-ji—the Ma's or mothers, single women, widows, and grandmothers who were able to take time away from their families. In all the time I spent at the temple I never even knew they existed. They stayed in the back, always out of sight, busy taking care of Maharaj-ji out of complete love and devotion. Sometimes he was very fierce with them. Once when they didn't bring his medicine on time, he said, "If you don't take care of me, I'll turn your minds against me."

It's Only Love

Maharaj-ji's teaching is love. That love stays with you wherever you are. The more open you are, the more you can receive the love. It's the beginning, the middle, and the end.

At first I was seeing him a lot through my heart in an emotional way, like having a good father who loved me so much, and I just kept basking in that affection. But I was stuck in an interpersonal, emotional, romantic kind of loving. It's not pure love, like Christ-love. I kept trying to make Maharaj-ji into a personality, and he wasn't. My mind was interfering with the power of his love, but I couldn't do much about it, because my mind was so dominant. He kept saying, "Ram Dass is so clever." I'm simpler now, which is nice. I'm still smart, but I'm not so clever.

I went through a transformation from personal to impersonal love for Maharaj-ji. At first I brought along all my old habits of personal love. Then I began to see how impersonal it is. He was just there, laughing behind it all. And it was still all love, so much I could barely stand it. It was anguish for a while, but I feel much closer to him now.

I remember once in Delhi we had found Maharaj-ji at the house of an old devotee named Soni, and we had all rushed there to his feet. We were all in ecstasy that we had gotten to him in the bedroom. I was made much of as a leading this and that, and everybody was fawning all over me. We went outside and were fed many sweets. I was standing by the door when Maharaj-ji came out of the bedroom to go to the car. He walked within six inches of me, but went right by me as if I were a lamp-post. There wasn't one iota, not a hint of recognition. This being, who was always patting me and doing all kinds of loving things, just walked by me as though he was passing somebody on the street. He wasn't even intentionally ignoring me; there was nobody "busily walking by." That took our relationship to a whole new level for me.

A Cup of Ocean, Please

The guru is just here. The guru is just sitting around doing nothing really, just manifesting. But what do you do? Can devotees do something to open themselves to the guru? Ramana Maharshi says, "from the point of view of the disciple, the grace of the Guru is like an ocean. If he comes with a cup, he will get only a cupful. There is no use complaining of the niggardliness of the ocean; the bigger the vessel, the more he will be able to carry."[11]

When I was with Maharaj-ji for long periods, I would have time to reflect about who he really was. We would sit across the courtyard and watch him. I'd be thinking, "Who is this?" "What are we about?" "What is this process?" Again the form started to become empty, really empty. I started to feel caught in some kind of tape loop in my mind, and I saw that I had to go deeper than the form and the linear human interaction. Maharaj-ji was so incredibly vast, yet I couldn't get to him as long as I kept seeing that form as real. So that reality gave way to a deeper level of being, where I kept feeling him surrounding me and the oceanic quality of his presence.

All I can ever ask of Maharaj-ji is to make me a pure instrument of his will. I just want to keep surrendering to him. I no longer even have a desire to be enlightened. I'm not interested in being done—it's not a realistic thing for me. It may happen or it may not, I don't know.

More and more I am less and less in evidence to myself. More and more I'm just whatever it is I am doing at the moment. It's just happening. I'm just action. I'm not acting self-consciously. But it's different from the unconscious action I've performed most of my life. All I want is to become like a finger on the hand of his consciousness, or like Hanuman, whom Maharaj-ji referred to as the "breath of Rām." I'm perfectly content to be the breath of Maharaj-ji.

Maharaj-ji is not going anywhere. As St. John says, "He that sent me is with me, he hath not left me alone. I do always the things that please him" (8:29). It's up to us to make the effort to reach up, to look within, to quiet our minds to make space for him. Then, as he said, "Bring your mind to one point and wait for grace."

a family man

Of MAHARAJ-JI'S LIFE much is unknown and much is conjecture. Dada said:

We do not know about Maharaj-ji's education, or the forms of sadhana he had undergone, or what guru he had. We only know that before the ashrams at Kainchi and Vrindavan were built he was moving all the time. For how many years he had been moving like that, how many places he had visited, how many persons he had initiated or delivered from their miseries, nobody can say. We have knowledge only about particular places or times, a small fraction of his life. I have met most of his very closest and oldest devotees and all agree that we have known only a part of his life. Although the life of Babaji was quite a long one, it was only since the sixties that he stayed at the ashrams in Kainchi and Vrindavan or places like Nainital. Even at the ashrams Baba would be running away at the first opportunity. Also, he might be sitting with us, he might be talking with us, but he could also be roaming, moving about in another place or another world at the same time. There are so many cases of Babaji being seen in two or three different places at the same time. His body might be in meditation, but he might not be in it.[1]

He began to appear regularly around Nainital about 1947. Older people have recognized him as the guru of their grandfather, which would suggest that he had had another body.

It was not until almost a decade after Maharaj-ji had died or left his body that we Westerners who had been with him in India began to hear credible stories about his having a family. There had been an arranged marriage when Maharaj-ji was about twelve. He left home soon thereafter and did not return for nine or ten years. What was it like for his family, having a husband or father who was a saint and a guru to so many people?

Thinking back, it made sense that almost all his devotees were householders. Though deeply respected by the *sadhus,* yogis, and other saints, he was primarily a householder guru. In India holiness is not confined to celibate *sadhus* or renunciates.

His family has enriched our multifaceted picture of Maharaj-ji, especially for those of us who were with him. Now that we have children of our own and have become householders ourselves, we are in awe that he was able to keep both the spiritual and the family worlds going simultaneously.

Maharaj-ji was a master of what in India they call *maya,* the projection of illusion. Occasionally he let slip hints of this power when he said things like, "I hold the keys to the mind." The separation of his family and spiritual lives was subtle. There was overlap between the two scenes, people seeing but not understanding. As the story has unfolded it became clear that these two strands of his life were indeed interwoven. A few devotees were aware of the family. And the family, although they were aware of Maharaj-ji's spiritual life, didn't make much of the guru business or comprehend the extent of his following.

Once Maharaj-ji returned home to his wife after being away. He put a handful of mustard seeds on his tongue. When he spit them out in his hand, they had all sprouted leaves. "See," he said, "the spiritual business is coming along."

Dharam Narayan, his second son, says he didn't really come to know Maharaj-ji as a saint until after his death. Dharam Narayan just knew him as a loving father who was there when he needed him. Maharaj-ji always behaved with him like another member of the family. When Maharaj-ji occasionally took relatives from his home village traveling with him and they met the devotees, he would make sure they had plenty of the delicious food and special sweets that were always around. They were quite satisfied with the treats and didn't pay much attention to the rest of what was going on, perhaps because Maharaj-ji was so casual about it.

Maharaj-ji was born Lakshmi Narayan Sharma on the eighth day after the new moon of the month of Margshirsh in about 1902 in his family's mud home in the rural village of Akbarpur, some distance from Agra. His family were landowners of the Brahmin caste. At his birth the astrologers predicted he would have the blessings of Lakshmi, the goddess of wealth.

His sons said that he was exceptional from birth: "He had no attachments. He was very generous and tried to help one and all, especially the underprivileged. He was very loving and affectionate." They said love and affection overflowed in his presence, and that they have not been able to provide as much love and affection to their children as their father did to them.

Maharaj-ji's father, Pandit Durga Prasad Sharma, was a learned man who was a great devotee of Hanuman, the monkey god, whom Maharaj-ji also worshiped. His father took him to Benares to learn Sanskrit when he was about six, and he spent a couple of years there before his mother, Kaushalya Devi, missed him so much that he was brought back home. She died of a sudden illness, possibly cholera, soon after, when he was about eight. His father remarried within a year to a young woman of eighteen or twenty. She and Maharaj-ji were in conflict from the start, probably because his own mother had so recently passed away and the new stepmother was trying to take the traditional reins of power as "mother" of the household.

When Maharaj-ji was around nine years old, one day he told his father that there would be robbers that night at their house. His father paid no heed and, sure enough, the robbers looted their house at gunpoint the same night.

When Maharaj-ji was twelve, his marriage was arranged. His bride, Ram Beti, was ten and, as was the custom, remained at her parents' home until three or four months after the marriage, and then she came to live at her in-laws' place in Akbarpur.

The friction between Maharaj-ji and the young stepmother continued, eventually culminating in an argument, after which Maharaj-ji was beaten by his father and locked in his room. Maharaj-ji escaped and left home. He was twelve or twelve and a half. He was not to return until 1924–25, nine or ten years later. Little is definitively known about those intervening years. The following sketch comes from Guru Datt Sharma, one of Maharaj-ji's old devotees.

Maharaj-ji first went to Udaipur in Rajasthan and got a job as a guard in a temple. Soon he moved on toward Gujarat and reached Rajkot. He started staying with a *mahant* (head of a large monastic order of *sadhus*). He was known as Lakshman Das during this time. The *mahant* was very impressed by Maharaj-ji and declared him to be his successor, but his decision did not sit well with his other disciples. When the *mahant* passed away, Maharaj-ji left to avoid a controversy.

He reached the village of Babania near Morbi in Gujarat, where he stayed at the ashram of a woman saint, Rama Bai. Maharaj-ji used to sit in a lake (*tal*) near the ashram, meditating under the water for hours at a time. He became known as Talaya Baba ("Lake Baba"). After spending considerable time at Babania, he started roaming around India on foot, which he did for the next eight years or so. Dada collected some additional stories about the Talaya Baba period of Maharaj-ji's *sadhana*:

Another clue came from Sri S. N. Sang, the principal of Birla College at Nainital and a great devotee of Babaji. . . . He narrated his first experience as a little school boy reading in a public school in the Punjab:

"The students used to have a camp for a few weeks in the mountains every year. We were in our camp in the Simla hills, collecting some flowers or running after butterflies, when we saw a man in a blanket passing by. We took no notice of him as there were so many persons coming and going. After a few minutes, a cowherd from a village in that area came running down shouting, 'Such a great saint has passed by and you did not run after him!'

"The question that we hurled at him was why he himself had not followed the saint. He said he had gone to call Santia (his wife) and other people in the village. When the people started going up the hill, we joined them. After quite some distance, we all came back as there was no sign of the man in the blanket.

"The cowherd began to talk of his boyhood days, when he had known that man in the blanket as Talaya Baba, the baba who lives in a lake. The cowherd said that he and the other village boys used to bring their cows and goats for grazing. They used to carry their food with them for the noon meal, as they would not return before the evening. After reaching a nearby lake, they would tie their food in a cloth and hang it on the branches of a tree.

"A baba used to live in that lake (talao) and was known by the name of Talaya Baba. Whenever they came there, they would see him in the water. He was very kind, and everyone used to talk highly of him as a sadhu, but he used to tease them a great deal. When they came for their meal at noon,

they would see that he had taken away their bag from the tree and had
distributed the whole of it to the people coming to him, or to the animals.
Then he would feed them in plenty with all kinds of delicious food—pure
halwa, laddoo, kheer—*they would never have imagined tasting so many*
sweets together. He would get the food by putting his hand on his head or
from the lake in which he was sitting. He loved them much and used to
talk to them when they were near him.

"*This was long ago. They were just small boys then, but he remembered*
everything about Talaya Baba."[2]

According to a *baba* who claimed to have accompanied him, sometime in the 1920s Maharaj-ji went on a *yatra*, or pilgrimage, following the

banks of the sacred Narmada River to the ocean, then returning up the other bank to the starting point, Amarkantak. A sixteen-hundred-year-old *baba* was the organizer of the *yatra*, and at the end of it he was said to have bestowed his *siddhis* on Maharaj-ji.

He is next heard of in the village of Neeb Karori. Maharaj-ji had an underground room or cave constructed where he did a lot of *puja, yogic kriyas* (or purifications), and *havan* (fire ceremony) and meditated. Someone used to leave a cup of milk at the mouth of the cave for Maharaj-ji every day. At one point the milk was not left for some days, and Maharaj-ji began to berate the *murti* of Hanuman that he worshiped for not providing him with sustenance.

Also from this time is the story of how Maharaj-ji became known as Baba Neeb Karori (or Neem Karoli Baba, as it later evolved). Since no one had given him any food for several days, hunger drove him to board a train for the nearest city. When the conductor discovered Maharaj-ji seated in the first-class coach without a ticket, he pulled the emergency brake and the train ground to a halt. Maharaj-ji was unceremoniously put off the train. The train had stopped near the village of Neeb Karori. Maharaj-ji sat down under the shade of a tree while the conductor blew his whistle to start the train.

The train didn't move. It sat there for hours. Another engine was called in to push, to no avail. Finally some passengers suggested to the railroad officials that they coax the *sadhu* back on board. The officials were initially appalled by such superstition, but after many frustrating attempts to move the train, they decided to give it a try.

Passengers and railway officials approached Maharaj-ji, offering him food and sweets. They requested that he board the train and resume his journey. Before giving an answer, Maharaj-ji ate his fill. He said he would board the train on condition that the railway officials promised to have a station built for the village of Neeb Karori. At that time the villagers had to walk many miles to the nearest station. The officials promised to do whatever was in their power, and Maharaj-ji finally reboarded the train. As soon as he was back in his first-class seat, the train began to roll.

Maharaj-ji said that the officials kept their word. Soon afterward a train station was built. Maharaj-ji said he didn't know why the train wouldn't move. He certainly had done nothing to it, but it was on that day that his "business" really got started.

During the years of Maharaj-ji's absence, his young wife led an austere and difficult life. As word of her husband's leaving home spread, the locals started teasing her. Some said that he had run away and would never come back or that he was dead. She had to listen to a lot of hurtful village gossip but could do nothing about it.

Ram Beti spent much of her time in worship. She would grind 250 grams (half a pound) of barley every day with the hand grinding stones of the time. With this flour she would make three *chapatis*. One she would offer to Shiva in the village temple, one she would give to a cow, and one she would eat herself. This is what she ate all those years Maharaj-ji was away. And she prayed to God continuously.

Someone from Maharaj-ji's grandmother's village saw a young man resembling Durga Prasad, Maharaj-ji' father, on the banks of the Ganges in Farrukhabad. Because the man knew Durga Prasad's son had run away from home, he informed the father, who went to Farrukhabad and discovered Maharaj-ji as he was going for his daily bath in the Ganges. He persuaded him to return home and take up his family responsibilities. Maharaj-ji had long hair like a *sadhu,* so he was taken for a haircut before he came home. This was in 1924–25.

When he first returned, Maharaj-ji stayed indoors most of the time. His powers were mostly hidden except for minor events, such as when his wife was unable to find something. Then he would tell someone to go behind the house, and the item would be found there.

Many *babas* and *sadhus* visited him at home, and guests were always welcomed and fed. His wife, though, who must have been more aware of his dual life than others, did not like hearing him addressed as "Baba" (an honorific for a holy man) and would get irritated with people who referred to him that way even after he left the body.

In general the saints and *sadhus* who visited were all respected and treated well. One named Keshavanand was given a warm welcome and treated in a manner befitting a saint. When another, known as Yogwale

Baba, came to visit, *chapatis* were made and offered to him with vegetables. As he did not eat *chapatis,* he asked for *paranthas* (fried flatbreads), which were prepared. The *baba* sat eating them in front of the fire as it was very cold. A passing farmer who saw him eating the *paranthas* commented that he and others worked for the whole day and got dry *chapatis*—why was this *baba,* who did no work and refused to eat *chapatis* coated with *ghee* (butter), now enjoying *paranthas*?

The *baba* heard this and felt so bad he threw the *paranthas* in the fire and got up to leave. Maharaj-ji asked the *baba* to please stay. He immediately asked for preparation of *puris* (another variety of fried flatbread). These were offered to him by Maharaj-ji with great respect. He ate these and was so impressed by Maharaj-ji's behavior that he fell at his feet. Later Maharaj-ji cited the maxim, *"Bhojan, Bhajan, Khazana Nari / Ye Sub Purdah Adhikari,"* meaning food, worship, wealth, and wife should all be kept private. Another saint who came to the village told a villager, one Shri Devi Ram, who was very close to Maharaj-ji, that Maharaj-ji was a *mahatma,* a great soul.

By all accounts Maharaj-ji was a loving and supportive husband and father who was present for all the important family events. His wife's sister says, "He loved his wife very much and ensured that whatever she desired was made available to her immediately. He would look after her in a manner that most husbands would not. If she took some decision, he would stand by her if he felt that she was right, even if this meant going against the entire village."

He did all she wanted except if he did not consider something right. A person came to the house asking Maharaj-ji's wife for some money for his son's release from jail. She refused, as this man was in the habit of asking for money on any excuse. Maharaj-ji was sitting upstairs and overheard the conversation and came down. The man said that his son was caught without a ticket on the train, and since he could not pay the fine, he was put in jail. Maharaj-ji gave him the required amount of money with tears in his own eyes. Later he told his wife of the feelings of a person whose son is put behind bars.

Three children were born in the ancestral home in Akbarpur, two sons, Aneg Singh in 1925 and Dharam Narayan in 1937, and a daughter, Girija, in 1945. Maharaj-ji paid particular attention to the education of his children, all of whom attended secondary schools and two of whom went to university. He did not differentiate between his sons and daughter, as did most families during that period, and insisted on the equal education for all the children. At times he personally escorted his daughter to school with an umbrella to protect her from the sun.

Maharaj-ji often taught his children with whatever was happening in the moment. Watching a family of birds in a tree he would say that as the mother bird feeds the baby birds, who fly away leaving their parents behind, we can learn detachment from the birds. He also used to relate stories from the *Ramayana*, particularly those about Sita and Anasuya.

He told stories and parables like that of a saint standing in the river who saw a scorpion floating by. He thought to save its life and picked it up from the water, but it stung him with its tail, causing immense pain, which he could not bear, so the scorpion fell back in the water as his hand recoiled. Again, the saint picked it up, and the same story repeated itself. Someone asked the saint why he kept doing this, when the creature was causing him so much pain. The saint said, "It is following its nature. When such a creature does not leave its nature, why should I leave mine?" Discomfort should not cause one to leave one's essential nature.

Although the family had servants, Maharaj-ji treated them with respect. He didn't consider any work insignificant. He would help the servant operate the *chara* machine used to chop the cow fodder because he felt it was a heavy job.

Wherever he was and whatever he was doing, his fingers were always moving, doing *japa*, repeating prayers. If anyone spoke to him he would say *Rām Rām,* as if he had been silently chanting *Rām Rām* all the time. He would lock himself in his room at Agra for days at a time, and no one dared disturb him except his wife.

Maharaj-ji arranged all of his children's marriages. At his daughter's wedding, he warned his son to get an alternate source of light. Indeed, the power went out and lanterns were used. After Maharaj-ji performed the ritual giving of the bride to the groom, he left the proceedings early. Siddhi Ma said he was locked in his room at Kainchi most of that day.

Maharaj-ji said one can reach God while fulfilling his or her duties as a householder. He was generally home for all the important festivals, which he would celebrate as the biggest landowner of the village. The villagers would come to the house, and at two of the major festivals, Holi and Diwali, he distributed five-kilogram (ten-pound) bags of wheat (a relative luxury) to the poor. When Maharaj-ji was present, a lot of people would gather around him, including many *sadhus*. He ensured that all were looked after. The atmosphere around him was full of fun and joy.

People came to him with all sorts of problems. He said that serving people is service to God. When he met with the village elders, he treated those of every caste with respect and love without discrimination. He said one should always think of giving more than one gets. In those days, during the Holi festival when people throw colored water on each other to remember Krishna's love play, people from the lower castes were not allowed to throw the color on people of higher caste. He was the first person in the village to break this restriction.

In many respects, Maharaj-ji was like any other father or elder of a family. The difference was that he was always very magnanimous in his approach and love flowed and poured from him. He always took special care in looking after his servants and the poor. Maharaj-ji loved to hear the *Ramayana* recited. Hearing the description of Sita alone in Lanka after she was kidnapped, tears would roll down his cheeks.

He started leaving home from Akbarpur for two or three days a month. As time passed, he would be gone for eight to ten days at a stretch, would come back and stay for a week, and then would be gone again. In 1962 the family moved to Agra, first renting, then purchasing a property. After his daughter's wedding Maharaj-ji's visits home to Agra and Akbarpur reduced drastically. When his wife had an attack of paralysis in 1972, however, he visited the family twice in Agra.

Dharam Narayan sometimes traveled with Maharaj-ji and visited him at the Vrindavan and Kainchi ashrams and at his Kumbha Mela camps in Allahabad or Haridwar. He would go basically to get spending money. Maharaj-ji gave him money, and he never bothered about anything else. If a spiritual thought crossed his mind or he heard of some miracle from devotees, Maharaj-ji would tell him that he was fooling everyone and Dharam Narayan didn't inquire further. Siddhi Ma was very much aware of the family and would look after the family members whenever they visited him.

Maharaj-ji's nephew was asked by his mother to go to the Vrindavan ashram to get some blankets. At the ashram he was mesmerized by the number of people and stood at a distance not knowing how to reach Maharaj-ji. Maharaj-ji shouted to him, inquiring about his mother and others. He told him to take the blankets his mother had sent him for. The nephew was surprised Maharaj-ji knew about the blankets without his uttering a word. Things like this happened constantly with family members but always seemed to get overlooked.

One year when his wife was not feeling well, Maharaj-ji moved the entire family to a rented house in Nainital for two months while he was in Kainchi. The family visited him from there.

On another occasion Maharaj-ji's daughter, Girija, came down with typhoid while he was away. The attending doctor said he couldn't help her, and the family was worried. Her maternal uncle went to Kainchi to tell Maharaj-ji. At first he looked worried, then he went into the Hanuman *mandir,* lit a lamp, and sat in the temple for some time. When he came out, he told the *pujari* to keep the lamp filled with *ghee* to keep it burning. Later, sitting with devotees, he said that this man was worried about his sick niece. He said nothing would happen to her and she would be all right. Girija recovered.

In essence, the family was content that he was a good husband, father, or relative, and no one bothered about anything else. From the first when Maharaj-ji came back home, the family knew there was something more to him. His wife used to question him a lot, but she never spoke and no one really knows what went on between them. Only Maharaj-ji knew how he kept the spiritual side and the family side of his life separate. This arrangement continued throughout his life, but both sides were happy, and nothing about the family surfaced in the large gathering of the devotees.

As the head of the landowning family in Akbarpur, Maharaj-ji was known and respected in the community. After India introduced democratic election of village officials, Maharaj-ji was elected headman of the village unopposed. He would sit under a neem tree on a raised platform, villagers would gather around, and he would resolve their problems. No *siddhis* were in evidence, though now some people say impossible things occurred and they did not realize it at the time.

Village life was not totally harmonious. Maharaj-ji wanted to get rid of the caste system, which was opposed by the higher caste people, including some of his own relatives. This created friction in the village. Later the headman post was reserved for a person from the lower castes. He ensured that a person named Bhoj Raj, or Bhoja, from a lower caste became headman despite the opposition.

He once asked his son Aneg Singh, "If I cut your finger, what color will your blood be?"

"Red," Aneg Singh replied.

He then asked, "If the finger of the sweeper's son is cut, what would the color be?"

"There would be no difference," his son replied.

Maharaj-ji said, "If there is no difference, then why differentiate? Go and play with the sweeper's son."

This was at a time when the caste system was firmly in place, and he was telling his children to break away from it and ensure equality for all.

In the Body

When you go to see a guru or a saint in India, it's traditional to offer fruit, flowers, or money. We often just brought Maharaj-ji apples or bananas. There was really nothing else you could give him. Maharaj-ji would take the fruits and throw them at people with astonishing accuracy. He really was a lot like a monkey. He had incredibly long arms.

Maharaj-ji's body was extraordinary. Its form kept changing, depending on who was looking at it, when, and what work he had to do with that person. There were times when he seemed tiny and agile, other times when he seemed a mountainous bulk, like the time that Dada's wife, Didi, tried to massage him and she couldn't reach over his body, it was so huge. There were other times when he seemed diminutive, and you wanted to protect him. His height changed as well as the immense expanse of his belly. If you've seen pictures of Nityananda, you will recognize that same barrel-like quality, which is perhaps an effect of the *shakti*. The luminous buttery quality of his skin was extraordinary. It was so soft and creamy, and it smelled like a baby's at times.

His eyes had long lashes, and they were usually half-closed. When you could see his eyes, they sometimes looked slightly crossed, as though one eye was seeing the world and the other was turned within. Only once when I was with him did he open his eyes fully and look directly into mine. The power of those eyes could take you into full *samadhi*. But to do that prematurely wouldn't liberate anyone; it would just create another high, so he masked that power. People couldn't bear that force, so he mostly kept his eyes half-closed behind those long lashes. The nail of his big toe was red as if painted with Mercurochrome. For the devotees it was like a lightbulb. But maybe he had an ingrown toenail.

He had incredibly flexible joints. He could join his hands behind his back and bring them up over his head to the front without ever disengaging his hands. He used to go to the children's ward of the hospital in Nainital and entertain the children with yogic tricks. He would put his arms flat on the floor, turn a somersault without lifting his arms, and then go back the other way. He demonstrated this facility to a group of about ten devotees, clasping his hands behind his back and bringing them to the front without letting go.

A doctor from Bombay who had been the bone specialist for Kennedy and Nehru came, and Maharaj-ji showed him his right arm, which bent the wrong way and could do all kinds of weird things. Maharaj-ji looked terribly concerned and asked the doctor about it.

The surgeon said, "Well, clearly you broke it when you were a child, and it never healed. It stayed loose in this way."

Maharaj-ji said, "Oh, isn't that interesting. What about this one?" And he did the same thing with the other arm, which made the doctor seem like a total fool. Maharaj-ji had a way with doctors, chiding them about what they thought they knew.

When Maharaj-ji first came to Nainital, he would walk over the roofs and up and down little ladders into the homes that are stacked on top of one another in the Nainital bazaar, the center of town. K.K. took me up on the top floor of his home and showed me how Maharaj-ji had climbed across the roofs to where a young Siddhi Ma was making "burries" (lentil paste dried on the rooftops for later use in the winter), how she had *pranamed* (humbly greeted him) and the loving quality of his smile.

Maharaj-ji went to the house of an old devotee, Sri Ram Sah. Siddhi Ma came and sang a *bhajan* so sweet that Maharaj-ji was in tears, and she was lost in the singing. It went, *"Sumiran karley mere mana . . ."* ("O my mind, remember . . ."). For a while after that Maharaj-ji would affectionately call Siddhi Ma *"mere mana,"* or "my mind," recalling the *bhajan.*

In each home the women would prepare a meal, as it was a blessing for them to cook for a saint. Once Maharaj-ji started at 6 A.M. and kept going until 11 P.M. He ate some twenty full meals, huge meals, with *puris* and rice and all that. He just kept eating and eating and eating. At each home he'd get up and leave after ten or fifteen minutes. He was serving all those people incredibly by doing that. On the other hand, during his last few years in the body he ate very little, hardly anything.

Maharaj-ji would develop illnesses that came and went with astonishing rapidity. He might come down with a high fever and be wrapped in blankets, and then an hour later it would be completely gone. He might take on something that would cause somebody else to die, like a massive heart attack, and it would go right through him. He took on a lot of stuff for other people. Mostly this was hidden. Few people ever knew that he was taking on their *karma.*

K.K. once went to see Maharaj-ji at Kainchi and found him huddled by a charcoal brazier, wearing a wool cap, sweater, and socks (which he never wore), sniffling miserably. He said, "Oh, K.K., I am very sick!" Instead of being sympathetic, K.K., who has a certain bad-boy quality at times, said, "Maharaj-ji, why do you bother trying to fool fools like us?" His cousin M.L., who was with him, was a bit offended by his presumptuousness, but Maharaj-ji took off the socks and cap and stopped acting like he had a cold.

I suspect that much of what Maharaj-ji did was not for us to see. There were times, many times in the last few years, when he would seem to go away even though sitting there. I think he spent a great deal of time in formless *samadhi* in his last years, in the back room where we generally weren't allowed to be with him. Once at Dada's home, when the *Ramayana* was being read, they stopped the reading and moved him out, because he was going into *samadhi*.

The first few years I was with Maharaj-ji, he was always doing *japa*, saying *Rām Rām Rām*, on his fingers. By 1970 he wasn't doing that so much. *Sahaja samadhi*, Maharaj-ji's state, is sometimes described as the *samadhi* that comes automatically, spontaneously, when one is in form and not in form at the same time, one foot in the world and one in the void. I think of *sahaja samadhi* as a state where you go in and out with each breath, where the universe is re-created with each breath, as the Buddha described. Imagine that inside Maharaj-ji is not time as we know it, but it's as if the mind moments have been spread out. It's both huge and tiny, so that each mind moment, of which there are trillions in each blink of an eye, is a full universe that is created, then ceases to exist, and then comes back in. In the same way that Buddha could label each one, Maharaj-ji could live within each one. In those cessations of existence is God, beyond any concept of God. Even the concept of God is still a mind moment—but in between those mind moments is where God *IS*.

At first when a person is going in and out of *samadhi*, those periods are very long. You enter into *samadhi* for periods of time on the physical

The great tree of Sahaja is shining in the three worlds; everything being of the nature of *sunya* (emptiness), what will bind what? As water mixing with water makes no difference, so also, the jewel of the mind enters the sky in the oneness of emotion. Where there is no self, how can there be any nonself? What is uncreated from the beginning can have neither birth, nor death, nor any kind of existence. This is the nature of all—nothing goes or comes, there is neither existence nor nonexistence in *sahaja*.

—*Bhusukupada*[3]

plane, like for three days, and then you come out. Then maybe it's in every night and out in the day. Finally it gets so that each moment is a full universe being created and destroyed. That ability to transcend time on this plane allows one to be both in God and in the world. It would seem to be at the same moment, although it's actually sequential, but the unit of time is so tiny that for all intents and purposes it's simultaneous. Maharaj-ji seemed totally relaxed, and yet there was always the tension of incredible energies and changes of levels. We saw so little of what he really was.

I think the greatest moment I ever had with Maharaj-ji was at sunset one day at Kainchi, when K.K., his cousin M.L., and I went out there. Ostensibly we were delivering some fragile things from Haldwani for Durga Puja at Kainchi. In the twilight sunset we just sat, and he was like Shiva. He lay down and started to snore, or what sounded like that, and he took me into states of ecstasy and bliss. I started to shake very violently and to go out and out, and he brought me down. He said, "He isn't ready." When we left, I turned back and watched him sitting there on his bench, just that living-*murti* quality of him.

Disappearing Act

In September of 1973 Maharaj-ji left the Kainchi ashram for the last time to go to Agra. As he got to the car leaving the ashram, his blanket slipped to the ground. A devotee picked it up for him, but he said, "Leave it. One shouldn't be attached to anything." It was folded and placed in the car. He traveled by the night train with only Ravi Khanna, a young devotee, attending to him. They picked up his second son, Dharam Narayan, in Agra, and stayed at the house of a devotee. Maharaj-ji complained of chest pain, and they saw a heart specialist, who examined him and said he was fine and just needed rest. They boarded the evening train returning to the hills, but got off soon in Mathura.

At the Mathura station Maharaj-ji went into convulsions, and they took him to the hospital in Vrindavan by taxi. The doctors there didn't recognize him, but diagnosed his condition as a diabetic coma, gave him injections, and put an oxygen mask over his face. After a short time he took off the mask, said it was useless, and said, *"Jaya Jagdish Hare* (Hail to the Lord of the Universe)!" several times. His expression became very peaceful, and he breathed his last. He had died. As he said when he left Kainchi the day before, "Today I am released from Central Jail forever." He was gone from that precious body we had all worshiped and loved, in which we had taken such delight.

Dada comments:

He wanted us to cut our attachment to his body. . . . The container, however precious or attractive, is not the substance we aim to acquire. We are told to set aside the container by taking hold of the contents. When we could not separate them, or failed to let go of the shell, he snatched it away himself and threw it off. The real Babaji is always with us and cannot be lost. Only the imitation one which stood before us creating illusions is gone.[4]

Though at the time it seemed like his *lila* ended, it has continued, in and out of many forms. His grace remains a constant invisible flow, like the solar wind, and the fragrance of his presence at the places of his *lila* can still be felt. Thinking of him is a channel for his love.

chapter nine

one in my heart

T HESE ARE STORIES of beings that open my spiritual heart. These beings are like luminous jewels of higher consciousness, beacons to seekers. They are mirrors for others and are themselves pure statements of the highest human evolution. Let their stories resonate and reverberate within you.

They have become it all, completed the circuit from the personal to the One. To gaze into the eyes of such beings or to hear of their lives resonates within each of us in a place where we *know*. These eyes are windows on eternity, a mirror of the Self that we share. These beings reflect in themselves the vast landscape that stretches between humankind and God, form and the formless. The kingdom of heaven *is* within them—Brahma, the formless source, *does* exist within each individual, and the sleeping giant within us stirs and is awakened by this resonance.

There's no formula for a realized being. The teachings of most of those portrayed here were simply an expression of their being or a response to the particular needs of their followers or questioners at a given moment. Some performed apparent miracles in their time on earth as a way to open people to receive their true gifts, their palpable peace, grace, love, wisdom, and compassion.

The beings here are certainly not the only ones to have become fully realized, just some of those who have crossed our path and inspired us. We offer them to you as examples, flashes in the spectrum of enlightened humanity at the nexus of the human and the Divine. This is a modest sampler of the Indian spiritual landscape.

When you're into bowling, you hang out with people who bowl. When you're into to physics, you hang out with people who enjoy solving physics problems. When you're attracted to your own God-being, you hang out with other beings in the spirit. These beings never forget who or why they are, or who you are. The mere recognition of their existence helps you to remember.

These saints up-level our understanding of the human condition. They change our perspective not only on the goal of human evolution, but also on how to get there, our view of *sadhana,* and why we do spiritual practices. They *are* the culmination of yoga, in union with the Beloved. Their lives are an expression of that divine love. May they help you on your journey too.

I had personal contact or *darshan* with only a few of these beings. Most of these accounts come from recollections of devotees, records of what these people said, and a few photographs. Few of them left much that could be called personal biography. It was of no consequence in their state of consciousness. There was not much left of what we understand as personality or ego. There was nobody home with any interest in self-narration.

The Lotus Rises from the Mud

Saints in India are still a ubiquitous part of the culture. Images of them adorn cabdrivers' dashboards, calendars, and shopkeepers' walls. The great saints or yogis are known as *siddhas,* or perfected ones. These great souls are beyond social norms. Their ways are mysterious and may seem irrational, their manifestations at times bizarre, yet they exude the nectar of divine love, deep peace, and oceanic presence.

Dada Mukerjee, who steeped himself in the love of saints, said:

> *Saints or sages are realized souls, those who have freed themselves from the doctrine of karma, fate or destiny. They are no longer slaves, no more at the mercy of birth and death. They take birth out of their own free and voluntary choice. Why do the saints and sages go on taking human form and undergoing all those hardships and trials that human beings have got to undergo? They take birth in order to help, to assist, to deliver, to elevate the downtrodden, the fallen, the helpless. I believe Babaji [Neem Karoli Baba] had that purpose.*
>
> *The methods of working of the different saints and sages are not the same. Some of them, some of the greatest ones, may be living in the dark caves in the Himalayas or in the forest, but even from there they are blessing humankind—their very presence goes on creating spiritual vibration, purifying the atmosphere. Other saints and sages may be living in human society. Some might be sadhus living in ashrams or mosques. Others might be wandering here and there. Some might be living as householders, never owning saffron clothes or matted locks. Babaji would talk about so many of them, each with different methods of working, but each and every one with the same aim—the showering of grace onto the people.*[1]

Siddhas take birth with no aspiration for themselves, no needs or desires of their own. Maharaj-ji had just one *dhoti* (a long cloth) and a blanket. They live for others. The life they lead is their *lila,* the divine dance or play they perform for seekers and devotees to create faith and love in hearts and minds. Blessings and grace flow naturally from them in an easygoing ordinary way, which is their *Ahaituki Kripa,* grace without reason, without cause, without getting anything in return.

These saints are based in Oneness. Their consciousness emanates from the *ātman,* the universal soul. While we aim toward the One, their consciousness already rests in Oneness while still in the world. They illuminate our path; they're provide a light for us to see where we're going.

That's where *darshan* comes in. It's a transmission from soul to soul. The ancient wisdom is experiential; it comes from voices and stories carrying the vibration of the soul. To tread on the path to the spirit requires wisdom beyond rational knowledge. *Siddhas* have firsthand experience of the universe. Their wisdom comes out of the One. The literal translation of *darshan* is "view," and *darshan* in that broad sense is the view these realized beings have from the One.

Compassion comes out of the One too, because they're com-passionate, *with* somebody else's passion. Compassion is not empathy. Empathy occurs between two separate beings when one person thinks sympathetically of another. Compassion is experiencing another's emotion as one's own with the wisdom of Oneness. Another person's suffering is one's own suffering. These saints are models of compassion. They are expressions of the One.

> A saint's heart melts like butter. No, it melts even more than butter. Butter only melts when you put it near the fire, but a saint's heart melts when anyone else's heart comes near the fire.
>
> —*Maharaj-ji*

You may want to read through this section, then work more intensively with the pictures. Open to a photograph of a realized being and stand the book upright on a table before you. Imagine you have gone from village to village, climbed the mountain, and entered a cave of the heart where just the two of you sit. Open yourself to receive a transmission from a being who has realized the true Self. Perhaps one picture or one story will provide the food your soul needs at this moment or direction for the next turning of your inner path.

Think of this book as part of the continuing dialog with your Self. The forms keep changing. The words keep changing, and nothing is changing. These beings exist in the infinite moment. You can keep turning pages, but on every page it *is*.

Martin Luther King, Jr., said, "I've been to the top of the mountain." These saints live on the top of the mountain too. The view from there is similar to God's view. From partway up the mountain, where we are, our life looks different from the way it looks from the top of the mountain.

Within the One there's no past and future; it's all available. God consciousness has no past, present, or future. The eternal present is another dimension that intersects ours, where all time just *is*. So when a fully conscious being looks at you, that being can know your past, present, and future.

Miracle stories are just stories. They may capture your imagination, but what they really give is a glimpse of that different reality of life in the *ātman*, the unitary consciousness of all things. Realized beings can play with the laws of nature, with the fabric of the phenomenal world to create as God would create. True *siddhas* are supreme and are bound by no rules. For them there are no differences; reality is undifferentiated truth, consciousness, bliss. But the real miracle is that they themselves exist— as human beings who are also absorbed in the One, yet who stay in form to help devotees and seekers on their way. Their *dharma,* their truth, is love, manifest in their constant care for their disciples and devotees. A realized being has the choice to return into the formless, yet chooses to stay in form to serve.

The great beings embrace and advocate the universality of the Spirit, the Oneness of God, in all its many forms. Ramakrishna, for instance, pursued and completed many *sadhanas* to demonstrate that all paths lead to the same place. He was a living statement of someone who adopted and worshiped many forms. Although the forms changed, he remained in his same ecstatic state of union.

Amid such immersion a *siddha* may retain only tenuous body consciousness. Ramakrishna would sometimes call for his pipe to smoke, because he needed to do something to stay in his body. He struggled to stay on the physical plane. Such beings may even lose the ability to experience anything through their senses.

People from different religious persuasions came to Maharaj-ji, and he would show an intimate understanding of the sources of those religions, as if he had been present or involved with the actual moments of their creation. Once we were talking about Christ and tears rolled down his cheeks. He said, "They killed him because he told the truth. You don't understand. Christ never died. He never died. He lives as the *ātman* in everyone. Christ and Hanuman are the same. They both serve God."

As one dives deeper into the realm of the spirit, there is similarity at the root of each religion. From the standpoint of universality, their founders are aspects of the same Being in different guises. It's like a change of sets and costumes for a different cultural context.

Consciousness, self-awareness, is what makes us human. It's the tool with which we work out our worldly problems, our personal, social, and political relationships. If consciousness is the arrow of human evolution, then these beings set the bar for all of our aspirations. Their unitary consciousness and the depth of their selfless love and compassion are the light at the end of humanity's tunnel. Their example of what is humanly possible reverberates through history.

The Buddha had a certain consciousness that today is reflected by the Dalai Lama as an honored public figure. Christ's indelible vision of Oneness is reflected by hundreds of saints and millions of churchgoers over two thousand years. People like Gandhi, Vaclav Havel, Oscar

Arias, and Nelson Mandela may not be fully realized, but they bring elements of that unity consciousness into public life. These people give us confidence and hope for the human race.

If we look at problems of the day through the lens of unity, we realize how much our consciousness is lacking. For instance, if we look at the environment from the soul's point of view, it's quite different than from the ego point of view. Doomsday scenarios of climate change mix up the ego's fear of death with the environmental issues. If we can have the clarity not to be fearful, we can see the problems facing our common home and approach them together. Saints who live in the *ātman* do not have fear; they have love and faith, but no fear.

Nation-states are like big egos, and entities like the U.N. are a cacophony of self-interested clamor. We truly need that unitary view from the top of the mountain to bring us together.

It Takes One to Know One

From our own limited view we often expect realized beings to behave as ego-based personalities like ourselves, though they may not. For our own comfort we try to reduce them to our own level, however inexplicable their behavior may seem. Someone will say, "Well, he's just a man, or she's just a woman," but it's not true in the same way we think of a man or a woman. Souls don't have identity like that; they're not men and women. A soul is not an Indian or a Westerner. Maharaj-ji saw us as souls; he didn't see us as egos.

In terms of who I thought I was, I kept thinking he was missing the mark. When he said, "Love everybody," I thought, "*I* can't love everybody. I'm not anywhere near that." But when you perceive yourself and others as souls, you bring love, truth, and compassion to your interactions with others. Then you are the mirror of their soul. A soul recognizes another soul.

Siddhis

We should understand that what we call a miracle in connection with a saint is simply their reality. To us their reality is a miracle. They see that level of causality where everything just *is*. They're living in a different time zone, the no-time-like-the-present zone, the eternally present moment. On the other hand, things that we take for granted they see as miraculous. A seed grows and blossoms into a flower, the wind blows— they live in that exquisite beauty of the universe moment to moment to moment. And that allows us to see our world anew.

A fully free being has all the power of the universe, the same power that Hanuman has to leap across the ocean, hold the sun, destroy armies of demons, or to do whatever is needed to accomplish God's work. These beings use incredible powers, but mask them by sowing confusion and doubt, as Maharaj-ji often did, or by exercising them behind the scenes, so you don't know their origin.

For those on the path who still think they're doing something, these powers, or *siddhis,* are distractions. People can get lost in using them for misguided purposes or to satisfy their own desires. (If you *think* you're a messiah, don't bet on it.) The universal advice is that if *siddhis* come, don't use them. If there's anyone there to use them, if there's any trace of ego, they will only cause trouble. Maharaj-ji was emphatic that *siddhis* should not be misused; he would sometimes say that other gurus used them like adolescent children or brought the Truth of the *dharma* down to the level of magic.

The eleventh chapter of the *Bhagavad Gita,* when Krishna shows the entire universe inside himself to Arjuna, is a demonstration of what a perfected being can manifest at will. *Siddhis* can be used to break through doubt.

Shirdi Sai Baba provides insight into this use of power to build faith. He had incredible *siddhis.* When he first came to the small village of Shirdi, people would have nothing to do with him, because he was so weird. One day he was begging, and the shopkeepers wouldn't give him any oil for his lamp. They watched as he poured water into the lamp and ignited it. That freaked them, so they started to worship him. His statement, "I give people what they want in the hope that they will begin to want what I want to give them," explains why a being deeply connected to God uses powers only to bring people closer to God.

Maharaj-ji had *siddhis,* but always acted as if he didn't. My yoga teacher, Hari Dass, wrote on his chalkboard that Maharaj-ji had given his *ashirvad* for my book. I said, "What is an *ashirvad*? And what book?" *Be Here Now* came out three years after that, and forty years later it's still selling. People still come up to say how it changed their entire life and opened them to a spiritual path. One blessing, and at least two million lives have been spiritually changed.

That's the power of the game at one level. With Maharaj-ji, only now and then out of the corner of your eye would you see a flicker of power. The bizarre thing is that when you tell it, it always has that element of confusion or doubt, so if you don't have faith you can reject it. You don't really know if he did something or if it just happened, a fantastic coincidence. But the greatest power is always love. Power can be used in the service of love, but not vice versa.

In the Egyptian tradition they say, "To act wisely in different periods of transition, one has to know the rhythms and laws of the cycles of the universe. This forms part of the true temple." That's how these powers manifest. It's not as though a realized being is sitting there thinking, "I'll use this power to blow this person's mind." Rather, such a being becomes so much a statement of the laws of the universe that when the moment is ripe, something happens. Ramakrishna says, "Dislodging a green nut from a shell is almost impossible, but let it dry and the slightest tap (from the guru) will do it."

As you meet these spiritual friends please keep in mind they are not what they appear. Appearances are just appearances. Let your own faith and longing guide you, not just your intellect; use your instincts and your heart as well. Remember that the path of devotion requires surrender, acceptance, just saying, "Yes!" If you are given a mango, just eat it and enjoy the taste. Don't bother about the size of the tree or how many years it took to grow—otherwise you will miss the taste, the essence of mango-ness!

ramana maharshi

Who am I? What happens when I die? We all ask ourselves that at one time or another. These questions lie at the core of our identity.

On July 17, 1896, a sixteen-year-old student named Venkataraman Iyer asked himself those same questions. He lay down on the floor of his uncle's study in the South Indian city of Madurai, held his breath, and pretended he was dying. Any one of us might have done something similar in our inquisitive years. He took it further:

One day I was alone in the first floor of my uncle's house. I was in my usual state of health. But a sudden and unmistakable fear of death seized me. I felt I was going to die. Why I should have so felt cannot now be explained by anything felt in the body. I did not however trouble myself to discover if the fear was well grounded. I did not care to consult doctors or elders or even friends. I felt I had to solve the problem myself then and there.

The shock of the fear of death drove my mind inwards and I said to myself mentally, without actually framing the words: "Now death has come; what does it mean? What is it that is dying? This body dies." And I at once dramatized the occurrence of death. I lay with my limbs stretched out stiff as though rigor mortis had set in and imitated a corpse so as to give greater reality to the enquiry. I held my breath and kept my lips tightly closed, so that no sound could escape, so that neither the word "I" nor any other word could be uttered. "Well, then," I said to myself, "this body is dead. It will be carried stiff to the burning ground and there burnt and reduced to ashes. But with the death of this body am I dead? Is the body I? It is silent and inert, but I feel the full force of my personality and even the voice of the 'I' within me, apart from it. So I am Spirit transcending the body. The body dies, but the Spirit that transcends it cannot be touched by death. That means I am the deathless Spirit." All this was not dull thought; it flashed through me vividly as living truth which I perceived directly, almost without thought-process. "I" was something very real, the only real thing about my present state, and all the conscious activity connected with my body was centered on that "I." From that moment onwards the "I" or Self focused attention on itself by a powerful fascination. Fear of death had vanished once and for all. Absorption in the Self continued unbroken from that time on.[2]

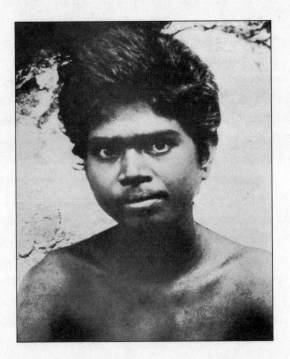

At that moment Venkataraman embarked on an inner journey through the layers of his own identity. He seized on and pursued the "I" thought, his actual sense of self, to its source:

The actual inquiry and discovery of "Who Am I?" was over on the very first day after a short time. . . . "I" was not dead—"I" was on the other hand conscious of being alive, in existence. So the question arose in me, "What was this 'I'?" I felt that it was a force or current working, despite the rigidity or activity of the body, though existing in connection with it. It was that current or force or center that constituted my personality, that kept me acting, moving, etc. The fear of death dropped off. I was absorbed in the contemplation of that current. So further development was issuing from the new life and not from any fear.[3]

Venkataraman had dissolved his ego self in the larger Self. Right in that moment he went through the whole liberation experience, and he was free. Sixteen years old. He didn't do any *sadhana,* he didn't sit in contortions and huff and puff, he didn't worship anything, he didn't make any pilgrimages, he didn't *do* anything. He just lay down on his uncle's floor and got enlightened. So, if you have an uncle . . . !

From that inner question, "Who am I?" which he came to call *atma vichara,* or Self-Enquiry, some force within him took over, and he was pulled into the Self on an inner journey. Later he came to be known as Ramana Maharshi. Ramana was a shortening of his original name, and Maharshi comes from *maha rishi,* great sage.

Of course, if you or I were to lie down on our living room floor and hold our breath contemplating death, the result might be different. You could say Ramana's soul was ripe for opening, or that divine grace entered the equation. Either way, his identification with his embodied self underwent a radical change.

In retrospect his experience of death was on a continuum with his life. Ramana's father had died a few years before, and it had a profound effect on the teenager. After the funeral he contemplated deeply the nature of his own awareness and where his father's identity had gone. That may have been the preliminary plunge into his own "I."

Otherwise Ramana had a normal happy childhood, although there were some hints he was unusual. He had a photographic memory, which helped him in school. He would sleep so soundly that no one could wake him. Once he was left alone in the house and locked the door as instructed. By the time the family returned he had gone to sleep. No amount of noise could rouse him to unlock the door. In play his cousins would beat him while he was sleeping, knowing he wouldn't wake up and would have no memory of it in the morning. At such times he was evidently completely oblivious of his body.

After his experience in the study, young Venkataraman remained inwardly absorbed. Usually a keen student, he became indifferent to his schoolwork, even though his uncle and brother kept after him. Six weeks after his initial experience, he surreptitiously left home and, with only a few rupees for train fare, headed to the sacred mountain Arunachala, a day's journey away.

Years later Ramana indicated that the presence of Arunachala hill had been in his consciousness since infancy. Sometimes called the "red hill," Arunachala is an ancient chthonic power place charged with spiritual energy. Hindus believe it to be an earthly embodiment of Shiva, a giant earth *lingam,* or phallus, an abode of many realized beings over the centuries. At its base in the town of Tiruvannamalai is an ancient Shiva temple. Ramana reached it on September 1, 1896, and went into the inner sanctum of the Shiva temple to have *darshan.* He never left Arunachala. The hill became his guru.

For the next ten years, until 1907, Ramana lived in silence, inhabiting first a subterranean room of the temple, then a succession of caves on the mountain. He was increasingly absorbed in a natural *samadhi* that had nothing to do with any practice. He wasn't trying to achieve anything, there was no goal, his state was unchanging. He was just *being*. There was no inside or outside. He felt no difference between himself and the universe. Later he said that, because he didn't talk, people said he was keeping *mouna*. Because he sat unmoving with eyes closed, they said he was meditating. But from his vantage point no one was doing anything; it was an unbroken flow of consciousness, just *here*.

He was so oblivious of his body that he didn't wash, his hair grew matted, his fingernails curled over, and he only ate when people put food in his hand. Ants nibbled his flesh, snakes and scorpions crawled over him. A few devotees were attracted by the magnetic aura of the young ascetic. One, named Paliniswami, cared for and protected his body for seventeen years while he lived in one cave. Ramana sat inwardly absorbed for such long periods he often needed help to stand up.

Once he answered a question by writing on the wall of the cave in Tamil, and someone realized he was educated. Eventually they got his name and village, and through word of mouth his family was contacted.

In 1907 Ramana broke his silence to instruct an especially ardent devotee, Ganapati Muni, himself a learned yogi who had many devotees. It was an indication of the compassion that colored Ramana's actions the rest of his life. Ganapati Muni was also an accomplished poet and scholar. Later he helped record Ramana's teachings, and it was he who bestowed the title Bhagavan Ramana Maharshi on the renunciate youth he now took for his guru.

The feeling of deep peace and joy in Ramana's presence was magical. Children would hike up to his cave to be with him, and after he began to speak again, he would play games like marbles with them. Pilgrims visiting Arunachala hill would seek him out, yet he remained so deeply absorbed in the Self, he was almost an appendage on the landscape of Arunachala. Word spread that here was a teacher of the

highest realization. He began to attract a ragtag cadre of renunciates who imitated his spartan life and wanted to stay near him.

Ramana's family found him. At first they tried to persuade him to return to civilization, promising he could pursue his contemplative life in relative comfort. They were eventually reconciled to the fact that he wasn't leaving Arunachala. They, too, were impressed by his spiritual state. After visiting and trying to bring him home to no avail, his mother came to live with him in the austere conditions on the hill and spent her last years with him.

In 1922 as she lay dying, he took her through her past and future births so she could get liberated. His mother's *samadhi* was a momentous event, and she was buried as a yogi in a tomb at the bottom of the hill. After her death Ramana moved down there with a few devotees, and they built a new ashram.

From 1922 to 1928, there were only two huts. One was a kitchen and the other general sleeping quarters constructed over the mother's *samadhi*. Ramana and his small circle of disciples continued their bare-bones life of renunciation. Once when robbers came, Ramana told his followers to open the door, so they could take what they wanted. There wasn't much to take.

Eventually an all-purpose hall was built with a bed where Ramana sat, gave *darshan,* and slept. It was open to anyone who came seeking *darshan* as well as squirrels, monkeys, and a cow, named Lakshmi, who got her pick of the food and fruit offerings. Gradually more buildings were constructed at Ramanashram, as it came to be called, to accommodate an increasing number of devotees.

Until the mid-1930s it was a very quiet scene. Ramana's younger brother, Nagasundaram, joined him and became a swami. He did the cooking, though Ramana also worked in the kitchen himself, coming in between 2:30 and 4 A.M. to cut vegetables and prepare breakfast. The saint allowed no special treatment and was himself a demanding, skillful cook.

During the day Ramana saw visitors, a cross section ranging from illiterate families to erudite scholars, comforting and counseling them in the several languages of South India. People asked advice on everything from spiritual matters to lawsuits and personal health. At times he would get a faraway look, and there would be extended periods during which everyone in the room would be lost in deep silence. By evening the silence grew pervasive, talk ceased, and peace bathed the room.

In later years the Maharshi attracted seekers from all over the world who came for his *darshan* at Arunachala. He taught in simple Socratic dialogues, the penetrating clarity of his words interlaced with gentle humor, deep affection, and his love for the Supreme. Although his method of Self-Enquiry is through the intellect, his devotional poems to Arunachala rank among the most beautiful and moving *bhakti* poetry. The record of his conversations in the *Talks* is an extraordinary document of spiritual transmission.

Within Indian philosophy Ramana Maharshi's teaching through Self-Enquiry is part of the path of *jnana*, knowledge, a nondual tradition that views material reality as illusion. His teaching came in answers to questions, responding to the needs of individuals on many levels. Some aspirants were ready for the direct path of Self-Enquiry he had himself undertaken. Others needed more mental preparation or to lighten their karmic burdens and attachments. He spoke to people wherever they were on their path. He said, "Each one thinks of God according to his own degree of advancement," and told people to "Worship God with or without form until you know who you are."[24]

The following exchange occurred with an English woman, M. A. Piggot, who came to the Maharshi after reading a popular account by Paul Brunton:

Q: *What are the hindrances to the realization of the true Self?*

R: *Memory chiefly, habits of thoughts, accumulated tendencies.*

Q: *How does one get rid of these hindrances?*

R: *Seek for the Self through meditation in this manner, trace every thought back to its origin which is only the mind. Never allow thought to run on. If you do, it will be unending. Take it back to its starting place—the mind—again and again, and it and the mind will both die of inaction. The mind exists only by reason of thought. Stop thought and there is no mind. As each doubt and depression arises, ask yourself, "Who is it that doubts? What is it that is depressed?" Go back constantly until there is nothing but the source of all left. And then, live always in the present and only in it. There is no past or future, save in the mind.*⁵

Though his method was *jnana,* he saw much in common with *bhakti,* of which he spoke lovingly: *"Bhakti* and Self-Enquiry are one and the same. The Self of the Advaitas (Nondualists) is the God of the *bhaktas."*[6]

Early in 1949 a small lump appeared on and was removed from Ramana Maharshi's arm. It returned and was diagnosed as malignant cancer. His followers were deeply distressed by the diagnosis. They asked him to cure himself for their sake, and he said, "Why are you so attached to this body? Let it go." When they started to cry and said, "Don't leave us, don't leave us," he said, "Where can I go? I am here." Although his illness must have been painful, he died as he lived, completely present and absorbed in the Self, radiating love and peace. He passed away on April 14, 1950.

Part of the mystery of this extraordinary realized being was his identification with the Arunachala hill. He thought and spoke of it as his guru, his inner Self, as the embodiment of Shiva. Once he set foot there he never left. He described Arunachala as the heart of the earth.

sri ramakrishna paramahamsa

Dwell, O mind, within yourself;
Enter no other's home.
If you but seek there, you will find
All you are searching for.

—Sri Ramakrishna[7]

Sri Ramakrishna was named Gadadhar (a name of Vishnu as "carrier of the mace") at his birth in 1836 to pious Brahmin parents in the village of Kamarpukur in the Hooghly District of Bengal. Both parents had visions of a divine child before his conception. From the first he cast a spell of sweetness over family and neighbors. The boy displayed a precocious

attraction to religion, memorizing ancestors, hymns to gods and goddesses, and tales from the Hindu epics. At the village school, studying
the great spiritual figures moved him so much that he would slip into a
trance and forget about his surroundings. As time passed, these trances
deepened into meditations that began occurring whenever a spiritual
mood overtook him.

At sixteen Gadadhar went to Calcutta to assist his elder brother who
was a priest and had opened a Sanskrit academy. Gadadhar loved dressing and making offerings to the deities and singing devotional songs. He
remained an indifferent student of the finer points of rituals, astrology,
and Hindu law, the erstwhile duties of a professional Brahmin priest.

His brother, Ramkumar, received a post as priest at a new Kali temple
and garden complex being built on twenty acres at Dakshineshwar, about
four miles north of Calcutta along the Ganges. It was the project of a
wealthy but low-caste widow of great piety, Rani Rasmani, who was much
devoted to Kali. She was assisted by her son-in-law, Mathur Mohan.

Mathur was deeply moved by the fervor and devotion of Gadadhar
and entreated him to join in the service of the deities, which included
Shiva and Krishna as well as Kali. Mathur seems to have been the one
who began to call him Ramakrishna. At first uncomfortable with a
temple scene that wasn't strictly Brahmin, Ramakrishna came to love
Dakshineshwar and its proximity to the holy Ganges. It became his real
home.

Though reluctant to become enmeshed in the formalities of Hindu
ritual, Ramakrishna finally heeded Mathur's pleas and became the priest
for the Kali shrine:

Into Her worship he poured his soul. Before him She stood as the
transparent portal to the shrine of Ineffable Reality. The worship in the
temple intensified Sri Ramakrishna's yearning for a living vision of the

*Mother of the Universe. He began to spend in meditation the time not
actually employed in the temple service. . . . Sitting before the image,
he would spend hours singing the devotional songs of great devotees of
the Mother. . . . He felt the pangs of a child separated from its mother.
Sometimes, in agony, he would rub his face against the ground and weep
so bitterly that people, thinking he had lost his earthly mother, would
sympathize with him in his grief.*[8]

Ramakrishna became desperate. He couldn't eat or sleep. Out of that
desperation came his first vision of the Mother. He said:

*I felt as if my heart were being squeezed like a wet towel. I was
overpowered with a great restlessness and a fear that it might not be my
lot to realize Her in this life. I could not bear the separation from Her any
longer. Life seemed to be not worth living. Suddenly my glance fell on the
sword that was kept in the Mother's temple. I determined to put an end
to my life. When I jumped up like a madman and seized it, suddenly the
blessed Mother revealed Herself. The buildings with their different parts,
the temple, and everything else vanished from my sight, leaving no trace
whatsoever, and in their stead I saw a limitless, infinite, effulgent Ocean of
Consciousness. As far as the eye could see, the shining billows were madly
rushing at me from all sides with a terrific noise, to swallow me up! I was
panting for breath. I was caught in the rush and collapsed, unconscious.
What was happening in the outside world I did not know; but within me
there was a steady flow of undiluted bliss, altogether new, and I felt the
presence of the Divine Mother.*[9]

That was only the beginning. His vision of the Mother took over
his normal waking consciousness. Uncertain whether he was living in
a hallucination, he felt burning sensations all over his body and other
strange manifestations. Fragile to begin with, his health went downhill.

His family sent him back to his native village, where his mother nursed him back to more robust health. Hoping to settle him down, they arranged for his betrothal, at age twenty-three, to a five-year-old girl from a neighboring village. As was customary in nineteenth-century Bengal, the actual marriage was postponed until the bride reached puberty.

Health restored, Ramakrishna returned to Dakshineshwar. The intensity of his spiritual journey, far from being dissipated, redoubled. A female tantric known as the Brahmani arrived at the temple (*tantra*, sometimes called the Left-Handed Path, uses external stimuli in its practices). On the instruction of Kali herself, he accepted her as a guru and proceeded under her guidance through an intricate series of practices from classical *tantra*. He mastered these rites in unusual fashion, ascending into *samadhi* and visualizing their outcome. At the culmination of his tantric *sadhana* he experienced the awakening of *kundalini*, the "serpent power" latent in the spine, rising to merge form and formless in the crown *chakra*. Later the Brahmani also guided him through the *bhakti* practices of Vaishnavism, and after mad longing he succeeded in having the *darshan* of Radha, Krishna's consort, and ultimately of Krishna himself. Moved herself by the depth of Ramakrishna's devotion, the Brahmani declared him an incarnation of God and became his devotee too.

Ramakrishna was hardly solemn or formal. He loved to sing, dance, talk, and joke with people. When singing devotional songs, he often became absorbed in an ecstatic *samadhi* state, losing all touch with the outside world. One of his nephews, Ramlal, who came to live at Dakshineshwar and to serve the Master (as everyone referred to him in later years), described Ramakrishna years later in 1931:

He was full of fun. Sometimes he made us laugh so hard that our stomachs would ache. Like a child, he would ask the devotees: "Well, I have actually seen and heard all these funny things. Is it wrong for me to tell you?"

The devotees would say: "No, sir. It is not wrong. Please tell us more. We love it."

When the Master would sing this song, "O Mother, this world is a marketplace of crazy people," he would dance this way. [Ramlal demonstrated how the Master would sing and dance in ecstasy.] When the Master was in a great mood, he would dance back and forth and also in a circle. When he would sing, "O Mother, you live in various moods," he would dance, clapping his hands, moving his waist, and keeping the rhythm with his feet.[10]

Worshiping the Mother, Ramakrishna became childlike, even at times childish. His nephew said: "The Master was usually in one of two moods. On some days he would observe all the traditional methods of purification; on other days he would completely ignore them. He would ask for food as soon as he returned from the pond in the morning and reluctantly wash his hands with water after eating. One day he explained: 'You see, Mother keeps me sometimes in the mood of a child, sometimes in the mood of a madman, and sometimes in the mood of a carefree soul.'"[11]

A mere touch from Ramakrishna could trigger transcendent experiences in others. One of his young devotees, Naren, who later became Swami Vivekananda, describes his second visit to Ramakrishna:

I arrived at Dakshineshwar at last and went straight to the Master's room. I found him deep in his own meditations seated on the smaller bed which stands beside the bigger one. There was no one with him. As soon as he saw me, he called me joyfully to him and made me sit down on one end of the bed. He was in a strange mood. He muttered something to himself which I couldn't understand, looked hard at me, then rose and approached me. I thought we were about to have another crazy scene. Scarcely had that thought passed through my mind when he placed his right foot on my

body. Immediately I had a wonderful experience. My eyes were wide open, and I saw that everything in the room, including the walls themselves, was whirling rapidly around and receding, and at the same time, it seemed to me that my consciousness of self, together with the entire universe, was about to vanish into a vast, all-devouring void. This destruction of my consciousness of self seemed to me to be the same thing as death. I felt that death was right before me, very close. Unable to control myself I cried out loudly, "Ah, what are you doing to me? Don't you know I have my parents at home?" When the Master heard this he gave a loud laugh. Then, touching my chest with his hand, he said, "All right—let it stop now. It needn't be done all at once. It will happen in its own good time." To my amazement, this extraordinary vision of mine vanished as suddenly as it had come.[12]

Ramakrishna was loving but relentless in pushing his young disciples into the arms of the Divine, by whatever route was right for each one:

Knowing Naren's inherent nature, Sri Ramakrishna instructed him in monistic Vedanta, which teaches that the individual soul and Brahman are identical. One day Naren was telling Hazra about Vedantic nondualism and his unwillingness to accept it. "Can it be," he said, "that the water pot is God, that the drinking vessel is God, that everything we see and all of us are God?" Naren laughed scornfully at the idea and Hazra joined in. While they were laughing, Sri Ramakrishna came up to them. "What are you two talking about?" he asked Naren affectionately; then without waiting for an answer he touched Naren and went into samadhi. Naren related the effect of the touch:

"At the marvelous touch of the Master my mind underwent a complete revolution. I was aghast to realize there was really nothing in the entire universe but God. I remained silent, wondering how long this state of mind would continue. It didn't pass off all day. I got back home and I felt just the same there; everything I saw was God. I sat down to eat and I saw that everything—the plate, the food, my mother that was serving it, and I myself—everything was God and nothing else but God. I swallowed a couple of mouthfuls and then sat still without speaking. My mother asked me lovingly: 'Why are you so quiet? Why don't you eat?' That brought me back to everyday consciousness, and I began eating again. But from then on, I kept having the same experience no matter what I was doing— eating, drinking, sitting, lying down, going to college, strolling along the street. It was a kind of intoxication; I can't describe it. If I was crossing a street and saw a carriage coming toward me I didn't have the urge, as I would ordinarily, to get out of its way for fear of being run over. For I said to myself: 'I am that carriage. There's no difference between it and me.' During that time I had no sensation in my hands or feet. When I ate food I

*felt no satisfaction from it; it was as if someone else was eating. Sometimes
I would lie down in the middle of a meal, then get up again after a few
minutes and go on eating. Thus it would happen that on these days I
would eat far more than usual, but this never upset me. My mother became
alarmed. She thought I was suffering from some terrible disease. 'He won't
live long,' she'd say."*[13]

In 1864 a stern renunciate named Totapuri, who had practiced austerities for forty years on the banks of the Narmada River to free himself
from attachment, stopped over at Dakshineshwar on his way back from
a pilgrimage to the mouth of the Ganges. He became Sri Ramakrishna's second guru in the flesh. Under his instruction Ramakrishna went
beyond the form of the Mother to the formless Brahman. Because he was
a child of the Mother, it was difficult for him to look beyond her. At one
point when Ramakrishna could concentrate no longer on the formless,
Totapuri poked a piece of glass between his eyebrows and said, "Meditate on this!" Finally, Ramakrishna entered into *nirvikalpa samadhi* (*samadhi* without form) for three days.

Early in 1868 Ramakrishna went on pilgrimage with his patron of
Dakshineshwar, Mathur Babu, and a large party to the sacred sites of
North India at Benares, Allahabad, and Brindaban. At each holy place
Ramakrishna had *darshan* visions of the deity. He saw things as they
were on the spiritual plane, like souls being liberated in the cremation
pyres in Benares, and met other great souls of the time, such as Trailanga
Swami. The journey brought out other sides of Ramakrishna too: "At
Vaidyanath in Behar, when the Master saw the inhabitants of a village
reduced by poverty and starvation to mere skeletons, he requested his
rich patron to feed the people and give each a piece of cloth. Mathur de-
murred at the added expense. The Master declared bitterly that he would
not go on to Benares, but would live with the poor and share their miser-

ies. He actually left Mathur and sat down with the villagers. Whereupon Mathur had to yield."[14]

Nine years after the betrothal, Sarada Devi, Ramakrishna's child bride, met him for the first time. She was fourteen and he thirty-two. He was visiting his family in Kamarpukur. In 1872, when she was eighteen, she and her father walked the eighty miles from their village to Dakshineshwar. She'd been hearing rumors about her husband's insanity and resolved to render "in whatever measure she could, a wife's devoted service."[15] She regarded this as her sacred duty. Ramakrishna in turn began instructing her in everything from housekeeping to meditation.

After a few months Ramakrishna performed a special *puja* to Kali, installing Sarada Devi as the living goddess. At the height of the ritual both went into a deep *samadhi* and their souls merged together. "After several hours Sri Ramakrishna came down again to the relative plane, sang a hymn to the Great Goddess, and surrendered at her feet, himself, his rosary, and the fruit of his lifelong *sadhana*."[16] In tantric terms his wife literally became the Divine Goddess. He was married to Kali on every level. Though never physical, the marriage to Sarada Devi became an extraordinary spiritual union.

Ramakrishna's single-minded dedication to his spiritual pursuit often carried him beyond the borders of conventional behavior. To get *darshan* of Krishna he adopted the persona of Radha and dressed in a woman's clothes and jewelry. He was frequently and unpredictably lost in ecstatic states. His emotion for God was intense. He was way outside the "normal" spectrum. After his years of *sadhana* and *samadhi* the remains of his ego were like a tattered prayer flag in the wind of the Divine.

The events of Sri Ramakrishna's life occurred more than a century ago, and we depend greatly on records and recollections kept by those who knew him. Fortunately some of his devotees and disciples were great scribes. Two direct sources are *The Gospel of Sri Ramakrishna,* which records conversations of Ramakrishna's later years through the eyes of a close devotee, "M" (Mahendra Nath Gupta), and *Ramakrishna as We Saw Him,* edited by Swami Chetanananda, with interviews and recollections from Ramakrishna's close disciples and devotees. The necessarily brief narrative here is largely drawn from them.

In the nineteenth century Calcutta was, along with Bombay, a cosmopolitan center of India. The British had recently consolidated their rule of the colony, and Western culture was on the ascendant. The earlier fervor of devotional Hinduism was being eclipsed by Western rationality from the Christian missionary schools. Ramakrishna, who was by no means politically or socially engaged, nevertheless influenced some key figures among Calcutta's intellectual circles, like Keshab Chandra Sen, leader of the Brahmo Samaj, a group actively synthesizing Hindu and Western values. The Master went to one of Keshab's gatherings and said, "People tell me you have seen God; so I have come to hear from you about God."

A magnificent conversation followed. The Master sang a thrilling song
about Kali and forthwith went into Samadhi. When Hriday uttered the
sacred "Om" in his ears, he gradually came back to consciousness of the
world, his face still radiating a divine brilliance. Keshab and his followers
were amazed.[17]

Amid such cultural upheaval, Ramakrishna attracted a small circle
of disciples he personally instructed. They became ambassadors of his
universal but still deeply devotional brand of Hinduism. There was also
a wider circle of devotees from all walks of life as well as a number of
female renunciates. After his passing, his wife, Sarada Devi, became the
revered mother for these devotees.

His inspiration kept spreading after his death. His chief disciple, Swami
Vivekananda (whose name means "bliss of discriminating knowledge"),
attended a Parliament of World Religions in Chicago in 1893. His break-
through speech caused a sensation. The charismatic young swami must
have been a dramatic infusion to the group of ministers, theologians,
and their wives. He went on to tour America and Europe several times.

It was not just inspiration, but pure delight in his company that attracted people to Ramakrishna. Even the disciplines of renunciation and
meditation were lighthearted:

The devotees would be so inebriated with pure joy in his company that they
would have no time to ask themselves whether he was an Incarnation, a
perfect soul, or a yogi. His very presence was a great teaching; words were
superfluous. In later years his disciples remarked that while they were with
him they would regard him as a comrade, but afterwards would tremble
to think of their frivolities in the presence of such a great person. . . .
Through all this fun and frolic, this merriment and frivolity, he always
kept before them the shining ideal of God-Consciousness and the path of
renunciation.[18]

The Ramakrishna Mission and Vedanta Society started by Vivekananda and the other swamis continues today in satellites all over India and around the world. But it all goes back to the sweet exalted soul living at a Kali temple outside turn-of-the-century Calcutta.

In 1885 Ramakrishna had a persistent sore throat. The devotees thought it had been brought on by too much talk or constriction in *samadhi*. The inflammation worsened and was diagnosed as cancer. The Master moved from the Dakshineshwar temple to a house and garden at Cossipore, where he led a more secluded life, though he was still giving intensive instruction to his young disciples and seeing many devotees. He persevered another year:

Sunday, August 15, 1886. The Master's pulse became irregular. The devotees stood by the bedside. Toward dusk Sri Ramakrishna had difficulty in breathing. A short time afterwards he complained of hunger. A little liquid food was put into his mouth; some of it he swallowed, and the rest ran over his chin. Two attendants began to fan him. All at once he went into samadhi *of a rather unusual type. The body became stiff. Sashi burst into tears. But after midnight the Master revived. He was now very hungry and helped himself to a bowl of porridge. He said he was strong again. He sat up against five or six pillows, which were supported by the body of Sashi, who was fanning him. Narendra took his feet on his lap and began to rub them. Again and again the Master repeated to him, "Take care of these boys." Then he asked to lie down. Three times in ringing tones he cried the name of Kali, his life's Beloved, and lay back. His eyes became fixed on the tip of his nose. His face was lighted with a smile. The final ecstasy began. It was* mahasamadhi, *total absorption, from which his mind never returned. Narendra, unable to bear it, ran downstairs.*[19]

anandamayi ma

The name Anandamayi Ma means "bliss-permeated mother." Nirmala Sundari Devi was born on April 30, 1896, in the village of Kheora in Tripura District of East Bengal, now Bangladesh. Instinctively attracted to ceremonies and chanting at the village temple, the child Nirmala saw figures coming out of the temple statues. At times she was found distracted, looking into space unaware of the world. Otherwise she was a sweet and helpful child, much loved by her family and neighbors.

In 1971 we were with Maharaj-ji at his ashram in Vrindavan, a pilgrimage place with many Krishna temples that's been a devotional center since the fourteenth century. Vrindavan has had a deep playful mood of love, ever since Krishna made love to ten thousand cowherd girls there. Anandamayi Ma was in residence at her ashram just a few blocks away. Maharaj-ji sent us to see her.

We didn't know what to expect. Anandamayi Ma's ashram is a more traditional Hindu scene than Maharaj-ji's. We all dressed up in clean white clothes for the occasion. There were a bunch of us, but because so many devotees were already there, we were lost in the crowd.

Anandamayi Ma was an ethereal, slight figure swathed in white, greeting devotees from a low platform. The atmosphere was oceanic, vast, and peaceful. It felt deeply familiar, like sitting at the kitchen table with your mother, but this was everyone's Mother. Any separation between Ma and ourselves seemed to dissolve in the quiet flow. We went back every day she was there.

During those few visits Anandamayi Ma touched a very deep, pure, simple, and loving space within me, a feeling of pure spirit. She's a real One, a rare One, an ancient One, the only One. In her presence you couldn't help but absorb something of the tremendous grace Indians have long attributed to such beings.

At that time she was in her mid-seventies and seemed frail, birdlike, like a leaf in the wind of time. Outwardly she was an aging lady surrounded by rather orthodox Hindus who were very protective of her and didn't like impure foreigners touching her feet or handing her offerings. Our pure whites didn't cut it with them.

Inwardly there was a deep current of *shakti,* or spiritual energy, flowing from her. She didn't care about social distinctions or being protected—that was from her devotees. As I sat before her, I began to realize why her followers were so intent on caring for her. She had so little ego, they were afraid she wouldn't take care of herself.

She walked and talked, laughed and sang, though once she kept silent for six months. She ate, though for a long time she ate only nine grains of

rice a day. Behind her eyes there was a detachment, like someone looking at you from a great distance or through a telescope. It was kind of a
puppet quality, as if there was nobody home. But simultaneously with
the emptiness you felt her completely engaged and present, full of concern and affection for the devotees and everyone around. Her moods
changed like weather.

My feelings in her presence were profound, subtle, and hard to put into
words. There was a tangible peace, a sense of completion and perfection, a
deep relief from the thoughts and daily concerns that constantly press on
the mind. Her every movement was *mudra,* a physical expression of the
totality of being in that instant. She opened the way for you to feel God.

Paramahansa Yogananda met Anandamayi Ma in Calcutta about 1946
and later invited her to his ashram in Ranchi. He recorded their encounter in his book *Autobiography of a Yogi,* including this dialog:

[YOGANANDA:] *"Please tell me something of your life."*

[ANANDAMAYI MA:] *"Father, there is little to tell."* She spread her graceful
hands in a deprecatory gesture. *"My consciousness has never associated
itself with this temporary body. Before I came on this earth, Father, "I
was the same." As a little girl, "I was the same." I grew into womanhood;
still "I was the same." When the family in which I had been born made
arrangements to have this body married, "I was the same." And Father,
in front of you now, "I am the same." Ever afterward, though the dance of
creation change around me in the hall of eternity, "I shall be the same."* [20]

My introduction to Anandamayi Ma came through Maharaj-ji. I knew
him as my guru, but I hadn't really reflected much on that caring maternal quality that is another aspect of the guru and such an integral
aspect of God in India. When Maharaj-ji said to see all women as the
Mother, it set off a sea change in my view of reality. Our Western Judeo-

Christian culture focuses so strongly on the Father, we tend to overlook the Mother. Anandamayi Ma was not a philosophical treatise. She was a living breathing woman for whom descriptions like "enlightened" or "realized" fall so short as to diminish her.

Anandamayi Ma's feminine qualities weren't just those of an individual woman. She was truly an incarnation of the divine Feminine, the Goddess. She embodied the qualities of the Mother that Maharaj-ji spoke of with such affection. She showed many different aspects of the Mother that Hindus revere.

I never actually saw Maharaj-ji and Anandamayi Ma together in the flesh, although once I had a vivid dream of both of them. In the dream they were like joyous, playful children. At the end they walked down a path holding hands like kids. I felt intense joy when I awoke.

I heard that one morning Maharaj-ji started berating the women at his ashram for not taking care of him: "You can't feed me. You people can't feed me or take care of me. I'm going to Ma. She'll feed me." He set off for Anandamayi's ashram and he kept saying, "She'll feed me. I'm going to see Ma. She'll feed me."

Maharaj-ji burst into the room at Anandamayi's, interrupting a big *darshan* sitting. He was like a child of five, with his blanket flying in all directions. He shouted at Anandamayi sitting there, "Ma! Feed me, feed me, Ma!" She just cracked up. Then they brought a huge meal. He tasted it, and then they passed it out as *prasad* to all the devotees. He was calling her Ma and she was calling him Father—Ma and Pa.

As with Ramakrishna, when Anandamayi was young the custom in those times of uncertain health and short lives was child marriage. Nirmala's was arranged while she was quite young. She lived with her brother-in-law's family, while her husband traveled to Dacca and elsewhere to find work. Eventually he found a position as manager of a private park in Dacca called the Shahbagh Garden. Nirmala joined him there, and they set up a household.

She maintained her duties as a Bengali housewife, cooking and cleaning, even though she would sometimes go into *samadhi* states, performing complex yoga *asanas* and *mudras* (gestures). At times she would roll on the floor in ecstasy, and the food would burn. Her awakening skirted insanity when she lost contact with the physical plane.

Her husband fortunately realized her extraordinary qualities. Ultimately he became her disciple. She was breathtakingly beautiful in those younger years, bathed in an unearthly radiance. She never became involved in the more down-to-earth aspects of marriage. Her God intoxication must have simply outshone all else. She later said her husband

never even had a sexual thought. Anyway, if he had even an unconscious urge, she went into *samadhi*.

Mother was staying on the first floor of the premises attached to Govindaji's temple. When the writer entered the room with two ladies with him, it was about 11 P.M. There was one electric light on. On entering

the room, they found Mother seated smiling, beaming with joy. Her whole
Body shone like a ball of dazzling light, making the electric bulb look
almost pale and red. Such wonderful radiance from a human figure was
beyond all our conception. Her body shone with such an intensely soothing
light that the whole room appeared to be filled with some divine, ethereal
presence.[21]

In Dacca Ma appeared to undergo intense bouts of spiritual practice. She later said she did not initiate these practices. Rather, they seemed to work through her. She said she was following her *kheyal,* which in the context meant a spiritual intuition or inner impulse. Affected by her obvious holiness, her transcendental states, and her luminous presence, devotees gathered around her. At the house there were frequent get-togethers for *kirtan.* Ma cooked and everyone shared *prasad.*

The sound of the divine Name affected her deeply. She would drop whatever work she was engaged in and fall to the ground in ecstasy. Sometimes she would lie motionless, but other times she would balance on her toes, hands raised and eyes fixed without a flicker. Sometimes she would bend into yoga *asanas* or *mudras,* either standing absolutely still or swaying rhythmically with her heaving breath.

Her dance might be gracefully undulating like a wave or whirling with incredible swiftness. Then her movement was like lightning, almost impossible to follow with the eye. Sometimes she would roll in ecstasy to and fro on the ground like a dry leaf driven before a storm. She was like a dynamo at such moments. The modest housewife who kept her face covered in front of strangers ran and danced oblivious to the world.

Danny Goleman (Jagannath Das) and I had gone for *darshan* at Anandamayi Ma's small ashram near Kankhal at Haridwar. We found Ma sitting on the steps of the little temple talking to the vice president of India. There were a couple of hundred other people. Finally the vice president left, and Anandamayi Ma went into one of the rooms.

Danny and I were talking and stayed behind until we were the last ones left in the *darshan* area. It was near dusk, food was cooking, and there was the sound of a conch and bells from the evening *puja*. Occasionally we'd see Anandamayi Ma, dressed in white, walking from one building to another, almost as if she were floating. Just seeing her filled us with waves of bliss.

Finally they told us to leave, because the temple was closing. We got up to go, and just then Anandamayi came out a side door and walked across the *darshan* area, right in our path. She looked as though she was sleepwalking. She hesitated just in front of us, looking past us, then stopped and allowed us to touch her feet. It was like being in the quiet of a deep forest and having a bird land on your shoulder or a deer come up and nuzzle you—a precious instant when you connect with something so pure, so untouched by the world, so elemental and free. It was a mysterious and intense moment. She continued on. We left the temple. There was no recognition; she didn't look at us. It was just *darshan*. We had touched something deep in ourselves. We had touched love itself.

> I do not wait for your spiritual fitness. Like the flowing Ganges I go on bestowing my compassion on all. This is my nature. This is my being.
>
> —*Unknown source*

From about 1927 Anandamayi, her husband, and a devotee called Bhaiji traveled about India leading a peripatetic life that she continued for the next fifty-five years. People all over India came in contact with her and came to depend on her for spiritual guidance. As she played out the *lila* of child, wife, and spiritual guide, she manifested from moment to moment the different aspects of the Mother: the peaceful serenity of Uma, goddess of dawn; the loving delight of Radha, Krishna's playful consort; Kali's protective fierceness; Sita's dharmic perfection; and the mystical energy of Shakti, the manifest cosmos.

She had no real personal identity. Sometimes she'd take on the qualities of some other pure saint who had lived in the locale where she was.

On her serene ocean, the restless mind relaxes, thoughts drift of their own accord to the stillness within.

—Unknown source

She would allow that aspect to come through her and would begin to walk and talk like that saint. Her powers of endurance and patience were extraordinary. She didn't get tired. As she said to Yogananda "I am the same," and that applied all the time and wherever she was.

Devotees were constantly trying to figure out and describe this amazing being in their midst. As she intimated on many occasions, she manifested to devotees according to their individual spiritual needs. She had no other agenda of her own, so it was really no wonder that everyone saw her differently. With a *pandit* she might discuss fine points of the Upanishads, with a poor farmer the impending marriage of a daughter, with a *sadhu* the course of his practice. She guided each person at his or her own level.

Ma wouldn't allow them to keep food overnight in the ashram. She made them cook and distribute everything and then beg or buy fresh food the next day. Once, one of her devotees kept an extra bag of flour in case Ma might want food during the night. About 9 P.M. she came out and started asking for *puris,* flatbreads cooked in *ghee,* or melted butter, which are delicious, but quite heavy and buttery. You might eat two at a meal. Ma started eating. She ate and ate and kept asking for more until she had eaten sixty-four puris. She said, "Don't you realize if I ate my fill, I'd eat the entire universe?"

shirdi sai baba

We know little of Sai Baba's origins. His name gives no hint. Sai Baba isn't even really a name. *Sai* is a Persian word for "saint," and *Baba* is Hindi for "father" or "grandfather," a term often applied to holy men. He looked like a beggar, but his ragged appearance and unpredictable behavior camouflaged a realized being of the highest order.

His early life remains a cloud of uncertainty. If the information is correct, he may have left home at the age of eight and undergone twelve years of austerities under the tutelage of a Sufi *fakir*, a Muslim mystic. Since he shifted easily between the Qur'an and Hindu rites and had devotees of every religious persuasion, that seems to fit.

He first came to Shirdi, a remote village in Maharashtra, about 1854, then left again. Sometime between 1868 and 1872 he returned and took up residence. He stayed continuously for half a century. Shirdi was six hours from the nearest railroad station. The only way to get there was by horse cart. It took considerable effort, especially in those days. There were no places to stay, no lights, and not even rudimentary comforts. After Sai Baba's *mahasamadhi* (his death) on October 15, 1918, Shirdi faded into obscurity until the 1960s and 1970s, when it again began to attract pilgrims.

When he first arrived, the villagers thought he was mad. He didn't fit any concept of a holy man. Sometimes he acted like a Hindu, but he also called on Allah. Only when they became aware of his extraordinary powers as a healer and his fathomless compassion for others did the villagers begin to honor him as a saint.

Gradually they realized they had among them, as another saint described him, a "jewel in a dung heap." "Nobody knew why he chose Shirdi as his abode. . . . If there was a personal reason it was as strange as the whole circumstances of his life: many years later, when he was already famous, he told a devotee to dig at the foot of the *neem*-tree where he used to sit on his first arrival there; a tomb was unearthed and he declared that it was that of his guru, not in this life but in a previous incarnation."[22]

Sai Baba would go out and beg for his food each morning. Though they thought he was a crazy *fakir*, some villagers took to feeding him, and he would stand in front of the same half dozen houses, later mixing their offerings together in a clay jar. He left the jar exposed, so animals could partake before he ate himself. He kept up this routine for the six decades he resided in Shirdi, right up until two days before his death.

There was a small Hanuman temple and a dilapidated mud-walled mosque (*masjid*) in the village. At first the temple priest wouldn't let him in, because he thought he was a Muslim. So the *baba* took up residence in the mosque. Later the same priest became greatly devoted to Sai Baba and served him the rest of his life. In 1885 when Sai Baba went into a *samadhi* trance for three days, he asked this priest to watch over his body. Some of the villagers thought he was dead and wanted to burn the body, but the priest zealously defended it.

Sai Baba slept on a narrow board some ten inches wide that was suspended from the ceiling of the mosque by flimsy rags. Lamps burned all night at either end. It was a mystery how he got on or off the board or, for that matter, kept from falling off.

Besides food, he needed only a little oil for the lamps, which he also used to beg from the local shopkeepers. When to tease him they refused to give him the oil, he returned unperturbed to the mosque. The villagers trailed him to see what would happen. He picked up a water pot and casually filled the lamps with water. They burned as brightly as if they'd been filled with oil. The awed villagers fell at his feet and pleaded forgiveness.

Over the decades more devotees made the pilgrimage to Shirdi, and he became the focus of village life. Many people came to regard him as their guru. He often spoke cryptically or in parables and circumlocutions. At other times he could be cosmically direct, such as once when he said to the devotees after worship:

Be wherever you like, do whatever you choose, remember this well that all that you do is known to me. I am the Inner Ruler of all and seated in their hearts. I envelop all the creatures, the moveable and immoveable world. I am the Controller—the wire-puller of the show of this Universe. I am the mother-origin of all beings—the Harmony of the three Gunas (qualities), the propeller of all senses, the Creator, Preserver and Destroyer. Nothing will harm him who turns his attention toward Me, but Maya will lash or whip him who forgets Me. All the insects, ants, the visible, moveable and immoveable world, is my Body or Form.[23]

This is strikingly similar to what Krishna says in the seventh chapter of the *Bhagavad Gita* and also in the ninth chapter, where he talks to Arjuna about devotion.

For Hindus a sacred bath at Prayag (modern Allahabad), where the Ganga (Ganges) and Yamuna Rivers converge, is very meritorious. Thousands of Hindu pilgrims journey each year at astrologically appointed times to perform this ritual.

Once Das Ganu thought that he should go to Prayag for a bath and came to Baba to get His permission. Baba replied to him—"It is not necessary to go so far. Prayag is here, believe me." When Das Ganu placed his head on Baba's feet, streams of Ganga and Yamuna water flowed out from Baba's toes. Das Ganu was overwhelmed with feelings of love and adoration and was full of tears.[24]

Sometimes Shirdi Sai Baba's temper flared. His moods could be mercurial, and at times his bizarre habits scared his devotees. People saw him vomit up his intestines, wash them out, and swallow them again, an extreme variation of a yoga *kriya,* or purification. On another occasion a devotee looked in and saw Sai Baba's limbs detached in different places around his room. He was about to report the murder to the police, but feared being implicated or becoming a suspect in the crime. The next day he saw Shirdi Sai Baba acting normally as if nothing had occurred.

Devotees petitioned constantly for his aid with health and other problems. When he first established himself at Shirdi, he was known as the local *hakim,* or doctor; he examined patients and gave out medicine. At first he gave some local remedies, but later he gave only *udhi,* or ash, from his fire, or *dhuni.* Treatment was invariably successful. People were saved from leprosy, bubonic plague, and blindness, not to mention more mundane intestinal and skin ailments. The lame walked, and infertile couples bore progeny. But most remarkable were the changes of heart as devotees left worldly ways to turn toward the spiritual.

Once while sitting with the devotees, Sai Baba suddenly plunged his arm into a blazing fire. Hastily they pulled him back, but his arm was badly burned. He explained he had saved the life of an infant that had fallen from the sling on its mother's back into a forge. Within days this was corroborated from a village some distance away. A doctor was brought from Bombay, but Sai Baba refused the medical attention and would allow only an herbal concoction and rags to be put on the burned arm. In a few days it was back to normal.

Other reports describe him further:

Sometimes in performing a miracle, he would say "I will do this." More often, however, his reply would be "Allah achcha karega" ("God will put it right") or "Allah Malik hai" ("God is the ruler"). It was a peculiar custom of his to refer to God as "the Fakir," and when refusing a request he would often say, "The Fakir will not let me do that" or "I can only do what the Fakir orders me to."

Sometimes he would explain that to prolong the life of a sick person would only cause prolonged suffering. Sometimes he would promise to bring him back in a new birth. Sometimes when asked to bless with issue, he would say that there was no child in that person's destiny (not that this always deterred him, for at least on one occasion he granted a child out of his own destiny, declaring that there was none in that of the petitioner). Sometimes he would give no explanation at all, but simply refuse, saying "Allah Malik hai" or "The Fakir [God] will not let me."

A woman's young son was bitten by a cobra and she cried out and begged Sai Baba for udhi, but he did not give it, and the child died.

H. S. Dixit, one of the oldest of the devotees, implored him, "Baba, her crying is heart-rending! For my sake revive her son."

Here again, as in the incident of curing a child's eyes with onion, it is striking to see that there was never the slightest doubt that he could do this.

Sai Baba replied, "Do not get entangled in this. What has happened is for the best. He has already entered another body in which he can do especially good work which he could not do in this one. If I draw him

back into this body, then the new one he has entered will have to die
for this to live. I might do it for your sake, but have you considered the
consequences? Have you any idea of the responsibility and are you
prepared to assume it?"[25]

Like a mother hen, Sai Baba gathered his disciples from near and far.
He took on both their spiritual and material care, sometimes alluding to
relationships over many lifetimes. Devotees thrived in his aura of love.
Under his wing they grew in devotion and surrendered to him as their
guru. In return he guided and took over responsibility for their spiritual
development.

To those who offer their love and put their faith in him, Sai Baba re-
turns blessings in great measure. He remains one of the best-loved saints
of India. You see his image on dashboards and storekeepers' altars all
across India because of his legendary generosity in using his powers to
aid his devotees. Many have faith that he is still present and exerting his
grace upon them.

jnaneshwar

Jnaneshwar (also called Jnanadeva) was a medieval saint of Maharashtra.
Because he lived so long ago, it's hard to distinguish between his actual
life and the stuff of legend. His name, Jnaneshwar, means "all-pervading
wisdom of God." He wrote a monumental commentary on the *Bhagavad
Gita* in popular Marathi, which is still so widely read it is simply called
the *Jnaneshwari*.

Jnaneshwar was born in 1271. India was being assaulted by Muslim
invaders, and there was political and spiritual upheaval everywhere.
In Europe Jnaneshwar would have been a contemporary of Meister
Eckhart, in Persia of Rumi, or farther west the Spanish Arab mystic

poet Mohi-uddin Ibn al-'Arabi. Apart from his deep spiritual attainment Jnaneshwar brought the great wisdom teaching of the *Bhagavad Gita* out of the Sanskrit provenance of Brahmin priests into a vernacular accessible to ordinary people.

He was a prodigy. He probably composed the *Jnaneshwari* in 1290, when he was nineteen. Sai Baba often recommended it to devotees. At twenty-five Jnaneshwar went into a deep meditation and never emerged. Though he died in his youth, he accomplished more than most saints do in a long life.

His body did not decay. In India this way of leaving the body is known as living, or *jivit, samadhi.* Eventually they built a *mahasamadhi* tomb around him and a temple over that. The inner sanctum of the temple is right over the tomb. It's like entering a powerful electric field. When you touch your head to the Shiva *lingam,* or phallus, that is the altar stone, it feels as if it's vibrating with *shakti,* energy.

Jnaneshwar's whole family were yogis. His father, Vitthalpant, was a householder saint; his older brother, Nivrittinatha (1273–97), was his guru; his sister, Muktabai (b. 1272), was a great mystic poet; and his younger brother, Sopana (b. 1273), was also an adept. All are revered as saints. You would think such a family would be honored by a culture so steeped in religious fervor. Instead, their life of the spirit collided with Brahmin orthodoxy and the caste system, and the family story is marked by tragedy.

Vitthalpant, a high-caste Brahmin, was the son of a prominent village headman. He married Rakhumabai, who was the daughter of a neighboring village headman and by all accounts loved him deeply. Vitthal was a deeply spiritual man who never felt cut out for family life. Much to Rakhu's dismay, before their home life was complete with children, Vitthal left on a pilgrimage. In Benares he was initiated by a great guru, Ramananda. Not mentioning his householder status, he took a vow of *brahmacharya,* celibacy, preliminary to *sannyas,* or renunciation.

As fate would have it, the guru Ramananda was invited to attend a ceremony at Nasik, a holy center not far from where Rakhu's family lived in Alandi, a holy town on the river Indrayani. En route he stopped overnight and, as befit a guru, was honored and fed by the village headman, Rakhu's father. Observing the telltale signs of Rakhumabai's married status at dinner, Ramananda blessed her to have children. When she burst into tears at this suggestion, having effectively been rendered a childless widow at fourteen, an interchange ensued in which he learned his new disciple was her errant husband. Promising to make good on his blessing, he ordered Vitthal to return and resume his family obligations. Jnaneshwar and his siblings were born some years afterward.

But all was not well. The local Brahmins, ruled by rigid caste conventions, decreed that Vitthal's vow had severed him from the Brahmin caste. Despite his guru's order, they wouldn't allow him and his young family back into the Brahmin fold. He and his family were shunned, literally outcasts, untouchables. Vitthal had no livelihood or prospects. His children were forbidden the sacred-thread ceremony bringing them into Brahmin society.

To our modern mind this sounds at most an inconvenience, but in that stratified hierarchic culture they were terribly stigmatized. No one would eat with them or even share water; no other kids could play with them. They had to live on the outskirts of the village. They had been thrust into outer darkness. Imagine the shame and desperation of a man aspiring to godliness, growing up as a privileged member of the elite priestly class, now unable to provide for his family and at odds with the elders of his own community.

Vitthal did his best. He took his oldest son, Nivritti, to another town where he had some remaining Brahmin friends for his thread ceremony. Returning on a jungle road, they encountered a tiger. His father told him to run. Nivritti found refuge in a cave where he met a yogi. Gahininath became his guru, training him in yoga, and Nivritti in turn instructed Jnaneshwar, who thereafter honored Nivritti as his guru.

Back home the family was still branded with untouchability. Hoping to expiate his sin and at least remove the stain from his children, Vitthal drowned himself in the holy river. His disconsolate widow died soon after. The children were orphaned and, though aided by grandparents, they were mostly left to their own resources. The holier-than-thou Brahmins were unrelenting.

Nivritti, now head of the family, took his siblings to Paithan, another Brahmin holy place, to obtain a "letter of purification" allowing the family to be reabsorbed into society. The priests were disinclined to provide relief until they came to realize these were not ordinary children. Jnaneshwar said, "When the power of God is here, even dumb animals can recite the Vedas." He laid hands on a passing water buffalo, which began to recite the Vedas. The priests reevaluated their judgment.

A period followed during which Jnaneshwar must have attained full realization and composed the *Jnaneshwari* commentary on the *Gita*. The *Jnaneshwari*, though written by a nineteen-year-old, is clearly the work of a highly evolved soul. The siblings apparently lived for some time with a Swami Satchidananda, an old friend of their father's, at his ashram in Nevasa near Nasik. There is a story that Jnaneshwar brought him back to life from a fatal illness.

Another story about Jnaneshwar and his siblings concerns a great yogi who came to see them at Alandi:

Changadeva was a great Siddha who lived for more than 1400 years, on the banks of the Tapi river. His preceptor was Vateshwar and from him he acquired a great many mystic powers. . . . Having heard about Jnanadeva's fame and glory as an incarnation of Lord Vishnu, he once

visited Alandi to meet Jnanadeva. He arrived at Alandi with a great
fanfare carrying large retinue and regalia; he himself was mounted
on a tiger and carried a live serpent as a whip to control the carrier.
Jnanadeva, his sister, and two brothers were sitting on the parapet [of
a stone wall] basking in the sun. Having come to know that a great
Siddha had come to their place, Jnanadeva desired to pay his respects and
welcome the guest. He therefore ordered the insentient wall to move in
the direction of Changadeva and, lo and behold! it moved and in no time
the whole company of Jnanadeva stood face to face with Changadeva.
The latter was bewildered with this miracle; his bloated ego pricked
and instantly he fell prostrate at the feet of Jnanadeva, realizing his
greatness.[26]

In an apocryphal story a couple of centuries after Jnaneshwar's
mahasamadhi, another Marathi saint named Eknath (1533–99) had a
vision in which Jnaneshwar came to him and said, "There's a tree root
growing into my neck. Would you please come and do something about
it?" Eknath opened the tomb, which he had to do by stealth at night because it would've been sacrilegious, and removed the tree root; he also
found a copy of Jnaneshwar's great work.

Jnaneshwar's four known literary works were all completed by the
time he was twenty-one. Our sense of his remarkable realization comes
from his words, though he himself criticizes their limited ability to
convey what he was expressing. Even in translation, *Amritanubhava*, or
"Ambrosial Experience," is unique poetry from the enlightened state, a
narration of the experience of realization from within. It is like a lingering fragrance of the sweetest flower imaginable.

THE UNION OF SHIVA AND SHAKTI

Thus have I paid my homage to the God and Goddess who are the limitless primal parents of the universe.

On the charming spot, the Lover Himself, out of overflowing love, becomes the Beloved, who is made up of the same flesh, and who eats the same food.

Out of deep longing they swallow each other, and again emit each other because they like to be two.

They are neither completely identical nor completely different. We do not know their real nature.

How strong is their desire to enjoy themselves! They become one through it and never allow their unity to be disturbed even in jest.

They are so afraid of their separation that, although they have given birth to the child in the form of the universe, their duality is not disturbed.

It is through God that the other is Goddess and without her the Lord is nowhere. As a matter of fact their existence is due to each other.

Oh! How sweet is their union! The great world is too small for them to live in, while they live happily even in the smallest particle.

Both of them are objects to each other. Both are subjects to each other. Both are happy in each other's company.

The essence of all void became Purusha through Her, while the Shakti got Her peculiar existence through the Lord.

Shiva Himself formed His beloved without whom Shiva loses His own personality.

Her form is the cause of God and His glory manifested in the process of the world. But Her form itself is created by Him out of Himself.

Blushing at Her formless husband and Her own graceful form, She adorned him with the ornament of the names and forms of the universe.

She is His form while Her beauty is due to him who is Her lover. They are enjoying the feast by intermingling with each other.[27]

bhagawan nityananda

The Vedas, the fount of Indian spiritual life, describe four states of consciousness: waking, dreaming, deep sleep, and *turiya,* which is a yogic state in which one no longer identifies with the body and neither sleeps nor dreams. Beyond that is a blissful apotheosis termed *turyatita,* "beyond *turiya,*" which is free from all delusion or expectation, One without a second, where all phenomena reside in the Self. You become the universe and the universe is in you. Bhagawan ("Lord") Nityananda (*nitya,* "eternal"; *ananda,* "bliss") lived in that state.

My guru, Maharaj-ji, said he knew Nityananda and that he was a "good *sadhu.*" Coming from Maharaj-ji, that was a great compliment, as much a cosmic understatement as when our Buddhist teacher, Munindra-ji, would call an enlightened being a "nice man."

How do you describe someone in words who is so completely beyond words and concepts? What can you truly know of such a being from the outside? Nityananda was considered an *avadhoot,* beyond body consciousness. In Mangalore during the 1920s or 1930s he described his state to some devotees, speaking of himself, as he always did, in the third person:

An Avadhoota has conquered death and birth. He has no consciousness of the body. An Avadhoota has gone beyond all Gunas (qualities). He is the

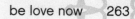

knower of the "Omniscient Light." He has no consciousness of the "I." . . .
When he comes to a village, he feels glad, whomsoever he may see. He has
no consciousness of duality though he moves here and there. He has no
hunger.

He eats plentifully if he gets plenty of eatables. If he does not get, he will not ask anybody. Those who give to him poison and those who give to him milk are the same to him. Those who beat him and those who love him are the same to him. To an Avadhoota, the universe is the father, the mother, and the relation. He becomes the universe and the universe becomes he. The universe is merged in him.[28]

Nityananda lived his life in a state of utter simplicity, devoid of personal possessions, completely detached. He spent much time in the jungle meditating, clad only in a loincloth, and that only to satisfy convention. He would bathe before dawn and ate little, for years only what others would feed him and then only fruits or vegetables. He didn't collect devotees, start organizations, teach, or write books. The power of his presence was complete in itself. He *was* at One.

Gestures, grunts, and sometimes a few words conveyed his often enigmatic communications to devotees, though he could expound at length, and sometimes gave instructions in dreams. The outpouring of his love and grace to those who sought him out came, as he would have said, automatically from God. Nor was the connection dependent on physical proximity or relative time; his influence extended to wherever someone thought of him, and though he left the body in 1961, it continues to the present.

Nityananda was a *siddha,* a perfected yogi, probably from birth, certainly from a very early age. His birth is shrouded in mystery, and his childhood is like a Bible story. The tale begins around the turn of the nineteenth century, about 1897, near Kanhangad in South Kannara District along the west coast of South India. According to one version, a woman of the untouchable caste returning from gathering firewood in the jungle came upon a male infant wrapped in a cloth, and gave (or sold) him to a childless friend named Uniamma. Uniamma happily adopted the child and named him Rām. She worked in the household of a local lawyer named Ishwar Iyer, a very devout man. (A variation, supported by Nityananda himself, has Uniamma finding the infant Nityananda on a riverbank protected in the coils of a snake.) The poor untouchable woman raised Rām as her own. Upon her death her employer, Ishwar Iyer, took in the orphan.

Although he had children of his own, Mr. Iyer developed a deep fondness for young Rām and became a kind of foster father to him. He took him on pilgrimages to temples and holy sites and passed on some of his own education, the boy's only schooling. On those trips he discovered young Rām could answer his most esoteric questions and satisfy his innate spiritual yearning. At home Rām was as mischievous as any child, but his games often took an unusual turn, such as when he dove into the neighborhood tank and did not come up for an unnaturally long time.

When Rām was about ten, his aging patron took him on pilgrimage to Benares. At some point during this trip the young Rām left Mr. Iyer, though he promised to see him again. Though little is known for certain about the next years, the indication is that Rām wandered in the Himalayas and became well known there as a great *kundalini* yogi. As promised, he came home when he was about sixteen. Mr. Iyer was so happy to see him he kept repeating, *"Nityananda, nityananda"* ("eternal bliss"), the name by which Rām became known thereafter. Not long after Nityananda's return, Mr. Iyer became very ill. He died with his head on Nityananda's lap. After his death Nityananda again went wandering, visiting pilgrimage spots and roaming farther afield through southeast Asia.

He returned and lived for some time meditating in a cave surrounded by the dense jungle where he had first been found, then moved to the site of an old fort along the sea coast at Kanhangad. The fortifications had caves that had been used by the soldiers, which Nityananda converted for meditation and an ashram.

In those early days Nityananda was known for a kind of monkey *tapasya*, standing erect and balanced high up in a tree. Devotees would come, and he would drop down leaves. A leaf would heal sickness or convey blessings. Though elusive and unpredictable, he became known as a healer and did a lot to help people, especially the poor:

One day a man who had lost his sight stood among the crowd beneath the tree. The others in the crowd eagerly picked up the leaves dropped by Nityananda and went home. Soon only the blind man was left. He continued pleading with the Master to restore his sight, explaining that as it was, he was not able to earn a living and so was a burden to his family. After a considerable time, Nityananda came to him and rubbed the man's eyes with leaves from the tree. No words were spoken, and no change was immediately apparent. However, on arising the next morning, the man was able to see and his sight remained restored.[29]

Later when he moved north of Bombay to a small town called Ganeshpuri, people lined up by the hundreds for a moment of his *darshan*. He rarely spoke. He'd just say, "Hunh!" and turn his head in certain ways. Some people learned to read his grunts and gestures and to interpret them. Someone would come and say, "Should I buy this stock, Babaji?" And he'd go, "Hunh," and they'd buy it and make a killing on the Bombay market. Some of these devotees got rich.

Nityananda's actions were sometimes so unconventional they seemed crazy. Once someone saw him follow a cow and, as it evacuated, catch the fresh dung and pop it in his mouth. Indians put such behavior within the context of holy madness, the unpredictable nature of someone beyond body consciousness.

Upending categories and concepts is just part of that manifestation. The actions of a realized being go beyond rational judgment or understanding. They may engender feelings of exaltation or revulsion that break down the judging ego. People felt the intense love and unity of Nityananda's being and that allowed even the most disorienting and bizarre behavior.

The difference between an insane person and divine madness is vibrational. With Nityananda so much *shakti* and love created an atmosphere that uplifted all who came within its subtle field. On the other hand, once I visited my brother, who was in a mental hospital and thought he was Christ. He said he was God.

So I said, "Well, I'm God too."

"No, you don't understand . . ." he objected.

All I could feel was his paranoia. I replied, "It's because you deny that the rest of us are God too that you're locked up."

Nityananda says:

The sense of equality is the greatest thing in this world. People go mad after shadows; very few are mad after the invisible (the subtle). True madness [for God] is very rare, it being found only in one among a lakh *(100,000) or two. Other people run mad after sixteen things in a* ghatika *(24 minutes). "I want this, I want that, this is different, that is different." Such is their mad talk. Entertaining various motives is madness. Greatness is madness. Practicing and seeing the reality is the opposite kind of madness. Liberation from birth and death is Divine madness. Those who have not realized the truth are mad after the gross [physical reality]. Everyone has one sort of madness or another. Thousands of people possess houses, diamond jewels, gold and property. They did not bring these with them at birth nor will they take these with them at death.*[30]

Nityananda built *dharmasalas* (pilgrim rest houses) and ashrams, created meditation caves and other projects, and planted trees. At Kanhangad, the old fort on the coast, the hill is tunneled with caves deep into the ground, some of which Nityananda dug with his own hands. For larger excavation projects and building roads he would also employ local laborers.

He paid the workmen every day in brand-new rupee notes. Sometimes he would pull the exact amount out of his loincloth. Sometimes the workers would file by, Nityananda would open and close his empty fist, and the exact change would fall into the worker's hand.[31] At other times he would say to the workmen at the end of the day, "On your way home pick up any rock in the jungle and your two rupees will be there." So they would leave and pick up a rock along the way, whichever one struck their fancy, and there would be their two rupees. There wouldn't be money under any other rock, just that one. They couldn't pick up two rocks and get twice as much. And the rupee notes were always new.

The local police got word of a naked *baba* with fresh rupee notes in his possession and became concerned about counterfeiting. An inspector and his sergeant came to see him and asked, "Babaji, where are these new rupees coming from?"

Nityananda also looked concerned and said, "Come! I'll show you."

They headed off down the road in the hot sun and soon he veered off into the jungle, finally arriving at a crocodile- and snake-infested swamp. Nityananda waded up to his waist into the swamp with the alligators, snakes, and bugs, reached down into the water, and came up with big bundles of fresh rupee notes, which he threw to the policemen. The currency was dry.

He said, "This is where I keep my press. Come in and see it!"

The terrified policemen bowed and apologized and ran out of the swamp. (In another encounter with the law he was jailed for vagrancy. The jailer observed him simultaneously inside and outside the jail and decided to release him.)

In his younger years Nityananda was a strange and galvanizing force, constantly moving about, with sometimes startling swiftness. Swami Muktananda related an incident in which a bus driver refused to pick up Nityananda along the road and drove on past him. At his next stop, miles away, there was Nityananda waiting for the bus. The driver took off and left him again. This occurred three times, until the shell-shocked driver acknowledged Nityananda and humbly offered to take him anywhere he wanted to go. Nityananda disappeared.

A railway ran near his ashram in the south near Kanhangad, and Nityananda would ride the trains, often accompanying the engineer in the locomotive. When asked for a ticket, he would pull masses of them from his loincloth. For one conductor Nityananda produced a garland of hundreds of tickets of all classes and asked the official to take his choice.[32]

Other stories are told about him as well:

The following is one of the few authenticated stories about this time period. The scene is Palani, where Lord Subramanya (a brother of Lord Ganesh in Hindu mythology) is the presiding deity. We must visualize the Nityananda of those days: looking like an eccentric vagrant, his body wire-thin as if lashed by severe austerities, but healthy and glowing all the same. Late one morning, he was ascending the last few steps to the sanctum at Palani, when the serving priest, having locked the doors of the shrine after morning worship, was coming down. Nityananda asked him to re-open the doors and have an arathi (light) waved before the deity. The priest was astonished that a vagrant would dare make such a request of a person of his status and curtly told Nityananda that the time for morning worship was over.

Nityananda went on as if he had not heard. The priest, expecting that Nityananda would walk around the sanctum and offer worship at the Muslim altar at the rear, was not concerned until he heard the temple bells ringing. When he looked back, he was dumbfounded to see the doors of the sanctum open and Nityananda sitting in the place of the deity with an arathi being waved in front of him by invisible hands. The vision vanished in an instant. Then Nityananda came out of the sanctum and stood on one leg for some time, with a steady yogic upward gaze. Apparently a lot of money was poured at his feet—whether by pilgrims or visitors or some invisible source is not clear. Nityananda, in any case, was accorded all the honors due to a Master. The pilgrims tried to persuade him to stay, but he refused. He gave all the money to the leader of the local sanyasis [renunciates] for a morning meal center (for serving one meal of rice porridge a day to the sanyasis). To complete the story, it was later learned that the local sanyasis had been praying to the Lord at Palani for some time to be provided with at least one meal during their stay.[33]

At Padabidri town (South) an arrogant money lender used to have a reckless drive in his dog cart through the narrow streets of the town, often injuring many pedestrians. One day when this money lender was on his usual reckless drive, he found Baba in his way. He stopped the dog cart, got down from it, and began to use the horsewhip on Baba's bare back with fury in flogging Baba with it. Baba remained quiet and impassive. To the astonishment of the onlookers, the rude money lender felt the agonies of his horsewhip stripes on his own back and felt his body burning with torrid heat, and he fell dead in the street.

Good for evil—Love for hatred.—At Udipi (South) Baba was first mocked, abused, and pelted with sand and stones, people taking him to be a madman. At the town's annual Rath Day (Chariot Day) celebrations, however, Baba in "retaliation" was seen throwing handfuls of sand at the Holy Chariot taken in procession in the streets. But to their fear and astonishment, the townspeople found that the sand falling on the Chariot got transformed into silver and gold coins. People who had abused and mocked Baba fell at his feet and begged for his pardon.

Baba, once during his stay with a businessman of Haleangdi town who had made a big fortune owing to Baba's grace, had been to the jungles nearby the town along with this businessman. There, in the jungles, Baba was seen by the businessman in communication with Sri Hanuman, who had a brilliant aura of light around him (and who is believed to have a perpetual life and who always stays invisible to the common eye in the Kali yuga, the current age, of the universe). Baba had warned the businessman ever to keep it to himself. The businessman was one day, however, tempted to speak it out to his wife. Baba, knowing the disclosure of the jungle incident by intuition, quietly walked out of his house, making straight to the Pavanje river, followed by the businessmen and others, who implored him to return, begging for his pardon. At that time the river was full of water, and no boat was available to take him across. Baba straightway walked over the surface of the river till he was across on its other side. The people who followed him and those on the banks of the river were simply stunned to see him walking across the water surface.[34]

About walking across the river Pavanje at full flood, it is clear Nityananda wanted to get to the other side, but since it was monsoon and the river was in flood, the boatman refused, perhaps because he did not wish to risk it for one person. Without a second thought, Nityananda then simply walked across. His own words are eloquent on the subject of the motives of spiritual masters. In 1953 when asked to explain the meaning of this unconventional incident Nityananda said:

> It is true that the Pavanje River was in flood at the time this one walked across, and that the boatman would not venture out. But it was not done with any motivation. It happened automatically—during the mood of the moment. But what is the use of all that? It only meant depriving the boatman of his half anna [few pennies]. One must live in the world like common men. . . . Once one is established in infinite consciousness, one becomes silent and, though knowing everything, goes about as if he does not know anything. Though he might be doing a lot of things in several places, to all outward appearance he will remain as if he does nothing. He will always remain as if he is a witness to everything that goes on, like a spectator at a cinema show, and is not affected by the pleasant or the unpleasant. To be able to forget everything and be aloof, that alone is the highest state to be in.[35]

It is not *bhakti* (devotion) to give a man some money or to give him a meal as charity. *Bhakti* is universal love. Seeing God in all beings, without the least idea of duality, is *bhakti*.

—Nityananda[36]

Nityananda's laconic and sometimes brusque exterior belied an ocean of boundless compassion for his devotees and indeed anyone who came before him. Although he described himself as a *jnani*, one on the path of knowledge, no better evidence exists than Nityananda himself for the convergence of *jnana* and *bhakti*, wis-

dom and love, in that final state of realization. Indeed, it was that loving capacity to help any who took shelter at his feet that attracted swarms of pilgrims and devotees, especially once he had settled in one place. Ganeshpuri was at first a remote jungle and hard to get to, but people by the thousands plied the road he built to stand in long lines for his *darshan*.

As he became known far and wide as a great healer, Nityananda would occasionally take others' painful conditions into his own body to accelerate their recovery. Seemingly incurable conditions were healed in his presence, though at times he refused to reverse the stream of an individual's *karma*:

Once a widow took her congenitally blind six-year-old daughter to the Master and pleaded for her eyesight to be restored. Nityananda said, "But the child has never seen light from its birth. Why are you insisting?" She nevertheless continued to plead. Nityananda then said, "Let the child ask what it wants." The mother told the child to ask for whatever she wanted, and the child said, "I would like to see my mother once." The Master made no response, and after a little time, he asked them to leave. It was the mother's custom to bathe the child first, then put her in a chair and go for her own bath. On this day as she came out of the bath, the little girl leapt up and ran to her, shouting that she could see. But her joy lasted only a few minutes; her blindness returned. Perhaps the Master did not wish to interfere with the irrevocable destiny of the child; perhaps any relief provided now would have interfered with the karmic law. However, since the mother was pleading, it appears he left it to the inner voice of the child to say what it wanted, and it came out spontaneously that she wanted to see the mother once. This wish was granted.[37]

Nityananda's being had and continues to have an extraordinary effect on those who seek his blessing, whether for material or spiritual benefit. Nor did he stint on giving to those who came for basic human needs, like food or health or money. Especially in the early days he would often cook and serve with his own hands great feasts (*bhandaras*) for poor children and the less fortunate. Money left as offerings to him by grateful devotees went thus toward feeding the poor. Such was the love of this outwardly simple man who could pass for a beggar, but was fully absorbed in the Oneness of everything.

deoria baba

Deoria Baba was a *bhakti* yogi who inspired millions on the path of devotion. He was probably India's best-known *sadhu*. We would see him at the *kumbha melas*, the great festivals of millions of *sadhus* and pilgrims, where crowds of people came for his *darshan*, gathering around his

bamboo and grass hut raised on stilts. Every hour or so he would emerge to give *darshan*. Sometimes he would pull blankets or food out from his hut; at other times he would distribute copies of his favorite text, the *Shrimad Bhagavatam*. At times, he would distribute far more items than could possibly have fit in his tiny hut.

Deoria Baba was also known as a *pandit*, one learned in the religious literature. He was a real yogi who taught only the path of love. We sometimes saw him when he came to Vrindavan to stay for several months each winter by the Yamuna River.

When he died in the early 1990s, he was documented to be over 150 years old and said by many to be more than 200. Of course, nobody else was alive who knew for sure. We met one of his numerous disciples, himself a highly respected guru, who was more than 90. Periodically, Deoria Baba retreated for months at a time into a cave in solitude, where he was said to regenerate his body by yogic processes. He lived naked, but would cover his private parts with a deer skin, which he also used as his seat. He held it about his waist in the rare moments when he stood to bless the throngs of devotees.

To see him gave rise to a feeling of natural majesty, like looking at the Grand Canyon or the Himalayas. There was a gentle sweetness to his manner that drew people. He addressed young and old alike as "children." His tender concern for the material and spiritual welfare of devotees was like that of a doting and forgiving grandparent. I saw him berate a rich man on the perils of possessions. He stood naked in his grass hut, speaking with the authority of a king who clearly lacked for nothing.

People came to him with mundane problems, hoping for health or wealth by the grace of his *siddhis,* or powers. Crowds of several hundred would wait humbly in the searing sun for him to emerge. Sometimes he would throw down sugar candy *prasad* through a trap door in the floor of his hut, sometimes endless handfuls of fruit; and sometimes he'd lower a leg through the trap door so people could touch his foot. Though he had devotees from all walks of life, he was primarily a *sadhu guru* to the wandering monks. He was held in the highest regard by millions of *sadhus.*

About Deoria Baba and Neem Karoli Maharaj-ji, Dada Mukerjee said:

After [Neem Karoli] Babaji had taken his samadhi, *Deoria Baba talked about him to his devotees on several occasions. He said, "He is free, a realized soul. How could he remain bound?" Then he said that Babaji's devotees had raised an enclosure around him thinking he could be held in that way. "How could this be possible? He might have stayed here for some time more, had there been no such enclosure."* [38]

Deoria Baba, himself a great saint, comes to Allahabad every year during the Magh Mela or the Kumbha Mela. A few years back he was here and some of his devotees who are well known to us came to our house for satsang. They said that the night before they had been sitting around Deoria on the sand, and someone came who said that he used to go to Neem Karoli Baba, but he is not there anymore, so he cannot go. Deoria Baba actually shouted at him, "What are you saying? Can such a saint go anywhere? He has done such kinds of tricks many times before! He is alive, and he always will be alive!" [39]

kumaon saints

Northeast of Delhi the Himalayan foothills surrounding Nainital and Almora, ascending from the plains to twenty-thousand-foot peaks, are known as the Kumaon Hills. Maharaj-ji frequented the area, which is a traditional abode of saints, *sadhus,* and yogis. The hill people are different from those who live on the plains, hardier perhaps, due to the rugged landscape or the ethnic mix that developed because the area was a crossroads for Tibetan, Nepali, and Chinese traders and foreign invaders going back to Alexander the Great. During the British Raj the ruling class coveted the hills to escape the stifling heat of the plains and established a summer capital for the northern province of Uttar Pradesh at Nainital.

Much of our knowledge of the great saints of the Kumaon has come from Krishna Kumar ("K.K.") Sah, who has experienced the *lilas* and has been steeped in the stories of these saints since childhood. Describing those early contacts, he said:

I heard these stories when I was just a young child. How was I dragged into that atmosphere by the devotees of these great saints, not just ordinary saints, but these very high saints? They happened to come and sit with me.

If you ask a child of this age about the stories of these saints, they will get bored. This is an age when most kids just want to play. I don't know how I fell in love with these saints. This is itself a miracle!

I was five or six years old when I met Neem Karoli Maharaj-ji. My father would not let me go to another house to see him by myself, but he allowed me to go with my nephew. People were sitting around with Neem Karoli Maharaj-ji. I thought that saints lived in the forest. I was wondering what kind of saint this was, coming to someone's house, and I asked my nephew about this. Maharaj-ji asked, "What is he saying? What is he saying?" My nephew was a bit embarrassed. "Tell me! Tell me!" So my nephew told him I thought saints lived in the forest and didn't come to people's houses. I said, "Will you come to my house?" Then and there he got up and came to my house. The fellow whose house we were in was quite upset.

That was my father's first darshan of Neem Karoli Maharaj-ji. When he got to the house, Maharaj-ji asked where the bed was that Hairakhan Baba had slept on, then he lay down on it. He asked my father about the mantra that Hairakhan Baba had given him, which no one but my father knew about. That was a turning point. Although he had met many saints, my father became a devotee of Neem Karoli Maharaj-ji right from that time. And it had a big impact on my life. Most people don't understand the feelings of the grace from these saints.

People enjoyed being with Maharaj-ji, but I think nobody ever enjoyed the kinds of things I have. Ninety percent of devotees were grown-ups, and even saints paid respect to grown-ups and elders. But I was just a child and anyone could have kicked me out for the liberties I took. That too was his grace, at every step. Once Maharaj-ji blessed (or cursed?) me that I should always remain like a child. So I have my own way of devotion.[40]

Three Kumaon *siddhas* were some of the greatest, but by no means the only saints of the area: Hairakhan Baba, Sombari Baba (or Sombari

Maharaj-ji), and Shri Bal Brahmachari Maharaj-ji. The lives of these great beings are mysteriously interwoven, and they all contributed to the atmosphere of the Kumaon Hills known as *siddha bhumi,* a place where perfected beings stay.

All had associations with K.K.'s family, and he told us these stories over the course of many years. K.K. is very particular about details and the reliability of sources. He's not responsible for any inaccuracies that have been brought in from others.

hairakhan baba

Hairakhan Baba was a *siddha* of almost mythic power who from about the 1880s until 1920 frequented the foothills and nearby jungles of the Kumaon area. His origins are mysterious. He was seen in the company of Tibetan lamas, sometimes wore Tibetan-style clothing, and used a prayer wheel. He became known as Hairakhan Baba after he miraculously appeared near the small village of Hairakhan. Hairakhan is named after a type of medicinal tree (myrobalan) used for digestive ailments. Saints often were given names according to place or circumstance, but sometimes no one really knew where they might have come from or their origins. Villagers said they saw a brilliant light over a nearby hilltop for several nights. It vanished, then reappeared closer to the village. Amid the light was the radiant body of a man of twenty or twenty-five years old, whom the villagers welcomed with reverence.

The saint was of such childlike character that he aroused deep maternal instincts in women. To him every woman was the Mother. Milk would start to pour out of women's breasts when he came near, even from those who had been dry for years. Sometimes he would drink from the breast, an occasional source of scandal. Once when he was doing this, a woman's husband came home and misunderstood the situation. The husband locked the door, left someone to guard it, and went to get the police. When they came back and unlocked the door, only the woman was in the room, and Hairakhan Baba was gone. The room had no other opening.

Gumani was a simple illiterate farmer who lived with his family outside the town of Haldwani at the base of the hills. By nature he was inclined to devotion, and he was quite detached from worldly existence. One day Hairakhan Baba came to his farm. Gumani accepted him as his guru. For an entire year Gumani served, fed, and took care of Hairakhan with great devotion, adding on to his hut so Hairakhan would have a

place to stay. Gumani's deep faith in Hairakhan was returned by the saint with miracles and great love. Once Gumani expressed a desire to bathe in the Sarada River some distance away. Hairakhan carried him there, flying through the air. Gumani's deep reverence and affection made him a legendary devotee, and he reportedly died in an exalted state.

A wealthy lawyer, *pandit* Bhola Datt, was riding to Haldwani when he passed Hairakhan sitting on a rock, laughing. The proud Bhola Datt thought Hairakhan was making fun of him, and he angrily confronted him. Hairakhan said he was not laughing at him, but because the temple bell at the Badrinath temple high in the Himalayas had fallen down and people were trying everything to get it back up without success. Bhola Datt thought the man must be crazy and decided he would go back and give him a thrashing if he was taunting him. When he stopped at the nearest train station to telephone, he got a return message that the temple bell had indeed just fallen, hundreds of miles away. How had this man known about it? Inquiring further, he realized he had met a saint and sought Hairakhan out again in the jungle to apologize. He became a great devotee and lived his last years doing *sadhana* at Hairakhan's ashram.

Hairakhan Baba's presence was first noted in the hills at the building of a dam at the Bhimtal lake. He was lifting heavy rocks and moving earth alongside the other laborers. After two or three weeks the foreman noticed he had not been collecting his pay like the other workers. At that point he disappeared. There had been several previous attempts to build this dam, but each time it gave way during the monsoon rains. This time the project was successful.

While he was staying up in the mountains near Almora, a man came who insisted that Hairakhan give him *darshan* of Bhagawan, the Lord. He wanted to see God. Hairakhan kept telling him to go away, but one day the man came back and kept demanding and yelling all day. Finally he started to abuse Hairakhan. Hairakhan sat the man down in front of him. A few moments later the man jumped up and ran off screaming into the forest. Hairakhan said the man would be mad for the rest of his life. All he had done was show him one part of one ray of the Divine Mother, but the man had insisted, so he had to do it.

Hairakhan left some written words, but his handwriting is in an unknown language. No one knows this language, though it appears to be a mix of ancient Pali or Nepali, possibly an ancient language called Brahmi; it could also be an archaic form of Hindi, Sanskrit, or Tibetan. People think that he must have traveled through Tibet. He spoke a mix of Hindi, Nepali, and hill dialects. Sometimes he would give blessings such as, "*Baba mansa phalegi* (The fruit of your desire will be fulfilled)," which can have different meanings depending on how it is interpreted.

On several occasions Hairakhan Baba appeared in more than one place at the same time. Some devotees went to a pilgrimage site for an auspicious occasion, and he said he would see them there. After traveling by the only available transport, they found him there awaiting them. When they returned home, the devotees there maintained that he had never left and confirmed that he had attended the ceremony there at the same time.

On the outskirts of Nainital there is a small temple at Sipahi Dhara where Hairakhan Baba performed a sacred fire-ceremony, or *havan*. As part of the ritual *ghee* is offered into the fire. On this occasion the *ghee* ran out, so Hairakhan used water for the oblations instead. The fire blazed up higher and higher. He also performed a similar fire-from-water *puja* at K.K.'s home.

The last time Hairakhan was seen in the body, he walked into a torrential mountain river at the confluence of the Kali and Gori Ganga Rivers at Askot near the Nepali border. The ruler of Askot helped to carry the palanquin with Hairakhan in it as a sign of respect. During the 1970s we met a woman, who was then about eighty, who had been there

when Hairakhan disappeared. She was a young girl at the time. She said they had gone up to the Gori Ganga, near the Nepali border. The devotees were with Hairakhan all on one bank. Hairakhan said to her, "Take my hand," and the next thing she knew she was on the other side of the river, and he was gone. Other observers said he walked into the river and disappeared. Some say he never left his body and is still alive and giving *darshan* to devotees.

In the 1950s he appeared to a Swedish artist, Niels Olft Cressander, and his wife in France, wearing European clothes, and then again in Russia, simultaneously in St. Petersburg (then Leningrad) and Stalingrad, to the husband and wife respectively. Subsequently, while living at Kasar

Devi near Almora, Cressander made a statue of Hairakhan that was installed near Kausani.

In 1958 at the inauguration of a new temple at the Hairakhan ashram in the jungle at Katgharia near Haldwani, a bright light appeared over the *murti,* the statue. Hairakhan was seen in the light, causing old devotees to faint in ecstasy.

Hairakhan once remarked he had seen the Mahabharata war with his own eyes. Some people thought he might be an immortal from that time, perhaps with a legendary jewel in his head. A man who belonged to the nearby village of Khurpatal was keen to test Hairakhan. He invited Hairakhan to come to his village and stay at his house. Once there, Hairakhan asked if the man would help him take a bath. He helped the saint to take off his clothes, then bathed and dried him, but in the process never once remembered to look for the jewel or other signs that he thought might be on his body. Hairakhan said, "Never test a saint."

As related by Hubba, an old devotee who was an uncle and neighbor of K.K.'s, one day Hairakhan went to visit Sombari Baba at Padampuri. Sombari got up and offered his seat to Hairakhan Baba as a sign of respect. Hairakhan Baba said, "Baba, I have a pain in my stomach, and I want some fresh milk." It was already nightfall, and the hill folk are very superstitious—no one milks a cow after sunset. Sombari sent someone to one of the farmhouses above the ashram. They found an old woman there who said, "Oh, I forgot to milk the cows. It is too late, now, but if anyone can use it, it is all right." And she sent the fresh milk, still warm from the cow. Was this done for Hairakhan Baba or was it a touch of grace for this old woman?

sombari baba

In Hindi Monday is Sombar, a day sacred to Shiva. Every Monday Sombari Baba used to feed people, cooking for numbers of devotees out of a single pot or reaching back into his cave and pulling out hot *puris* and other food. He was very humble and self-deprecating. He referred to his devotees as children and said it was only attachment that brought them together.

He was born in Pind Dadan Khan, a village along the Jhelum River in the Northwest Frontier Province of Punjab in what is now Pakistan. His father was a judge. Not much is known about his early life, although he was apparently educated. He may have had a Sufi guru in Kashmir.

In the Kumaon Hills Sombari Baba made ashrams at the confluence of rivers. His two ashrams at Padampuri and Kakarighat were isolated, lonely places, one in deep forest and the other along a riverbank. Traveling between them he occupied caves, also near rivers. He would bathe two or three times a day even in the depth of the Himalayan winter and in spring when streams filled with icy meltwater. His only covering was a loincloth and a thin cloth over his upper body. He left his body in 1919 at Padampuri. A couple of photos were taken of him. Others were attempted, but they wouldn't come out without his permission. Once the glass in a camera lens cracked.

Sombari Baba told a young man not to leave the ashram, because it was late and he'd have to walk back through the jungle at night. The man did not heed his advice and went anyway. He was mauled by a tiger up in the mountains. Another time Sombari told a devotee not to take a train leaving that night. That person didn't go, and there was a big train wreck that claimed many lives. These *lilas* of saints may be hard to understand—they are teachings in the moment for those involved and one needs some faith and insight to feel them in the heart.

A rich person from Kashipur, Lala Radhey Shyam, was brought to Sombari in a litter chair. He was very sick and almost on his deathbed. He had heard about Sombari Baba and expressed a wish to have his blessing before death. He had lost much of his body weight and had been unable to eat more than a teaspoon of milk a day for weeks. Sombari said,

"Take him down and bathe him in the river." It was an icy mountain stream. His companions protested, "But Babaji, that will kill him!" He told them to do as he said. Then he went in and cooked a full meal of rice and vegetables with *ghee* and forced it into the man's mouth. The man revived and lived another forty years, long enough to see six grandchildren.

Sombari Baba allowed an old devotee, Govinda Ram Kala, to stay at the Padampuri ashram. One evening Sombari gave him three potatoes and told him to eat all of them. He went down to the river and ate one, and then another. Afterward he said he felt as though he was in the seventh heaven of the gods. He was transported to the realm of gods and goddesses just by eating those potatoes.

Meanwhile a *sadhu* came who begged Govinda Ram for food. Now, Sombari had told him specifically to eat all three potatoes, but still he gave the last one to the *sadhu*. When he came back, Sombari asked, "Well, did you eat all of them?" Govinda Ram related the whole story and said, "Maharaj-ji, just eating two of them I was full." Sombari didn't say anything.

Govinda Ram said later that, by eating just the two potatoes, he had received as much as he could hold spiritually. He felt if he ate the third potato, he would leave his body or become one with God. The third potato might have been liberation, but he didn't know what would happen and he wasn't ready. He didn't have the capacity to "digest" it.

Of course, this was all Sombari Baba's *lila,* his play. That is the beauty of saints. They do something, and they let the devotee do something. They find out whether he or she obeyed or not, then they keep quiet. They don't commit. Nobody really knows what would have happened with the third potato except, certainly, Sombari. One can only watch and surrender to the moment.

In the summer Sombari stayed in Kakarighat, where it was exceedingly hot. In the winter he would stay at Padampuri, where it was extremely cold. He went for the opposite of comfort. Traveling between them he would stop at Khairna and then at the cave in Kainchi where Neem Karoli Baba's ashram is now. As far as is known, he came to Padampuri first. His *ishta deva* (personal god) was Shiva, and he made Shiva temples. Wearing only a thin cotton cloth even in winter, he would smoke *charas,* hashish, in a clay *chillum,* or pipe. He was *purna siddha,* fully perfected, always one with God. He had no need of *puja* or *sadhana.* Whatever he did of that was done for devotees. That is a quality of the *siddha.*

He used to make a kind of *roti,* or bread, in the fire, small thick *chapatis* called *tikkar* that he would bake in the coals of the fire. He would make two each day and break them in half. One half would go to the cow, one half to the crows, and one half to the fish; then he would eat the last half—half of one *tikkar* each day.

As part of K.K.'s father's job as Circle Inspector of Police, he was given two or three horses, and when he went on tour he would see Sombari at Kakarighat or Padampuri. K.K.'s father treated him as if he were a family elder and consulted him on every detail of life, even how to get his daughters married. When K.K.'s father would get ready to leave Padampuri, Sombari would say, *"Hare,* Bhawani Das, your girls will be waiting for you to come, and they will be asking what this *baba* has sent for them." Then he would send some special *prasad* for the sisters (K.K. wasn't born yet).

Urba Datt Pande related this story about his father, a local man who during the British Raj was a clerk for the Divisional Forest Officer in Nainital. It was a good post, and he was nearing retirement. The British officer, his wife, and Pande were returning on horseback from Almora to Nainital. He mentioned to his English boss that he wished to stop to have *darshan* of the saint at Padampuri. The Englishman said that he wanted him back in time for work in Nainital. He warned him he might lose his job, if he did not return in time. He went for *darshan* anyway, even though it was late in the day. But he was also nervous about his job, so he hurried along.

On his arrival Sombari Baba had him make a *chillum,* then bathe in the river and prepare food. Pande started really worrying about getting back in time. It was so late when he finally left, he was sure he'd lose his job. Sombari said, "Don't worry!"

He found the British officer and his wife where the Padampuri trail rejoins the horse trail to Nainital, their way blocked by two huge cobras that were causing the horses to rear and had delayed them more than an hour. As soon as Pande arrived, the cobras left. The British officer was so grateful to him for saving their lives that not only did he get to keep his job, but the officer arranged for a large plot of land near Almora to be granted to him, which is still in his family.

Near the turn of the twentieth century, K.K.'s brother-in-law, Indra Lal (I.L.) Sah and a friend were walking from Nainital to their high-school history exams in Almora, the school district center. There were no roads in those days, and they were traveling on the footpath that connected the hill communities. It was a two- or three-day walk. I.L. describes his first encounter with Sombari Baba:

Early one spring afternoon when I was still in my teens more than six decades ago, I set out on foot with a couple of friends from Nainital to Almora to sit for a high school examination. In the evening we stopped at Khairna overnight at a wayside shop before going on in the morning. We were preparing to sleep when the shopkeeper, an elderly person, came and suggested that we have darshan *of a* sadhu *before going to Almora in the morning.*

It was a dark spring night, pleasantly cool. With our guide we crossed a hanging bridge and a sandy waste to the lonely cave where the sadhu *stayed. The river was flowing softly nearby. It was quite a large cave, with one dim lamp and a small fire burning in the front.*

A gruff voice from the river bank called out that we were trespassing across the boundary of the ashram with our shoes on. In the dark none of us had noticed a line. We apologized, and retraced a few steps and took off our shoes. The Baba directed us to go in and sit near the fire and await his return. Our guide told us that the Baba goes to the river to feed the fish several times each day.

Sombari Baba came and sat near the fire opposite us. He was of short stature and advanced age, with matted locks and ash-smeared body. He enquired about our parents and about a prominent mela (festival) in our town. Then he related to us the story of a king who has everything to *indulge his senses in, but never found real peace and joy. He gave us prasad and before we left the ashram, our guide asked him to bless us to achieve success in our exams. Sombari Baba said that one who works honestly and diligently is always successful.*

We returned and had sound sleep. Although at the time I understood little of Sombari Baba and the life he led, the sacred peace and quiet that pervaded the ashram was my first unforgettable experience before entering life.[41]

As he slept, I.L. had a vivid dream of the history exam. He saw a question about the second Panipat War, one of the battles for Delhi. He remembered the questions on waking and told his friend about the dream. His friend ridiculed him and said that battle was unimportant and unlikely to be in the exam. I.L. studied the questions he had seen in the dream. When they got there and received their exam questions, the whole exam paper was as I.L. had seen it. For the next few minutes he sat there stunned, thinking about Sombari, not knowing how to begin.

The exam monitor noticed his bemusement and asked why he was sitting idle. So he got serious and started writing. Once he started, he finished quickly. Coming out of the examination hall his friend said, "Oh, I.L., you were correct." They both understood Sombari's blessings.

For the rest of his life I.L. was attracted to saints and had a deep appreciation of their wisdom and love. This was his entry into the spiritual side of his life.

shri bal brahmachari maharaj-ji

K. K. Sah reports the appearance of Brahmachari:

About two years after the moksha *(liberation/death) of Sombari Baba, in 1921–22 a saint appeared known as Bal Brahmachari Maharaj-ji near a cave*

*at Padampuri. Sombari Baba before leaving this world had predicted this
saint appearing in his golden youth, and the devotees regarded him as an
incarnation of the Baba. He lived there in a secluded cave and later visited
other places. . . . There was an aura of light around him. . . . This Yogi
was of a very high stage and was a perfect "Siddha" in Pranayam Yoga.
He never revealed himself nor his yogic powers, but the devotees benefited
from his silent blessings and grace. Almost all the devotees of Shri Sombari
Baba and Shri Hairakhan Baba used to visit him frequently for his Darshan
whenever possible. . . . He withdrew from this life in 1959 at Almora.*[42]

Before he left the body, Sombari Baba intimated that he was going and
that another would come in his place. When his devotees asked how they
would know him, Sombari said, "He'll play with you." When a youthful
yogi appeared in a cave above the ashram at Padampuri, it seemed as
though he had been there for some time, although no one really noticed
his presence for a while and he kept disappearing. He was a *bal brahmachari*, celibate and absorbed in God from birth. At first he would play with
the local children and avoid adults, but eventually he kept company with
the adults too. He took up some of the same practices that Sombari Baba
had done, such as meditating and practicing *pranayama* in Sombari's six-
by-six-by-five-foot underground box, going into *samadhi* for two or three
days at a time.

Most of Sombari's devotees in turn became devotees of Brahmachari
Maharaj-ji. After a few years they decided they had to make an official
decision about his legitimacy, so all the devotees of Sombari got together
to decide for sure whether he was or he wasn't Sombari. By that time
they had a regular *darshan* scene going with him. It was very informal.

Brahmachari used to play cards with them, mostly Trumps, which re-
sembles Gin Rummy. He termed the cards his "fifth Veda" (there are four
Vedas), using them as a subtle teaching tool with the other card players. It

was not gambling, which he frowned upon, recalling how much trouble it got the Pandava princes into in the *Mahabharata*, when they gambled away both their kingdom and their sister.

The devotee to whom Sombari had said, "He'll play with you," hadn't been around much. He came and was playing cards with Brahmachari, when suddenly he remembered what Sombari had told him. He had an epiphany.

Another Sombari devotee, one Devidatt Kabdwal, who was known for being very particular and having a keen analytical mind, also watched and tested Brahmachari. When he acknowledged Brahmachari, that confirmed it for others too. Kabdwal later went to Jaipur and got a marble *murti* (statue) made of Sombari Baba to be installed at Padampuri. It's still there and feels as though it has life.

At the time there was no motor road from the railhead at Kathgodam to Padampuri. The marble *murti* came by bus up to Bhowali in a heavy box stuffed with cotton. Snow started when the *murti* arrived at Bhowali, continuing more and more heavily. There were still many miles to go on the foot trail to Padampuri. About ten men were taking turns carrying the *murti* box on their shoulders together a few at a time. They had to climb uphill to Champhi/Matiyal and then continue on the forest trail to Padampuri. When the men were totally exhausted, Brahmachari came and said, "What happened? Is it too heavy? All right, let me try." And he just put it on his shoulders and started walking. It was unbelievable.

Brahmachari lived for some time in a *kuti* (small house) built for him in an orchard owned by K.K.'s family along the road from Nainital to Bhowali. At Brahmachari's instruction an underground box like the one at Padampuri was constructed when a second story was added onto the *kuti*. He would have devotees close him in this box, which had only one door, and tell them to return after three or four days (no food or anything else). It was underground *samadhi*. After some days they would come and open it again. K. C. Tewari described how they would go and knock on the door, and Brahmachari would open it a little to see who it was. Tewari said there was so much light coming from Brahmachari, they couldn't look at him.

Nityanand Misra, a local historian, had been suffering from mental depression and one day was just standing around the bus station in Nainital feeling purposeless. A schoolteacher friend, D. D. Joshi, who was a devotee of Brahmachari, saw him and asked him to accompany him to see Brahmachari at Jokhiya. As they walked the six kilometers to the *kuti*, Misra was filled with confusion and tension. He decided he needed some real solutions for the many questions in his mind.

On arrival they saw Brahmachari and sat with him. As Brahmachari talked to the other devotees, a strange thing happened to Misra. When he got home, Misra related how he had received clear answers without asking Maharaj-ji anything, just listening to what he said to others. All his problems were solved, and the tension and depression were gone from his mind. Misra became a devotee and later described an extraordinary meeting that occurred in about 1941 in Lucknow, the state capital of Uttar Pradesh. Brahmachari was staying at Clay Square in Lucknow, where he had a small *kuti*, a hermitage, at the home of a devotee. Anandamayi Ma was also in Lucknow and came to visit him. Brahmachari wasn't there when she came, and she left. On returning, Brahmachari said that they had to go visit her because she had come all the way there. Anandamayi was staying on the other side of the Gomati River some distance away. About ten people set off with him in a *tonga*, a horse cart.

When they got there, Anandamayi and Brahmachari got into a spirited conversation that lasted a long time. She was asking him questions and he was answering. Devotees who accompanied him said they had never seen him talk so much or with such animation. Then Neem Karoli Maharaj-ji just happened to come by too. He reportedly said, "The Ganges is flowing. Draw as much water from the Ganges as you can put in your vessel," meaning everyone should carry away from such an amazing exchange whatever his or her spiritual capacity allowed. Witnesses to this event said they had never seen saints of this caliber come together like this.

Brahmachari Baba was playing cards with some devotees, their usual four-handed game of Trumps. His partner in the game was very nervous, because his wife was having an operation in the hospital. It was a very delicate operation. Brahmachari Baba had him play cards with him despite his anxiety, but wouldn't let him talk about his wife. They were playing partners, and at one point in the game he exclaimed, "It's done.

It's done." Everybody thought he was talking about the game, but about ten minutes later a runner came from the hospital with news that the operation was over and was a success. Brahmachari Baba stood up and looked at the man and said, "You have no faith. I told you I would take care of everything."

Although Brahmachari mostly dressed in ordinary hill clothing, K.K. said that when he traveled or went out, he dressed like a prince. He wore a fine suit and boots and a turban and carried a walking stick. In those days the local buses were run by a cooperative called the K.M.O.U. (Kumaon Motor Owners Union), and the front seat was reserved for dignitaries. They always booked it for him. When Brahmachari was leaving K.K.'s *kuti* for the last time, he was accompanied by a party of ten and he was dressed in his princely garb.

On another occasion Brahmachari met Neem Karoli Maharaj-ji at the Clay Square in Lucknow. He prostrated himself flat on the ground in *dunda pranam,* a gesture of the deepest respect. The devotees who had come with him were surprised. He said, "You people have no idea who he [Neem Karoli] is." The two saints were closeted in the *kuti* for a while. When they emerged, the devotees described them as glowing like the sun.

Brahmachari held a small *bhandara* at K.K.'s *kuti,* attended by only a few people. One of his devotees was sitting to the side, feeling a bit disappointed. Brahmachari came up to him and said, "I know what you're thinking. If I wanted, the cars would be lined up to Delhi. But that's not good for someone who is still doing *sadhana.*"

When Brahmachari left his body, Neem Karoli Maharaj-ji said, "He had you all fooled. He was the greatest yogi on the earth in this time."

credits and permissions

Grateful acknowledgment goes to the following photographers for the use of their work in this publication:

Page v: Maharaj-ji. Photo by Balaram Das.
Page xviii: Maharaj-ji, Rameshwar Das, and Jagannath Das.
Page xix: Maharaj-ji. Photo by Mohan Baum.
Page 8: K. K. Sah and Maharaj-ji.
Page 10: K. K. Sah's brother Harish and sister Bina. Photo by Rameshwar Das.
Page 11: K. K. Sah and Ram Dass. Photo courtesy of K. K. Sah.
Page 27: Ram Dass and Maharaj-ji. Photo by Rameshwar Das.
Page 29: Westerners with Maharaj-ji. Photo by Rameshwar Das.
Page 33: Ram Dass. Photo courtesy of Ram Dass.
Page 39: Eating on the veranda. Photo by Rameshwar Das.
Page 50: "Nainital High" group photo at Evelyn Hotel, Nainital. Photo courtesy of Rameshwar Das.
Page 53: Ram embracing Hanuman.
Page 55: Maharaj-ji with women touching his foot. Photo by Balaram Das.
Page 58: Ram Dass and Maharaj-ji. Photo by Rameshwar Das.
Page 67: Tewari and his granddaughter, Puja. Photo by Rameshwar Das.
Page 72: Bhagavan Das. Photo by Ram Dass.
Page 75: Maharaj-ji. Photo by Balaram Das.
Page 87: Swami Muktananda. Photo by Rameshwar Das.
Page 99: Maharaj-ji.
Page 106: Maharaj-ji. Photo by Rameshwar Das.
Page 108: Hanuman murti at Kainchi. Photo by Rameshwar Das.
Page 135: Ram Dass and *sadhu*. Photo courtesy of Ram Dass.

Page 137: Hari Dass Baba and Ram Dass. Photo courtesy of Ram Dass.

Page 140: View of Kainchi from Ram Dass's window. Photo by Ram Dass.

Page 145: Ram Dass. Photo by Rameshwar Das.

Page 147: Ram Dass. Photo by Rameshwar Das.

Page 149: Lama Foundation commune buildings. Photo by Rameshwar Das.

Page 161: Maharaj-ji.

Page 165: Maharaj-ji. Photo by Balaram Das.

Page 171: Dada Mukerjee. Photo by Rameshwar Das.

Page 183: Sah family with Maharaj-ji. Photo by Rameshwar Das.

Page 187: Maharaj-ji. Photo by Balaram Das.

Page 189: Jivanti Ma, Siddhi Ma, and Maharaj-ji.

Page 197: Maharaj-ji as young *sadhu*, Lakshman Das.

Page 199: Maharaj-ji's early days in Nainital.

Page 222: Ramana Maharshi.

Page 226: Ramana Maharshi.

Page 229: Ramana Maharshi.

Page 235: Sri Ramakrishna.

Page 238: Sri Ramakrishna.

Page 242: Anandamayi Ma. Photo by Rameshwar Das.

Page 245: Anandamayi Ma.

Page 247: Anandamayi Ma.

Page 254: Shirdi Sai Baba with devotees.

Page 263: Nityananda.

Page 266: Nityananda.

Page 273: Nityananda.

Page 275: Deoria Baba. Photo by Rameshwar Das.

Page 280: Hairakhan Baba. Photo by K. K. Sah.

Page 283: Hairakhan Baba.

Page 289: Sombari Baba.

Page 296: Maharaj-ji with Dada Mukerjee. Photo by Rameshwar Das.

Grateful acknowledgment also goes to the following for the use of their work in this publication:

Pages 6–7: "Living Flame of Love" by St. John of the Cross, original translation by Mirabai Starr for *Be Love Now*. Printed with permission.

Pages 23, 121, 158–59, 176: From *Hsin-Hsin Ming: Verses on the Faith Mind*, by Seng-ts'an, translated by Richard B. Clarke, Zen teacher and founder of the Living Dharma Center, P.O. Box 304, Amherst, MA 01004. Reprinted by permission.

Page 49, first paragraph: From *In Praise of Vallabh* by Gopaldas, translated by Shyamdas, Pratham Peeth Publications, 2002. © Sacred Woods 2002. Reprinted with permission.

Page 51, last paragraph: From the *Yugal Gita of the Bhagavat*, translated by Shyamdas, Pratham Peeth Publications, India. Reprinted with permission.

Pages 101–2, 233–34, 234, 234–35, and 236–37: From *Ramakrishna as We Saw Him*, edited and translated by Swami Chetanananda, Vedanta Society of St. Louis, St. Louis, 1990. Reprinted with permission by Vedanta Society of St. Louis.

Pages 173–74, 177–78, 192–93, 196–97, 211, 214, 276–77: Passages from Dada Mukerjee, *By His Grace* and *The Near and the Dear* reprinted with permission from *By His Grace: A Devotee's Story*, Dada Mukerjee. © Hanuman Foundation 1990, 2001.

Pages 266–67, 268, 269, 270, 272, 273–74: From *Nityananda: The Divine Presence* by M. U. Hatengdi and Swami Chetanananda, Rudra Press, Portland, Oregon, 1984. Reprinted by permission.

Pages 277–78: From K. K. Sah, personal communication, courtesy of K. K. Sah.

Pages 288–90: From Indra Lal (I. L.) Sah, personal diary, courtesy of K. K. Sah.

Pages 290–91: From *Uttarakhand, The Holy Himalayan Region*, newspaper article by K. K. Sah in *The Pioneer Hill Supplement*, 1970.

Page 292: Illustration of Brahmachari Maharaj-ji courtesy of K. K. Sah.

notes

Chapter One: The Path of the Heart

1. Larry Brilliant, *Fierce Grace* 46:20, Lemle Pictures, 2001.
2. St. John of the Cross, *Living Flame of Love,* trans. Mirabai Starr (unpublished).
3. Tulsi Das, *Sri Ramacharitamanasa* (Gorakhpur: Gita Press, 1968), Sundara Khanda, p. 30.
4. Dr. Martin Luther King, Jr., quoted on The King Center, www.thekingcenter.org/ProgSources/.
5. Seng-ts'an, *Hsin-Hsin Ming: Verses on the Faith Mind,* trans. Richard B. Clarke (Buffalo, NY: White Pine Press, 2001).

Chapter Two: Excess Baggage

1. Tukaram, trans. S. R. Sharma (Bombay: Popular Book Depot, 1962), p. 11.

Chapter Three: To Become One

1. Krishna Das, *Pilgrim of the Heart* audio series, and personal exchange.
2. Tulsi Das, *Sri Ramacharitamanasa* (Gorakhpur: Gita Press, 1968), Uttarakanda, Doha 103a.
3. F. Max Müller, *Ramakrishna: His Life and Sayings* (New Delhi: Rupa, 2006), #89, p. 118.
4. Swami Nikhilananda, trans., *The Gospel of Sri Ramakrishna* (New York: Ramakrishna-Vivekananda Center, 1942), p. 399.
5. Gopaldas, *In Praise of Vallabh,* trans. Shyamdas (Vrindaban: Pratham Peeth Publications, 2002), introduction.

6. Raihana Tyabji, *The Heart of a Gopi* (New Delhi: East-West Publications Fund, 1971), p. 24.
7. *Yugal Gita of Bhagavat,* trans. Shyamdas (Vrindaban: Pratham Peeth Publications, forthcoming).
8. Jayadeva, *Gita Govinda,* trans. Monika Varma (Calcutta: Writers Workshop, 1968).
9. Tulsi Das, *Sri Ramacharitamanasa* (Gorakhpur: Gita Press, 1968), p. 280.
10. Ansari of Herat, 1006–1089 CE.

Chapter Four: Darshan

1. Kabir, *One Hundred Poems of Kabir,* trans. Rabindranath Tagore and Evelyn Underhill (Madras: Macmillan, 1970), 76 (III. 48, *Tusurat nain nihar*).
2. Kabir, *One Hundred Poems of Kabir,* 22.
3. Jnaneshwar, Amritanubhava.
4. Ramana Maharshi, *Talks with Sri Ramana Maharshi* (Tiruvanamallai: Ramanashramam, 2006), p. 165.
5. Shah Latif, in *Sufis, Mystics, and Yogis of India*, ed. K. M. Munshi (Bombay: Bharatiya Vidya Bhavan, 1971), p. 151.

Chapter Five: Guides

1. Kabir, *One Hundred Poems of Kabir,* trans. Rabindranath Tagore and Evelyn Underhill (Madras: Macmillan, 1970), p. 54 (XLVIII, 1.107. *calat mansa acal kinhi*).
2. Swami Vivekananda, "The Experience of Cosmic Consciousness," in Swami Chetanananda, ed. and trans., *Ramakrishna as We Saw Him* (St. Louis: Vedanta Society of St. Louis, 1990), p. 63.
3. Swami Vivekananda, "The Experience of Nirvikalpa Samadhi," in *Ramakrishna as We Saw Him,* p. 70.
4. Swami Ramdas, in *Servant of God: Sayings of a Self-Realised Sage, Swami Ramdas,* compiled by Susunaga Weeraperuma (Delhi: Motilal Banarsidass, 1999), p. 205.
5. Swami Nikhilananda, trans., *The Gospel of Sri Ramakrishna* (New York: Ramakrishna-Vivekananda Center, 1942), p. 129.
6. Ram Dass, *Miracle of Love* (Santa Fe: Hanuman Foundation, 1979), p. 363.

Chapter Six: Remover of Darkness

1. Hakuin, *Zazen Wasan: Song of Zazen.*
2. Jnaneshwar, *Amritanubhava,* trans. Ramchandra Keshav Bhagwat (Madras: Samata Books, 1985), p. 122.
3. Ravi Prakash Pande, *Divine Reality: Shri Baba Neeb Karori Ji Maharaj,* 2nd ed. (Kainchi: Shri Kainchi Hanuman Mandir and Ashram, 2005), #245, pp 202–3, combined with version from Krishna Das.
4. Seng-ts'an, *Hsin-Hsin Ming: Verses on the Faith Mind,* trans. Richard B. Clarke (Buffalo, NY: White Pine Press, 2001).
5. William Shakespeare, *As You Like It,* Act 2, scene 7, ll. 139–43.

6. F. Max Müller, *Ramakrishna: His Life and Sayings* (New Delhi: Rupa, 2006), #123, p. 127.

7. Swami Abhayananda, *Jnaneshwar: The Life and Works of the Celebrated Thirteenth-Century Indian Mystic-Poet* (Olympia, WA: Atma, 1989), chap. 2, vv. 61, 64–69.

Chapter Seven: The Way of Grace

1. F. Max Müller, *Ramakrishna: His Life and Sayings* (New Delhi: Rupa, 2006), #154, p. 134.

2. Seng-ts'an, *Hsin-Hsin Ming: Verses on the Faith Mind,* trans. Richard B. Clarke (Buffalo, NY: White Pine Press, 2001).

3. Paltu Sahib, quoted D. Sarma, p. 150.

4. Swami Nikhilananda, trans., *The Gospel of Sri Ramakrishna* (New York: Ramakrishna-Vivekananda Center, 1942), pp. 680–81.

5. Dada Mukerjee, *By His Grace: A Devotee's Story* (Santa Fe, NM: Hanuman Foundation, 1990), p. 82.

6. Seng-ts'an, *Hsin-Hsin Ming.*

7. Kabir, *One Hundred Poems of Kabir,* trans. by Rabindranath Tagore and Evelyn Underhill (Madras: Macmillan, 1970), I, p. 1.

8. Mukerjee, *By His Grace,* p. 161.

9. Gampopa, *Jewel Ornament of Liberation.*

10. Ravi Prakash Pande, *Divine Reality: Shri Baba Neeb Karori Ji Maharaj* (Kainchi: Shri Kainchi Hanuman Mandir and Ashram, 2003), #182, pp. 189–90.

11. Arthur Osborne, *Ramana Maharshi and the Path of Self Knowledge* (Newburyport, MA: Red Wheel/Weiser, 1995), p. 142.

Chapter Eight: A Family Man

1. Dada Mukerjee, *By His Grace: A Devotee's Story* (Sante Fe, NM: Hanuman Foundation, 1990), p. 169.

2. Dada Mukerjee, *The Near and the Dear* (Sante Fe, NM: Hanuman Foundation, 2000), pp. 130–32.

3. Bhusukupada, *Bauddhagan O Doha* No. 43.

4. Mukerjee, *The Near and the Dear,* pp. 40–41.

Chapter Nine: One in My Heart

1. Dada Mukerjee, *By His Grace: A Devotee's Story* (Sante Fe, NM: Hanuman Foundation, 1990), p. 169.

2. Arthur Osborne, *Ramana Maharshi and the Path of Self-Knowledge* (York Beach, ME: Samuel Weiser, 1970), pp. 18–19.

3. A. R. Natarajan, *Timeless in Time: Sri Ramana Maharshi* (Bloomington, IN: World Wisdom, 2006), p. 13.

4. Ramana Maharshi, *Bhakti Marga and Yoga Marga,* ed. Sanjay Lohia (Bangalore: Ramana Maharshi Centre, 2004), pp. 34, 36.

5. M. A. Piggot, quoted in Natarajan, *Timeless in Time,* pp. 107–8.

6. Ramana Maharshi, *Bhakti Marga and Yoga Marga,* p. 40.

7. Swami Nikhilananda, trans., *The Gospel of Sri Ramakrishna* (New York: Ramakrishna-Vivekananda Center, 1942), p. 475.

8. Nikhilananda, *Gospel of Sri Ramakrishna*, Introduction, p. 13.

9. Nikhilananda, *Gospel of Sri Ramakrishna*, pp. 13–14.

10. Swami Chetanananda, ed. and trans., *Ramakrishna as We Saw Him* (St. Louis: Vedanta Society of St. Louis, 1990), pp. 43–44.

11. Chetanananda, *Ramakrishna as We Saw Him*, p. 45.

12. Chetanananda, *Ramakrishna as We Saw Him*, pp. 61–62.

13. Chetanananda, *Ramakrishna as We Saw Him*, p. 63.

14. Chetanananda, *Ramakrishna as We Saw Him*, p. 137.

15. Nikhilananda, *Gospel of Sri Ramakrishna*, p. 37.

16. Nikhilananda, *Gospel of Sri Ramakrishna*, p. 37.

17. Nikhilananda, *Gospel of Sri Ramakrishna*, p. 43.

18. Nikhilananda, *Gospel of Sri Ramakrishna*, p. 47.

19. Nikhilananda, *Gospel of Sri Ramakrishna*, p. 72.

20. Paramahansa Yogananda, *Autobiography of a Yogi* (Los Angeles: Self-Realization Fellowship, 1968), p. 457. In a footnote to the passage quoted the author notes: Anandamayi Ma does not refer to herself as "I"; she uses circumlocutions like "this body," "this little girl," or "your daughter."

21. Unknown source.

22. Arthur Osborne, *The Incredible Sai Baba* (New Delhi: Orient Longman, 1970), p. 2.

23. Gunaji, *Sri Sai Satcharita* (Bombay: Sai Baba Sansthan, 5th ed., 1969), pp. 13–14.

24. Gunaji, *Sri Sai Satcharita*, p. 19.

25. Osborne, *The Incredible Sai Baba*, pp. 40–41.

26. Sri Jnanadeva, *Amritanubhava*, trans. Ramchandra Keshav Bhagwat (Madras: Samata Books, 1985), p. 137.

27. Jnanadeva, Amritanubhava.

28. Bhagawan Nityananda, *Chidakash Geetha* (S. Kortright, NY: Eden Books, 1981), #55, p. 12.

29. M. U. Hatengdi and Swami Chetanananda, *Nityananda: The Divine Presence* (Portland, OR: Rudra Press, 1984), p. 29.

30. Nityananda, *Chidakash Geetha*, #51.

31. Hatengdi and Chetanananda, *Nityananda*, p. 50, paraphrased.

32. Hatengdi and Chetanananda, *Nityananda*, p. 41, paraphrased.

33. Hatengdi and Chetanananda, *Nityananda*, p. 28.

34. D. R. K. Gaurishankar, *Master Key to Peace: Bhagawan Nityananda*.

35. Hatengdi and Chetanananda, *Nityananda*, pp. 31–32.

36. Nityananda, *Chidakash Geetha*, #44.

37. Hatengdi and Chetanananda, *Nityananda*, p. 30.

38. Dada Mukerjee, *The Near and the Dear* (Sante Fe, NM: Hanuman Foundation, 2000), p. 121.

39. Dada Mukerjee, *By His Grace*, pp. 159–60.

40. K. K. Sah, personal communication.

41. Indra Lall (I.L.) Sah diary, courtesy of K. K. Sah.

42. K. K. Sah, "Uttarakhand: The Holy Himalayan Region," *The Pioneer Hill Supplement*, 1970.